# Introduction to Deep Learning
## Black/White version

Prof. Dr. Jürgen Brauer

August 2018

Introduction to Deep Learning
1st Edition, August 2018.

Note:
This is a black/white version of the original book version
which uses colors in some figures. It allows for lower
printing costs and therefore a lower final price. However,
some details might be recognized better in the color version.

Prof. Dr. Jürgen Brauer
University of Applied Sciences Kempten.
Bahnhofstr. 61
87435 Kempten (Allgäu), Germany
www.juergenbrauer.org

# Contents

# What is Deep Learning?

## 1.1 "How are they called? Neutrons?"

Let me start this book with a small anecdote - a short part of a discussion I had with my flatmate during my study times at the University of Bonn. Once I sat with her at dinner in our shared flat ...

Jürgen: What have you done today?

Christine: I learned the whole day for my oral exam tomorrow in psychology.

*She studied towards a magister degree where you have to choose a major and two minors. Psychology was one of her minors.*

Jürgen: Did you know that I changed from University of Trier after my intermediate diploma to University of Bonn since I am very interested in neuroscience? They have an department of neuroinformatics here.

Christine: What do you do in neuroinformatics?

Jürgen: You simulate the functioning of biological neurons with the help of artificial neuron models and connect many of them to artificial neural networks.

Christine: What are these neutrons?

Jürgen: They are called neurons! Christine, you really should know what a neuron is if this is the evening before your oral exam in psychology! Neurons are the building blocks of our brains! They are the basis of all mental processes.

*She rapidly finished her dinner, then went to her room to read into the topic. After some minutes the door openend and she asked:*

Christine: How are they called? Neutrons?

Jürgen: Protons!?

Christine: *grins at me*

Jürgen: Neurons! They are called neurons! Not neutrons!

*@Christine: please fogive me, that I make this conversation public. You were really a funny flatmate.*

## 1.2 Convolutional Neural Networks drive the boom

**Your brain has many of them.** Probably you already know that the field of Deep Learning (often abbreviated by DL in the following) is heavily inspired by the biological neurons found in our brains. In 2009, a study [1],[35] showed, that the human brain has about 86 billion of these neurons (!), which is less than the number estimated and taught before (100 billion neurons). Interestingly, the study also showed that humans do not differ from other primates in the sense, that their cerebral cortex has a proportionally larger size. The cerebral cortex is the brain region that plays a key role for higher mental functions as attention, perception and language. Only 19% of all human neurons are located in the cerebral cortex, which is the same ratio as for other primates and rodents.

**Artificial Neural Networks (ANNs).** In the field of Deep Learning the function of these neurons is modeled by simple computing units, called neurons as well. These *technical neuron models* are then connected with each other to so called *artificial neural networks*. At this point another important idea is borrowed from nature, namely the way they are connected to each other. From neuroscience it is known, that in some parts of the brain, biological neurons form "layers of neurons", in the sense, that neuron connections are mainly from one layer to another and only sparsely between neurons in the same layer. This observation lead to idea of *feed forward neural networks (FF)*. If further, a certain technical neuron model is used which is called *Perception* and each neuron in layer $i$ gets its input from *all* neurons from the previous layer $i - 1$, these artificial neural networks are called *Multilayer perceptrons (MLP)*. This *fully connected* criterion does not hold in general for all FFNs.

**ANNs are not new.** Now the MLP model is not new. Already in the 1980s MLPs were a popular approach to machine learning. However, the model was not suitable in practice to solve the important machine learning tasks of image classification and object localization and after some hype about neural networks, the machine learning community moved to other techniques, as, e.g., *Support Vector Machines (SVMs)*.

**CNNs are the drive of the boom.** The responsibility for the new boom of the field has to be attributed mainly to a variant of feedforward neural networks, which is called *Convolutional Neural Network (CNN)* and was introduced by LeCun [27]. CNNs do not only use Perceptrons in the so called *convolutional layers* and the *classification layers* at the end of the network, but they also use other simple computing elements, as, e.g., a maximum operation in the *pooling layer*. Probably the key factor for the success is the insight, that using a hierarchy of neuron layers, where the neurons represent more and more complex features as we go up in the hierarchy of layers, can simplify all pattern recognition tasks, such as classification and localization of objects in images.

**Receptive fields.** Furthermore, another important idea from biological visual systems was stolen: the computing elements have *receptive fields* similar to biological neurons. This means that they do not get the input from the whole image area, but from small restricted regions in the image. What this means is that in lower layers many local classifications are made and the classification results are propagated to the next layer which again does not get its input (indirectly) from the whole image but from a subarea of it.

**Missing ingredients.** However, LeCun presented his work [27] already in 1989! Why did it need more than 20 years to start the boom? The common understanding in the community is that at least the following further ingredients were missing:

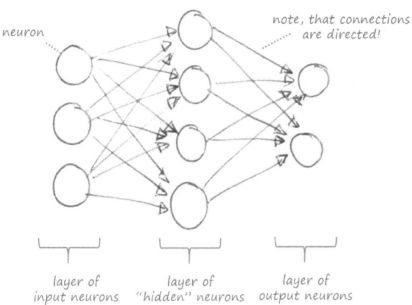

Figure 1.1: A feedforward neural network (FFN) model steels two important ideas from nature: 1. Brains use simple computing elements, called "neurons". In a FFN their functionality is roughly modeled by technical neuron models, as, e.g., Perceptrons. 2. Neurons form "layers" in brains in the sense that neurons within a layer are only sparsely connected with each other and densely between layers. Note, that in real brains these connections can go to many previous and following layers, whereas in a standard FFN the connections only go to the next layer.

**1. More data.** The datasets that CNNs are currently trained on are really large. In the 1980s storage restrictions did not allow to store datasets with millions of images. Now, storage space for millions of images is not really a problem any longer. Furthermore, large sets of images can be collected easily from the WWW.

**2. Faster computing hardware.** Even if enough data storage and large datasets had been available in the past, the computing power to process these datasets simply was not available. With the development of faster and multi-kernel CPUs and GPUs it is now much easier to train a CNN consisting of many layers with many neurons.

**3. Better transfer functions.** The technical neuron models used *transfer functions* to model the neuronal firing rate in dependence of its input activity. It was shown in an important paper by Krizhevsky et al. [24], that a transfer function called *Rectified Linear Unit (ReLU)*, gives better results than the transfer functions usually used before and equally important, that this transfer function is much faster to compute.

**4. Regularization techniques.** Regularization techniques are techniques that guide or modify the learning process in a helpful way. Artificial Neural Networks can suffer from a problem called *overfitting*, which means, that they steadily increase their performance on the data set used for training, but show a poor performance on new data. A technique called *dropout* is now a standard regularization technique for addressing and solving this problem.

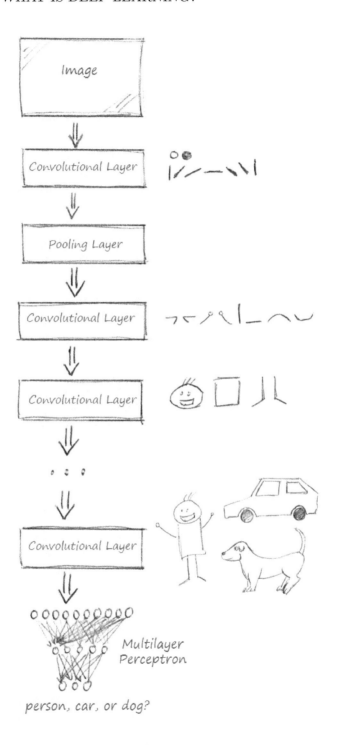

Figure 1.2: A convolutional neural network consists of a cascade of convolutional and pooling layers. Early stages typically detect features as edges, then line contours, at later stages then parts of objects or (not necessarily) even complete objects.

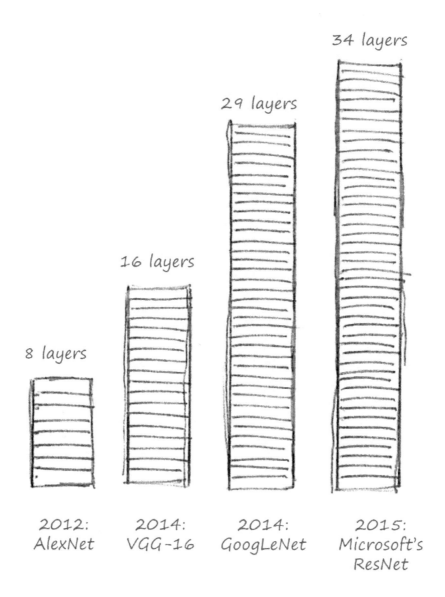

Figure 1.3: Going deeper. For important CNN models presented by research teams in the last years more and more layers of neurons have been used.

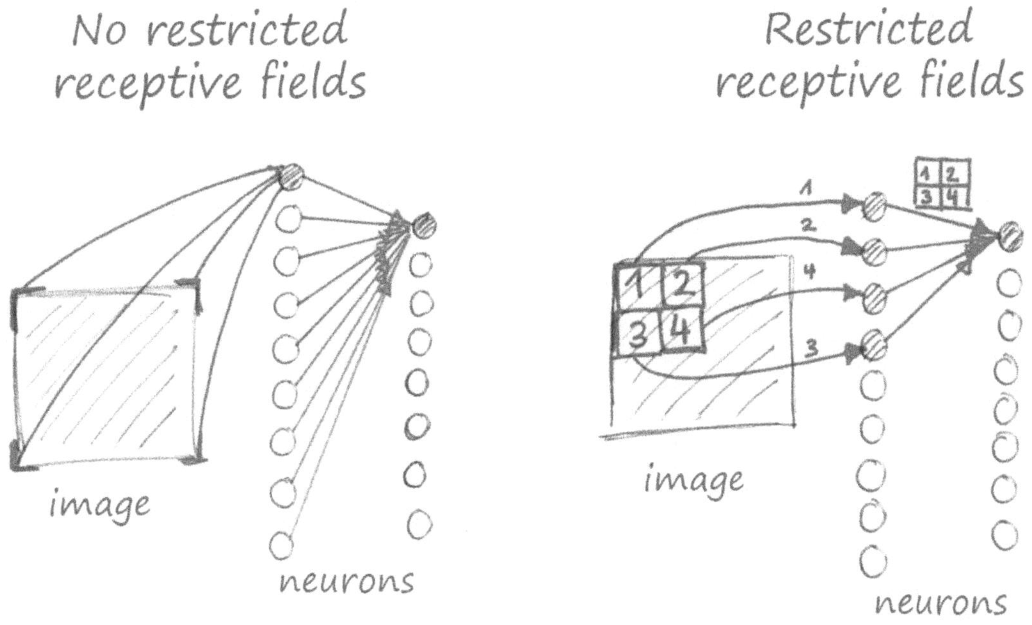

No restricted
receptive fields

Restricted
receptive fields

image

neurons

image

neurons

Figure 1.4: The principle of receptive fields is another important idea that is used in CNNs and which is clearly inspired by nature. It means that a neuron does not get its input from all other neurons from a previous layer, but just a small subset. This allows first to classify locally and communicate the classification result to the following neuron, which combines classification results from several previous neurons and for this has an larger effective receptive field.

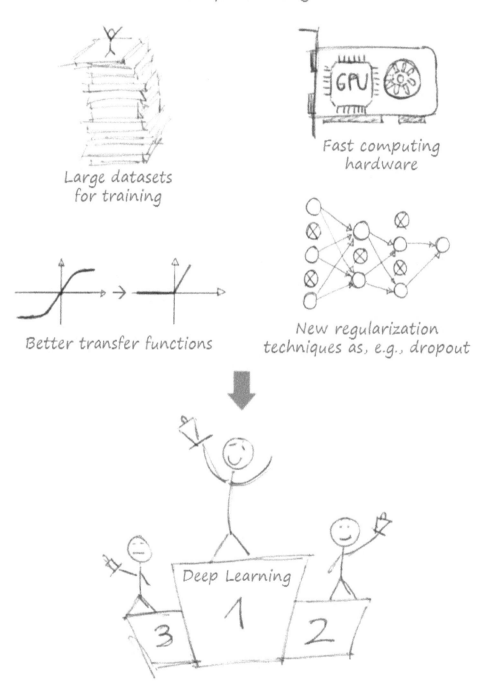

Figure 1.5: Convolutional Neural Network were already invented in 1989 by LeCun. However, the success came only about 20 years later due to some missing ingredients.

## 1.3 Deep Learning without neurons

**Cascade of non-neuronal classifiers.** Currently, the most important principle exploited in CNNs is the hierarchical representation of the image information within a deep cascade of layers of neurons, which gave the field its name *Deep Learning*. The first layers learn simple edge or color contrast feature detectors. The next layers can detect primitive shapes. Higher levels then combine these shapes to form object parts or even complete object representations. But, it is important to understand, that this principle is not necessarily connected to neural networks. The neurons in today's CNN convolution layers perform a simple operation (a convolution), which is basically nothing more than a classification of the input coming from its receptive field. It can also be considered as a compare operation, which compares the input with a pattern prototype stored in the neuron's weights. No one has said that these classifiers have to be neurons. So, a hierarchy of local non-neuronal learning classifiers should in principle work as well! With this claim I want to underline my opinion, that it is not the neurons that have led the field to success, but it is the usage of a hierarchy of feature classifiers.

**Neurons as a glue for models.** This does not mean that we should forget the neurons and start building new models without neurons. Modeling information processing and information representation with the help of neural networks is still a promising approach to tackle the problem of building a *strong AI*. A strong AI is an artificial intelligence with general knowledge as opposed to a *weak AI*, an AI without general knowledge, but very competent in some niche, e.g., playing chess or Go. If different research groups share a common base, namely neural networks, for building individual models that solve problems as, e.g., object localization, object and scene classification, object tracking, attention mechanisms, learning of movements for a robot, etc., there is a better chance that we will be able to "glue" these models together as an artificial brain and put it into a robot one day. For sure, gluing" different models together will be one of the most trickiest part and will often mean combining existing neural models into a new model that is different from the individual models.

## 1.4 Neuroscience as a treasure for machine learning

Here is another personal anecdote:

**My proposal: We should learn hierarchical representations.** In 2006 I was looking for a position to do a PhD thesis. My impression was (and still is) that there were a lot more principles from nature that we could exploit for artificial neural networks. So I wrote a two-page proposal for a PhD thesis topic which I wanted to work on. Some of the main ideas were the 1. unsupervised learning of feature hierarchies by exploiting local synaptic learning rules (CNNs use supervised learning and non-local learning rules) where the learning rules were supposed to be driven just by the massive correlation information inherently in spatio-temporal data (image, videos, music, etc.), 2. the usage of spatio-temporal correlation information across sensor modalities for realizing what today is called 'sensor data fusion', and 3. the usage of so called *spiking neurons*, which are biologically much more plausible. I sent this proposal to the German neuroscientist Prof. Christoph von der Malsburg. It seemed to me that he was someone who had devoted his life to neurosciences [30] and that he should recognize the importance of these ideas. And he really helped me! Since he had no positions at this time, he sent my proposal to one of his colleagues who called me on the phone. After some discussion at the phone an interview followed and finally he offered me a PhD position at the newly founded Frankfurt Institute of Advanced Studies (FIAS). Unfortunately, there was no full 100% payment for PhD students at this time and due to some financial obligations I had (I bought a car and all furnitures for my first flat by the help of a credit), I had to reject the offer.

**Neuroscience as a treasure.** What do I want to tell you with this anecdote? First, if you are searching for a PhD position or if you have an interesting idea for a master thesis, do not hesitate to sent your ideas to persons which could have similar interests and ideas and understand that you are the right person. Second, in my eyes, neuroscience is a treasure and there are much more ideas that we can borrow from nature to build better pattern recognition systems! There is now a common agreement in the machine learning community that borrowing the idea of hierarchical representations was the right step. The natural question arises: Are there any other cool ideas that we could exploit?

**Self-organization as another important principle.** I think there are plenty of similar ideas - even if the majority of these principles have not yet been identified or understood. Let me give you an example: Another principle which has been understood already quite far is the principle of self-organization. The benefits have been shown in a neural network model, called the *Self-Organizing Map (SOM)*. Here, neurons show a characteristic connection pattern with neighbored neurons. If we consider a single neuron, the connections to nearby neurons are excitatory and connections to neurons that are far away are inhibtory. This (Mexican hat function alike) connection pattern allows a limited set of feature detectors to distribute their representation possibilities efficiently among the space of possible inputs. Interestingly, this principle has not yet been exploited in the context of CNNs!

**"Deep Learning" is not a good name for the field.** With this in mind, it is clear, that the name "Deep Learning" is actually not very appropriate if we think

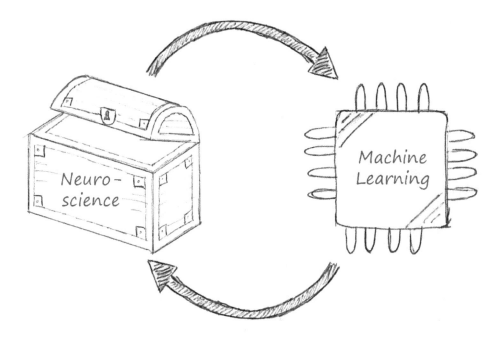

Figure 1.6: An stronger interplay between neuroscience and machine learning could help to harvest and understand more fruitful ideas than just the idea of hierarchical representations and receptive fields used in CNNs.

of a new field in machine learning that 1. uses neurons as its basic computing units and 2. tries to exploit more principles than just hierarchical representations from the biological role model in the nearby future. What would be a better name for the field? I have one. We could call the field "Neural Networks"! Awesome, or?

**"Neural Networks" as a taboo word.** Why isn't it called "Neural Networks"? Since there were so few successful applications of classical neural networks between 1980-2010, the term had become a taboo word. After working for many years as a software developer in the field of medical informatics, I started a PhD thesis at Fraunhofer in 2009. The task was to develop a new approach for 3D human pose estimation based on monocular images. I was free to choose the approach, but it was clear, that Neural Networks were not considered at all! It was the time of interest point detectors and local feature descriptors as SIFT and SURF. It was the time of RANSAC, the HOG detector, Support Vector Machines, Bag of Words, Deformable Part Models (DPM), the Implicit Shape Model (ISM), etc. But it was not the time when people were open for Neural Networks. The then head of the departement for object recognition at Fraunhofer told me in my interview "You can do everything here! [Pause] But no Neural Networks!". It is interesting to see how quickly things changed in the last years. In March 2017 I visited my old colleagues. They told me, that they now heat their offices in the winter with Nvidia graphics cards + Deep Learning algorithms. Is it cold? → `python train_cnn_using_imagenet_on_gpu.py`

**Future of the field: We need a shift from supervised to unsupervised learning.** Furthermore, the field of Deep Learning drives towards a dead end. In order to come up with better models, we need more and more labeled data, since the current standard training approach is a supervised one, i.e., for each input pattern, we need a desired output pattern. However, providing labeled training data is expensive and it is hard to scale: What if we do not want 1 million training images, but 1 billion? Billions of training images are easily available. A single TV-channel, e.g., provides more than 2 million training images per day (25 frames/sec * 60 sec/min * 60 min/h * 24h/day = 2,16 million frames/day). So 100 TV-channels, already give us more than 1.5 billion training images per week. Ok, I am not sure, if we really can learn something from Home-Shopping-TV images, but let us assume, we can ;-) (Of course we can, it is perfect spatio-temporal data with full of tasty correlations in the data!) We cannot label this amount of data in a useful way. Not even with Amazon's Mechanical Turk platform. Nevertheless, the answer is nearly obvious: I definitively remember, that my mother never labeled the TV series I was watching. I could ask her questions as, e.g., "What is this?" and I got some labeling information that I could use to connect the activity patterns in my brain with high-level entity concepts but she really did not provide me bounding boxes or a list of all objects present in each frame. Therefore, we need new learning rules that allow to learn mostly in an unsupervised way just as humans do with an additional small pinch of supervised learning. We could, e.g., try to learn nearly all layers unsupervised, then use just some few manually labeled examples to connect the activation patterns of neurons in the higher levels with the categories interested in.

## 1.5   About this book

**Neural networks without neurons.** During my studies of neuroinformatics at the University of Bonn I had to read the book "Neural Networks for Pattern Recognition" by Christopher M. Bishop [4]. It is an excellent book about neural networks. However, Bishop presents the whole topic without *ever* using the term "neuron" as far as I remember. E.g., he does not talk about "hidden neurons" in a Multi Layer Perceptron, but calls them "hidden units". It shows a certain attitude: We actually do not need the biological motivation and background if we talk about technical neural networks. The idea, models and mathematical formalisms of distributed representations and computing using simple "units" can be developed without drawing analogies to biological neurons.

**Neural networks with neurons.** In this book I want to introduce the topic of Deep Learning and neural networks by adopting exactly the opposite position. The reasons are mentioned above. In my eyes, the field of Deep Learning and neural networks can make major advances if there is a continuous exchange between neuroscience and machine learning. For this, the book will present also some interesting facts from neuroscience and will not just present only technical neuron models.

Figure 1.7: In the supervised learning scenario for each input pattern (here: images of numbers), a label is needed ("This is a four!"). In the unsupervised learning scenario only input patterns are available.

# Deep Learning:
# An agile field

## 2.1 Exponential growth of interest

**Google Trends.** Have a look at Fig. 2.1. The data was retrieved from Google Trends in September 2017. Google Trends provides information about how often search terms were entered (in a popular search engine which name I will not mention here). However, Google Trends does not provide absolute numbers of searches but normalizes the data using the maximum number of searches in the time period investigated. This simplifies comparisons. Therefore, the scale on the y-axis ranges from 0 to 100, where 100 means the maximum number of searches that has ever been recorded for the search term.

**Enormous growth of interest.** The diagram plots the data of two search terms for the last 13 years. Support vector machines (SMVs) are *the* example for a classical machine learning classifier. In 2004 search queries for "support vector machine" were much more frequently than for "deep learning". But around 2012 things turned and in the last five years the interest in "deep learning" has increased enormously world-

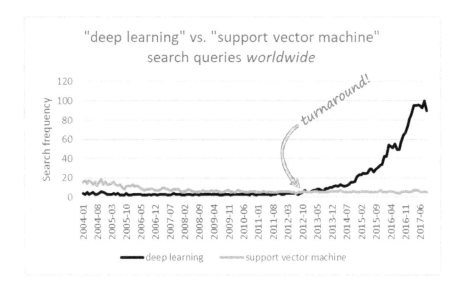

Figure 2.1: Strong growth of interest in DL *worldwide* between January 2004 and September 2017. [Data source: Google Trends]

wide. In September 2017, "deep learning" has been entered 18 times more often than "support vector machine".

**US before Germany.** This change did not happen at the same time everywhere in the world. Compare Fig. 2.2 and Fig. 2.3. These figures show the frequencies of the two search terms between September 2012 and September 2017 restricted to search queries coming from the United States and Germany respectively. The comparison shows that the topic of Deep Learning gained more interest than SVMs in the United States around 2013, while the same change happened in Germany about a year later.

**Computer Vision before NLP.** Also the change did not happen in every machine learning subfield at the same time. In the subfield of computer vision a DL model presented by Alex Krizhevsky et al. [24] won the ImageNet Large Scale Visual Recognition Challenge (ILSVRC) of that year. In the subfield of Natural Language Processing (NLP) the revolution came later as the following quote by Christopher Manning [31] from Stanford University suggests:

> "Deep Learning waves have lapped at the shores of computational linguistics for several years now, but 2015 seems like the year when the full force of the tsunami hit the major Natural Language Processing (NLP) conferences."

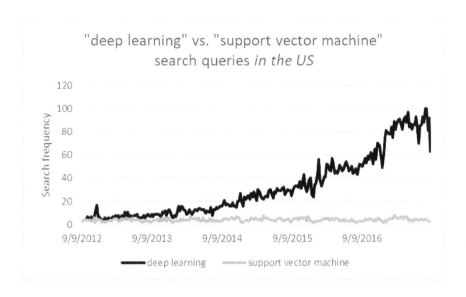

Figure 2.2: Strong growth of interest in DL *in the US* started around 2013. [Source: Google Trends]

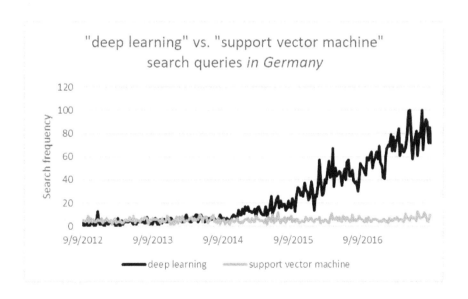

Figure 2.3: Strong growth of interest in DL *in Germany* started around 2014. [Source: Google Trends]

## 2.2 Acquisition of DL startups

Here is another personal anecdote that fits to the title of this section:

**Another personal anecdote.** At the beginning of the year 2016 I was torn between the idea of continuing my job as a professor and the idea of joining the Deep Learning hype by accepting a job in industry. It is interesting to see that many other people have similar ideas now. People at Quora ask, e.g., *"Should I quit my job and spend 3 years to learn machine learning and deep learning if I have about $200k in savings?"* or *"Is it worth it to quit my USD $150K software developer job to study machine learning and deep learning?"* (neither I had $200k in savings nor a salary of $150k, so it should have been easier for me to quit my job). When I stumbled upon the website of a young start-up called MetaMind I became really interested. They developed Deep Learning models for computer vision and Natural Language Processing (NLP) and the CEO, Richard Socher, a former Stanford Ph.D. student of Andrew Ng, seemed to be excellent in both fields. I finally applied. And indeed, I got an invitation for a skype interview with Caiming Xiong and Richard Socher. In order to prepare for the interview I went again to their website and read a notice: "Metamind joins Salesforce" which meant that this young start-up had been acquired by Salesforce in the meantime. By the way, Richard gave me two weeks for a very interesting coding task on sentiment analysis, but my job at the University was so demanding that I could not find even a minute to work on it. The only time slot since I started my job as a professor in my daily schedule that is not filled with work is 12 a.m. to 6 a.m. and usually reserved for sleep (which is important for learning and forming memories). So I took back my application. Nevertheless, Richard was very friendly and said I could resume my application whenever I wanted. Very good style!

**What do I want to tell you with this anecdote?** Also at the level of companies you can see that the field of Deep Learning is an extremely agile field. Maybe you apply for a young start-up as well that will be acquired already in some months by one of the big players.

Over 250 private companies focusing on artificial intelligence (AI) have been acquired between 2012 and mid 2017 [6] by corporate giants like Apple, Intel, Google, IBM, Samsung, Ford, GE, and Uber. Many of them use Deep Learning techniques.

### Google

Google, e.g., acquired DNNResearch in 2013 for about $5 million [42]. DNNResearch was a small Canadian start-up founded by three researchers: Prof. Geoffrey Hinton from University of Toronto and two of his graduate students, Alex Krizhevsky and Ilya

Figure 2.4: A large number of Deep Learning start-ups have already been acquired by the usual suspects.

Sutskever [26]. It allowed Google to offer its Google+ Photo search just six months after the acquisition.

Another important acquisition by Google was DeepMind Technologies - a British company. Google paid about $650 million in 2013 [42]. Facebook was also interested in DeepMind Technologies but Google won the race. DeepMind actually has no concrete products, but focuses on AI research using Deep Learning techniques. Well known research results are so called *deep reinforcement learning* algorithms for learning (Atari) video games from scratch and the *Neural Turing Machine*: a neural network model that is able to use a tape as an external memory, similar to the Turing machine model used in theoretical computer science. In 2016 the company made headlines when its program *AlphaGo* beat a human professional Go player. The game was invented in ancient China more than 2500 years ago and none of the computer programs before ever reached the professional play level.

In 2016 Google acquired the French visual search start-up Moodstock located in Paris which focuses on providing DL based image recognition functionality on mobile devices by the help of an API. Recently, Google bough Halli Labs, an only 4-month-old Indian AI and machine learning (ML) startup, located in Bangalore.

There are a lot of other DL technology based companies Google acquired. The list is really long [43]. Three further examples of Google's acquisitions in 2014 are Jetpac (city guide for over 6000 cities based on automatically analyzing Instagram photos) and the two spin-offs from University of Oxford: Dark Blue Labs (specialized in DL for understanding natural language) and Vision Factory (DL for visual object recognition).

## Intel

Three startups were acquired by Intel in 2016 alone:

Itseez, which was founded "already" in 2005, developed a suite of DL based algorithms to realize Advanced Driver Assistance Systems (ADAS), e.g., for detecting when a car drifts from its lane or to brake automatically, when a pedestrian crosses the road.

Nervana was acquired by Intel for approximately $408 million [12]. Nervana developed a DL framework called "Neon", which is an open-source python based language and set of libraries for developing deep learning models, but the acquisition also brought talented chip designers to Intel, since Nervana was developing a custom ASIC - which is called the Nervana Engine. The chip is optimized for DL algorithms by focusing on operations heavily used by DL algorithms.

Movidius is specialized on low-power processor chips for computer vision and deep-learning. One if its products that has been released in July 2017 is the "Neural Compute Stick" (NCS): an USB stick which contains Movidius' Myriad 2 processor. This is a *Vision Processing Unit (VPU)* that allows to accelerate vision and deep learning algorithms. In contrast to a *Graphics Processing Unit* (GPU), a VPU lacks specialized hardware for, e.g., rasterization and texture mapping, but provides direct interfaces to grab data from cameras directly and allows for massive on-chip dataflow between the parallel processing units.

### Facebook

In 2012 Facebook announced its acquisition of the Israeli facial recognition company Face.com. The company developed a platform for facial recognition in photos uploaded via web and mobile applications. The technology continued in Facebook's internal project DeepFace, a deep learning facial recognition system created by a research group at Facebook.

Mobile Technologies, the maker of the Jibbigo translation app, and a leader in speech recognition and translation was acquired by Facebook in 2013. Jibbigo was the world's first speech-to-speech translation app when it was launched in October 2009.

In 2016 Facebook bought Zurich Eye, a spin-off of ten researchers of the ETH Zurich that concentrates on developing a solution for providing accurate position information for robots to navigate in indoor and outdoor environments using camera and inertial measurement unit (IMU) data.

### Apple

Perceptio was acquired by Apple in 2015. It used the DL approach to develop a solution for smartphones, that allows phones to classify images without relying on external data libraries, i.e., to be online.

In 2017 Apple paid around \$200 million to acquire Lattice Data [11], a firm that develops algorithms to turn unstructured data such as text and images into structured data. Lattice Data is located in Menlo Park, California and tried to commercialize a Stanford University research project known as "DeepDive".

Apple also bought the Israeli startup RealFace in 2017, a cybersecurity and machine learning specialized in automatic face recognition.

## 2.3 Hardware for DL

**The need for AI accelerators.** Computation time has become a major issue for the DL business. Even with several CPUs and GPUs large models are trained on the order of several days or even weeks. For this, *AI accelerators* are being developed by different companies that try to speed up the training and inference step of DL models by focusing on the most frequently used operations used in DL models or by taking into account the special memory access patterns. For neural networks, e.g., the memory access pattern is very good predictable and differs from graphics algorithms, e.g., by the fact that it is more important to keep temporary variables on-chip (*scratchpad* *memory*).

**Another personal anecdote.** As a student I worked two days per week at the University of Bonn as a student assistant in different projects (Retina implant, Growing-up robots) at the department of neuroinformatics. One day I helped to bring some stuff to the basement and my diploma thesis supervisor said: "Look Jürgen! This is an old neurocomputer, called SYNAPSE. Prof. Anlauf from the other department helped to build it." This old neurocomputer was a piece of neuroscience history and now it stood there with a lot of dust on it. What a pitty! He continued: "If you want to speed-up neural networks and you have 5 years, you can choose between two alternatives. Either, you invest 5 years to develop a new special chip for speeding up neural networks which is then restricted to some few models. Or you wait for 4 years, buy the newest hardware at that time for a fraction of the costs and you have still a year to develop any kind of neural network model in the remaining time on that hardware and the resulting speed will be the same compared to the first alternative." I am not sure, whether my old diploma thesis supervisor is still right with his prediction. Regarding the past I would say: he was right. But things seem to change now, since a big player is investing a lot in his own *AI accelerator* platform. I will not give you the name of this big player.

## Google

**The Tensor Processing Unit is being revealed.** At the Google I/O in May 2016 it was made public that Google had designed a custom ASIC (Application-Specific Integrated Circuit = "a special chip") that was developed specifically for speeding-up their machine learning applications. Norm Jouppi, perhaps the most important head during the development of this new chip, revealed in a post [18] at the same day that these custom ASICs had been deployed in Google data centers already a year before this Google I/O announcement. The new chip was named *Tensor Processing Unit (TPU)* and it was also revealed, that AlphaGo was already powered by TPUs in the matches against the Go world champion, Lee Sedol. So the Deep Learning algorithms that won against the Go world champion already ran on special hardware.

**Simple design. Fast development.** Only recently [19] details have been published about the internals of a TPU. The development time was extremely fast. The design, built and deployment in data centers needed only 15 months. The TPU was designed to be a co-processor similar to the old *Floating Point-Units (FPUs)*, connected to the CPU by a PCIe I/O Generation 3 bus with 16 lanes. In order to simplify the hardware design and testing, it was decided that the TPU does not fetch the instructions by itself from the memory. Instead, the CPU has to send the instructions to the TPU into an instruction buffer. Internal function blocks in the TPU are connected by 256-

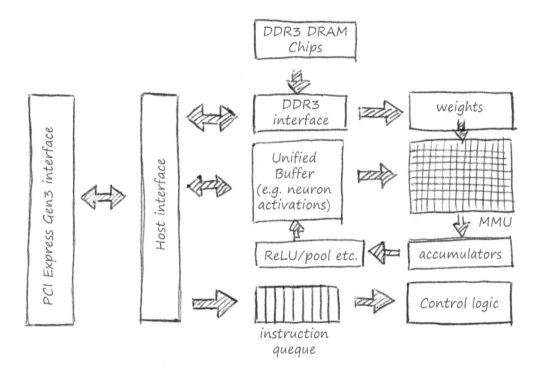

Figure 2.5: Schematic sketch of the function blocks of a Tensor Processing Unit (TPU). TPUs are optimized for matrix operations as, e.g., multiplying a matrix of neuron activations with a matrix of weights.

*byte*-wide paths!

**Matrix Multiplication Unit.** The heart of a TPU is the *Matrix Multiplication Unit (MMU)*. It contains a huge number of simple units which are called *MAC (Multiplier-Accumulate)*. A single MAC unit computes the product of two numbers and adds that product to an accumulator. The MMU of a TPU contains 256x256=65536 of such MACs that can perform 8-bit multiply-and-adds on signed or unsigned integers. Since matrix multiplications and convolutions are currently the most important operations for deep neural network models, the design of the TPU was optimized to speed-up exactly these operations.

**Data flow.** The input for the MMU are two memory structures, called "weights" and "unified buffer" (e.g. containing activation values of neurons). The 16-bit product outputs of the MACs are stored in a third memory structure, called "accumulators". These outputs are then transmitted to a unit called "activation" which can perform the non-linear transfer function of a neuron (such as ReLU, sigmoid, etc.) and pooling operations. The results are then stored in the unified buffer again.

**TPU block diagram.** A simplified schematic block diagram of a TPU can be found in Fig. 2.5. Note that according to the floor plan of the TPU die, the most chip area is taken by the MMU (24% of the chip area) and the "unified buffer" (29% of the chip area) for storing neuronal activations.

**2nd generation TPUs and Cloud TPUs.** The second generation of Google's TPUs were presented in May 2017 [7]. While the first generation TPUs were designed for inference (application of already trained models) and not for training of new models, the second generation TPUs were designed for both training and inference. A single 2nd generation TPU now provides 180 TFLOPs (180 TFLOPs = 180.000.000.000.000 = 180 trillions of floating point operations / second) and can be connected to a "pod" of 8x8 TPUs, which provides even 11,5 PFLOPs (= 11.500.000.000.000.000 = 11.5 quadrillions of floating point operations / second). These new TPUs are now also available for the public through the *Google Compute Engine* and are called *Cloud TPUs*.

## Nvidia

Many chip manufacturers want to have a piece of the cake with the title "Deep Learning boom". Nvidia announced in May 2017 [10] to offer a new computing platform soon, called *Nvidia Tesla V100*, that provides 120 TFLOPs [10]. For embedded systems such as robots and drones, the *Nvidia Jetson* TX1 and the new TX2 computing boards can be used. Since an important application for DL algorithms are *Advanced*

*Driver Assistance Systems (ADAS)*, Nvidia also tries to offer products for this market segment with the help of the *Nvidia Drive PX* and the new *Xavier AI Car Supercomputer* board announced in January 2017.

## 2.4 Software for DL

**Computation graphs.** Nearly all major deep learning software libraries such as TensorFlow, PyTorch, CNTK, Theano, etc. are based on *computation graphs*, i.e., you specify a sequence of operations that your input data (sometimes called "Tensor") flows through and each of these operations is represented by a node in the graph. Thereby, you define a forward pass for the network. *Automatic differentiation (AD)* is then used to compute the derivatives of functions that are stacked on each other. This allows to realize the backward pass in a computation graph, in which the derivatives of the functions are computed with respect to their different parameters. Then a small step into the direction of the negative gradients can be made in order to minimize some *loss function*. This approach is called *gradient descent*.

**Theano.** Theano is named after a Greek mathematician, who may have been Pythagoras' wife. Technically, Theano is actually not a machine learning library, but a numerical computation library for Python which makes use of NumPy (Python library for support of large, multi-dimensional arrays and matrices). Theano has been developed at Yoshua Bengio's machine learning lab at the University of Montreal with the goal to support rapid development of efficient machine learning algorithms. It is possible to use another library, called *Keras* on top of Theano.

**Keras.** Keras can be seen as a comfortable interface (a front-end) for machine learning programmers which can work with many different machine learning libraries as back-end. Currently Keras provides support for using MXNet, Deeplearning4j, Tensorflow, CNTK or Theano as a back-end.

**Caffe and Caffe2.** Caffe is a deep learning framework developed by Berkeley AI Research (BAIR) and open-source as well. It was originally created by Yangqing Jia during his PhD at UC Berkeley. It was written in C++ and provides interfaces for Python and MATLAB. Caffe2 was announced by Facebook in April 2017. It is developed by the team of Yangqing Jia, who now works at Facebook.

**TensorFlow.** TensorFlow was developed by the Google Brain team, first only for internal use at Google. Before, the closed-source library DistBelief was used. TensorFlow was then released under the Apache 2.0 open source license on 9 November 2015. Version 1.0.0 was released on 11 February 2017. However, although it is not even two years old at the time of writing this text, TensorFlow is now one of the most popular GitHub repositories and perhaps the most widely used library for Deep Learning with a lot of examples in the web.

**Torch and PyTorch.** Torch is a machine learning library with an API written in Lua. It is used by large companies such as Facebook and Twitter. Facebook open-sourced PyTorch, a Python API for Torch, in January 2017. It is therefore quite new and still in the Beta stadium.

*3*

# The biological role model: The Neuron

## 3.1 Your brain - A fascinating computing device

**My first brain dissection.** I really moved from Trier to Bonn to continue my studies of computer science there since they had an department for neuroinformatics and I had developed a passion for neuroscience. I was still a student in 2001, when I took part at a hands-on workshop about macroscopic brain structures at the University of Frankfurt. The goal was to give researchers in neuroscience the possibility to really hold the brain structures in their own hands which they are investigating and modeling in their daily work. The leader of the course was surprised when I registered for the course and said to me: "Oh, you are the first computer scientist that takes part in our course!". I was surprised as well since it was such a fascinating opportunity for computer scientists interested in neuroscience. Real brains were provided! In the program of the course it was mentioned to take one's white coat with to the course. Unfortunately, most often computer science students do not wear white coats. Do you wear a white coat while programming? So I borrowed one from the course leader. We started by opening the dura mater, the outermost layer of three membranes that envelop the brain. Each day new brain structures were dissected by the course participants and their presumed functions. Seeing and holding the different brain structures directly in my hands was a profound experience. It was like opening the tower of my first personal computer when I was a pupil and observing these many cables and electronic components on the motherboard. You do not really know what they do. Nevertheless, I have the feeling that it helps to see and touch things in order to start the process of understanding. However, I will never forget the obtrusive smell of formalin that was used to preserve the brains. Open desktop towers really smell better...

Figure 3.1: This is me as a student in 2001, taking part in a hands-on course on brain structures at the University of Frankfurt. Yes, it is a real neural network that I am holding in my hands! [Source: private photo archive]

**Neurons are quite small.** There are a lot of brain structures that can be distinguished already by the human eye without using a microscope. Nevertheless, all these different brain structures use the same building block: Neutrons! ... Uhm ... Neurons! You cannot see these neurons with your own eyes. They are too small. You need a

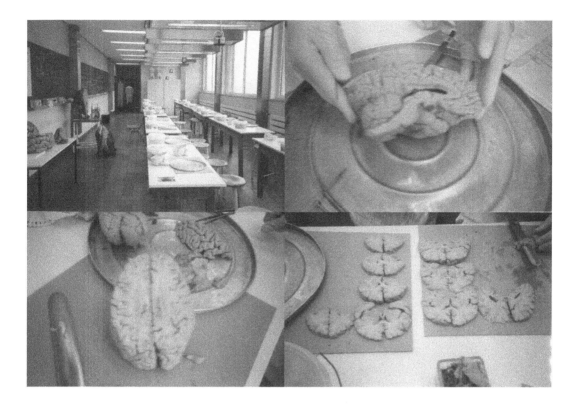

Figure 3.2: Some more impressions from my first brain dissection [Source: private photo archive]

microscope. However, there are very different neuron types. Depending on the neuron type the size and form varies largely. The most important part of a neuron, the neuron's soma (cell body), can have diameters between 5 $\mu$m and 100 $\mu$m (remember: 1000 $\mu$m = 1 mm). Take a tape measure and observe how large 1 mm is. In a cube of this side length (1 mm$^3$) you can find roughly between 20.000-40.000 neurons (see [40], p.18) depending on the brain region you consider! See Fig. 3.3 to be impressed how dense neurons can be packed due to their small size.

**Neuronal tissue.** These neurons connect to each other and thereby build a dense tissue. The part of the tissue that we can see with our own eyes and that is gray are mainly the cell bodies of the neurons (*gray matter*), while the white looking part of this tissue are the axons (*white matter*). This neuronal tissue is able to do all the magic that we would like to do with computers but what we cannot nowadays. Imagine that this tissue allows you to enter visual information to some of these neurons in that piece and it will compute whether it is the face of your mother or your girl

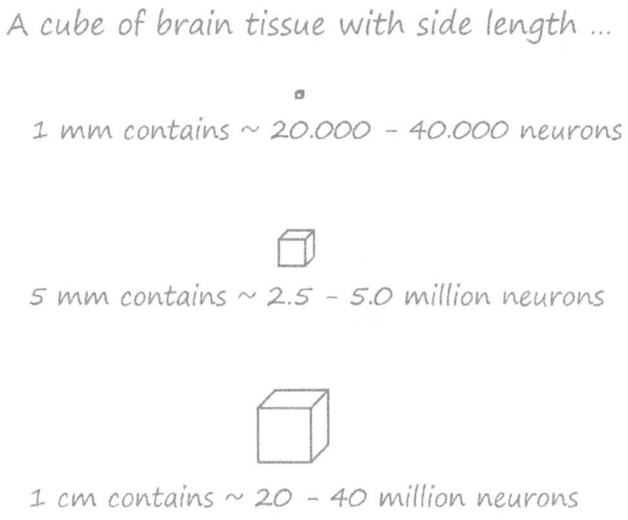

A cube of brain tissue with side length ...

1 mm contains ~ 20.000 - 40.000 neurons

5 mm contains ~ 2.5 - 5.0 million neurons

1 cm contains ~ 20 - 40 million neurons

Figure 3.3: Neurons are very small. Therefore a large number of neurons fit into small volumes.

friend. Imagine that another piece of tissue allows to output electrical signals that will activate muscles in our arms such that we can play a melody on a piano. Imagine that some other piece of neural tissue allows to analyze smells ("Hey! This smells like formalin") and another piece associates smells with experiences ("Hands-on workshop on brain structures").

## 3.2  Structure of a neuron

**A neuron can be divided into three parts.** The structure of a typical neuron is shown in Fig. 3.4. It can be divided into three parts: the *dendrites*, the *cell body (soma)* and the *axon*. The *dendrites* of a neuron can be considered as extensions of the cell body. The shape of the set of dendrites resembles a tree. For this, it is not surprisingly that the set of dendrites is also called the *dendritic tree*. The dendrites offer contact points (so called *synapses*) for the input signals from other neurons (*axodendritic synapses*). For this, it can be considered as the neuron's main input interface. However, it is also possible that a neuron establishes a connection to another neuron directly at its soma. In this case the connection is called an *axosomatic synapse*. Note, that there are even further types of synapses, e.g.: axosecretory synapses secrete directly into the bloodstream and axoaxonic synapses emit neurotransmitter into the extracellular fluid. The *cell body* or *soma* is responsible for the generation of proteins (large biomolecules) that are needed for the correct functioning of the nerve cell. The *axon* is a special extension of the soma that starts at the so called *axon hill* and typically branches out similar as the dendritic tree. The endings of the axons are called *axon terminals*.

## 3.3 Signal processing by action potentials

**Resting potential.** Imagine you measure the voltage between the inner part of the cell and its surrounding medium with the help of a voltmeter. You would recognize that the voltage is about -70 mV when there are no incoming signals. It is called the *resting potential* of a neuron whereby the inner of the cell is negatively charged compared to the extracellular environment. It is the result of different concentrations of ions in the fluids on both sides of the cell membrane which is generated by so called *ion pumps*.

**Threshold potential and action potential.** The input signals for a neuron come in as electrical signals at different positions of the dendritic tree. These individual electrical signals flow towards the soma and change the membrane potential of the cell. The incoming signals can increase or decrease this membrane potential and these changes sum up if the signals come in approximately at the same time. Now, something very interesting happens if the membrane potential is decreased such strongly that it reaches a value between approximately -50 mV and -55 mV! When this so called *threshold potential* is reached, voltage-gated ion channels will open and initiate a characteristic flow of ions. The membrane potential will change in a characteristic manner and will always show the same curve of change as depicted in Fig. 3.5. This signal will move along the axon into the direction of its endings, the synapses. It is called an *action potential*, or *nerve impulse* and mostly *spike* (due the spiky form of the curve of the change in the membrane potential). We also say: the *neuron fires*.

**Action potentials always show the same form.** Note, that this signal always has the same form! Thus it is actually a binary signal: Either the signal is present or not. However, the *firing rate*, i.e., the number of spikes a neuron fires per second, can be very differently. It cannot be arbitrary large, since there is a *refractory period* in which the neuron cannot generate a new action potential. Since an action potential spans a time period of about 3-4ms, maximum firing rates of about 250-330 spikes / second result.

## 3.4   Synapses

**The connection between two neurons.** Synapses are the connections between two neurons, see Fig. 3.6. However, there is a small room between the ending of the synapse of the sending neuron (*presynaptic neuron*) and the contact point of the receiving neuron (*postsynaptic neuron*), e.g., some location on the dendritic tree of the receiving neuron. This small room is called the *synaptic cleft*. This is true for the most synapses which are called *chemical synapses*. However, there is also another type of synapse - the *electrical synapse* - which works differently.

**Conversion of an electrical into a chemical signal.** Here is what happens if an action potential arrives at the end of a chemical synapse:

1. The action potential reaches the end of the axon of the presynaptic neuron, the *axon terminal*. It opens ion channels that allow positively charged $Ca^{2+}$ ions to enter.

2. Due to the increase of ions inside the axon terminal vesicles with neurotransmitters fuse with the membrane of the axon terminal. The neurotransmitter flow out of the vesicles into the synaptic cleft.

3. Neurotransmitters bind to neurotransmitter specific receptors at ion channels at the dendrite of the postsynaptic neuron. This opens the channels and lets certain ions that can pass the channels flow into the dendrite, thereby changing its membrane potential.

So the electrical signal (the action potential) at the presynaptic neuron will be converted into a chemical one that passes the synaptic cleft and will then result in a new electrical signal in the postsynaptic neuron.

**Effect on postsnaptic neuron.** The effect upon the postsynaptic neuron can be *excitatory*, a decrease of the membrane potential, or *inhibitory*, an increase in the membrane potential. A decrease of the membrane potential is also called an *Excitatory PostSynaptic Potential (EPSP)*, whereas an increase in the membrane potential is called an *Inhibitory PostSynaptic Potential (IPSP)*. However, whether the release of the neurotransmitters will lead to an EPSP or an IPSP is not determined by the presynaptic neuron or by the neurotransmitter, but by the type of receptor that is activated.

## 3.5 Neuronal plasticity

**Why this complex process?** But why did nature event this complex process of transferring an electrical signal from one nerve cell to another? Why does the axon terminal not just grow into the dendrite of the subsequent neuron and let the action potential jump directly to the subsequent neuron? Why this transformation of an electrical signal into a chemical one and back to an electrical signal?

**Synaptic plasticity as a subtype of neuronal plasticity.** The answer is that the synapse is the place where learning happens since the strength of the signal transmission is adjustable! This fact is called *synaptic plasticity* and it is a special case of a larger phenomenon called *neuronal plasticity*.

**Potentation vs. Depression.** If the presynaptic and the postsynaptic neuron fire approximately at the same time, the impact of future action potentials of the presynaptic neuron onto the postsynaptic neuron can grow in the sense that the EPSP or IPSP will become stronger. This process is called *potentiation*. If pre- and postsynaptic neurons do not fire simultaneously, this impact can also become weaker, which is called *depression*.

**Short-term vs. long-term plasticity.** Depending on the time scale on which these changes last, *short term potentiation/depression (STP/STD)* is distinguished from *long term potentiation/depression (LTP/LTD)*. Short term plasticity processes as STP and STD are changes that last for tens of milliseconds to a few minutes, while long term plasticity processes as LTP and LTD can last for hours, days or even a whole life. Some long term plasticity seems to have happened in my brain: I can still remember my hands-on course on brain structures that I participated in 2001.

**How is synaptic plasticity realized?** These synaptic plasticity effects seem to be achieved by nature with the help of a large set of different processes. For potentiation, e.g., at the presynaptic side, more neurotransmitters can be released, while at the postsynaptic side additional ion channels and receptors can be provided. For releasing more or less neurotransmitters at the presynaptic side and thereby increasing or decreasing the *strength of a synapse* different changes can be made responsible. E.g., the number of locations where the vesicles can fuse with the membrane and release their neurotransmitters into the synaptic cleft can be changed. Also the number of neurotransmitters stored in the vesicles in the axon terminals can be changed. Even the number of calcium channels at the axon terminals can be varied.

**The synaptic weight as data storage.** The impression arises that nearly all parameters of a synapse are modifiable in order to strengthen or weaken the synaptic transmission. This *strength of a synapse* seems to be an important or perhaps the most important place in the brain where information is stored.

**Structural plasticity.** However, the term neuronal plasticity does not only subsume synaptic plasticity processes, but also structural changes. E.g., the so called *dendritic spines*, the locations at the postsynaptic neurons that can be contacted by the axon terminals of the presynaptic neurons, can change their size. There can even be new synapses generated (*synaptogenesis*) or pruned (*synaptic pruning*) if synapses are not used. Axons can sprout new nerve endings.

## 3.6 Spike-Timing Dependent Plasticity (STDP)

**How is the synaptic weight changed?** If synapses are the place in brains in which information is stored, an important research questions arises: When exactly happens potentiation and when is depression initiated at a synapse? What is the synaptic learning algorithm or procedure that determines whether the synaptic strength is increased, decreased, or kept as it is?

**Hebbian learning as a key idea.** An early theory regarding this synaptic learning procedure stems from Donald Olding Hebb. Hebb was a professor for psychology at McGill University in Montreal / Canada. In his book "The Organization of Behavior: A Neuropsychological Theory" [16] Hebb wrote:

> *When an axon of cell A is near enough to excite cell B and repeatedly or persistently takes part in firing it, some growth process or metabolic change takes place in one or both cells such that A's efficiency, as one of the cells firing B, is increased*
> *(page 62 in his book [16])*

This important idea how learning at synapses could work influenced and inspired many neuroscientist that came after Hebb. It is called *Hebbian theory*, *Hebb's postulate* (there were no clear physiological evidences for this postulate at his time), or simply *Hebb's rule*.

On page 70 Hebb formulates the idea with other words:

> *The general idea is an old one, that any two cells or systems of cells that are repeatedly active at the same time will tend to become "associated", so*

*that activity in one facilitates activity in the other.*
*(page 70 in his book [16])*

Hebb was really good in generating postulates in 1949. He also postulated the following:

> *The most obvious and I believe much the most probable suggestion concerning the way in which one cell could become more capable of firing another is that synaptic knobs develop and increase the area of contact between the afferent axon and efferent soma ("Soma" refers to dendrites and body, or all of the cell except its axon)*
> *(page 62 in his book [16])*

As we know from the section about neuronal plasticity above, Hebb's postulate was correct: synapses can indeed grow and even new synapses can develop.

**The synaptic weight change curve.** It needed some decades for the development of neuroscientific measurement techniques to proof Hebb's postulate. But today we know, that Hebb's postulate is correct. In a work in 2001 [3] the exact synaptic weight change curve could be measured. It was shown that the relative timing of the spikes that occur at the presynaptic neuron and the postsynaptic neuron is crucial: If the postsynaptic neuron fires shortly after the presynaptic neuron has fired, the synaptic strength will be increased. If it is the reverse, i.e., the presynaptic neuron fires shortly after the postsynaptic neuron has fired, the synaptic strength will be decreased. Further, if the time difference between the pre- and postsynaptic spikes is more than ca. 80 ms, the strength of the synapse will not change.

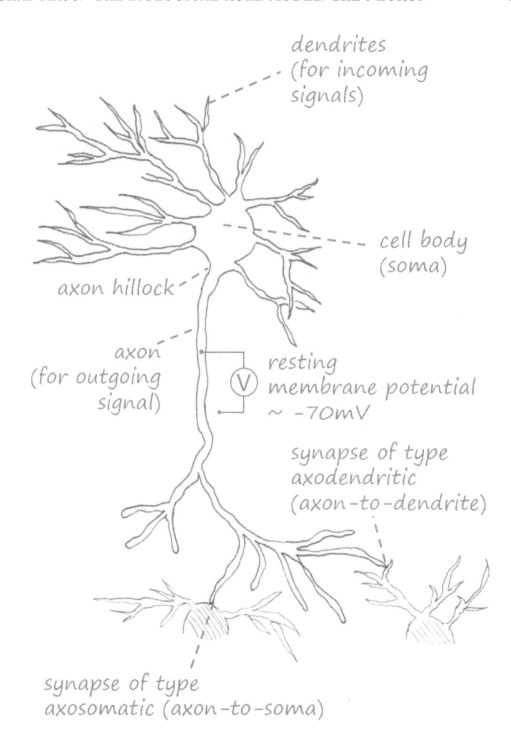

Figure 3.4: Structure of a neuron.

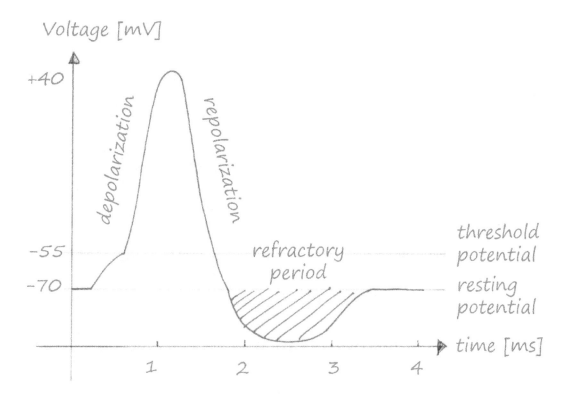

Figure 3.5: The action potential of a neuron is a characteristic change of the membrane potential that automatically happens if the neuron's membrane potential is decreased below the the threshold potential. It always shows this form! This is the signal which neurons send to subsequent neurons.

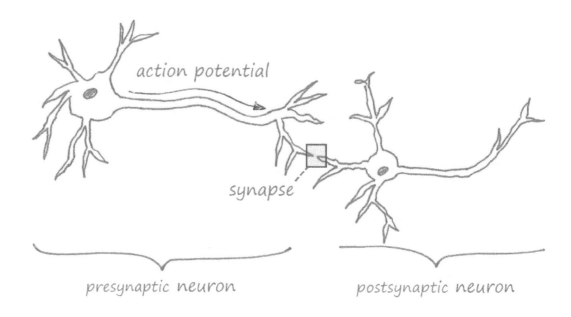

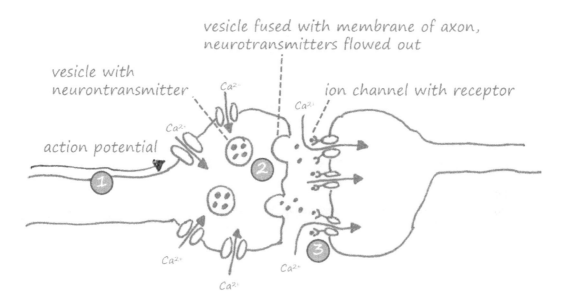

Figure 3.6: Structure and processes of a chemical synapse - the connection between two neurons.

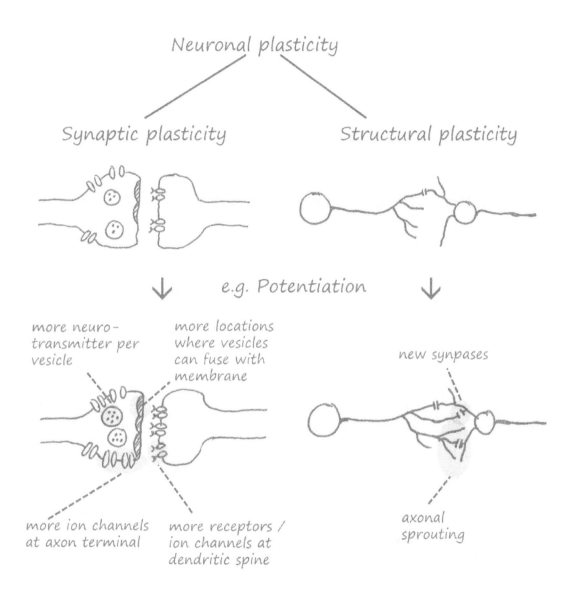

Figure 3.7: Neuronal plasticity can mean changes of the synaptic transmission strength, but also structural changes as new synapses or axonal sprouting.

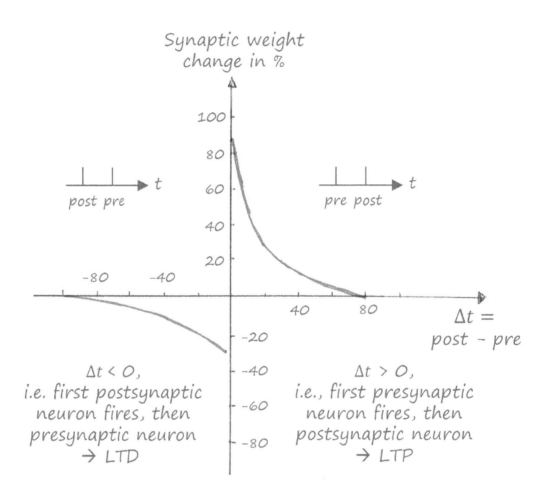

Figure 3.8: Spike-Timing Dependent Plasticity (STDP) curve (schematically drawn): If first the presynaptic neuron fires, then shortly after that the postsynaptic neuron, a long-term potentiation (LTP) process will increase the strength of that synapse. If first the postsynaptic neuron fires, then the presynaptic neuron, the transmission strength of the synapse will be decreased by a long-term depression (LTD) process.

# The many faces of a neuron

## 4.1 What is the function of a biological neuron?

**We should have some idea what a neuron does.** In order to develop a technical model of a biological neuron that can be used in simulations and artificial neural networks, we need to have some idea of what the function of a neuron is. What is just an artifact of how biological systems implement information processing with brains (also called "wetware") and can be neglected in a technical model and what is the core function that a biological neuron realizes? It is similar to the question of the function of legs. Legs consist of bones, tendons and muscles. Their function is to give an organism the ability of locomotion. However, it is not necessary to implement the function of locomotion exactly as nature does using bones, tendons and muscles. We can use servos, springs and aluminum parts to build artificial legs for robots.

**Wrong intuitions are taught.** In popular science presentation sources we can often read a <u>wrong</u> description of the function of a neuron:

> *"Neurons are a special type of cell with the sole purpose of transferring information around the body"* [20]

Such wrong statements unfortunately lead the understanding of the reader into a wrong direction ("Aha! So a neuron is a cable for signals!"). Ask yourself: If all these 86 billion neurons act as cables in your brain and just transfer signals from one neuron to the next, where does the actual computation happen?

**Remember what we already know about biological neurons.** However, with the knowledge about some details of biological neurons from the previous chapter it should not be too difficult for you to postulate another theory of the function of a neuron! First, give it try! Then read the following.

We know that neurons receive signals from other neurons with the help of their dendritic tree and that these signals can increase or decrease the membrane potential of the neuron. Only if a certain threshold of the membrane potential is reached, a new signal will be generated and be transferred to many other neurons using the neuron's axon. So the neuron accumulates information from many other sources and "makes a decision" to inform other neurons or not.

## 4.2   Neurons as spatial feature or evidence detectors

**Detecting coincidence of spatial patterns.** Have a look at Fig. 4.1. Imagine there is a receptive field for neurons 1-3 of size 7x7. However, only the inputs to neuron 1-3 are drawn that are largely excitatory. All the other (non-drawn) inputs are assumed to have neither an EPSP or IPSP effect onto the neurons. Imagine that neuron 1 spikes if the three "pixels" (photoreceptors) that form a small horizontal line are present and correspondingly neuron 2 and 3. Now imagine that the synaptic weights to neuron 4 are set such that only if neurons 1-3 spike roughly at the same time, neuron 4 will spike as well. In such a scenario, neuron 4 would only spike if the spatial pattern that forms a "seven" is present. Thus neurons can function as a spatial feature detector.

**A neuron is not just an AND gate.** It seems that a neuron is very similar to a logical AND gate, right? In the above example neuron 4 only fires,

```
if (neuron-1-spikes) AND (neuron-2-spikes)
AND (neuron-3-spikes)
```

However, we could also imagine another set of synaptic weights such that neuron 4 already fires if only two of the neurons 1-3 spike. In this case, neuron 4 would detect also other spatial patterns than just a "seven". Then the logical function that neuron 4 realizes could be described similar to:

```
if (neuron-1-spikes AND neuron-2-spikes) OR
(neuron-1-spikes AND neuron-3-spikes) OR
(neuron-2-spikes AND neuron-3-spikes)
```

But we could also imagine another setting (see Fig. 4.2) with such strong synaptic weights between neurons 1-3 and neuron 4 such that a large firing rate of only one of these three neurons 1-3 could already be sufficient to let neuron 4 spike. For this, it is more appropriate to think of the neuron as a spatial pattern (or feature) detector that accumulates evidence from different sources where the evidence is a continuous value (encoded by the firing rate) and the pattern detection result is encoded as a continuous value (the firing rate) as well. In this sense, a neuron can be thought of an evidence detector, which can signal evidence for a certain pattern if enough conditions are met.

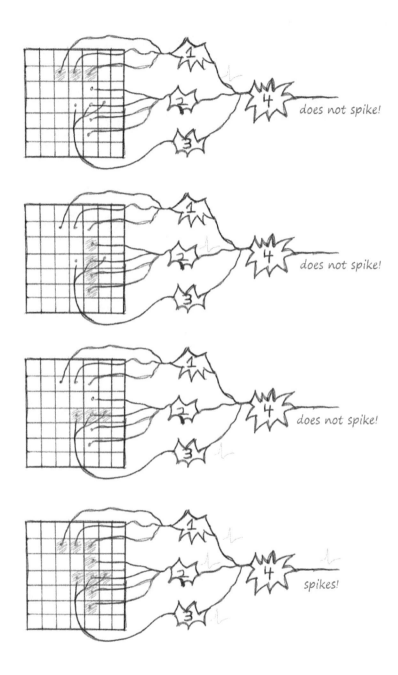

Figure 4.1: Neurons 1,2 and 3 fire, if certain vertical or horizontal lines are visible. However, neuron 4 only fires if neuron 1,2 and 3 fire roughly at the same time. Thereby neuron 4 is able to detect a spatial pattern that corresponds to the number seven.

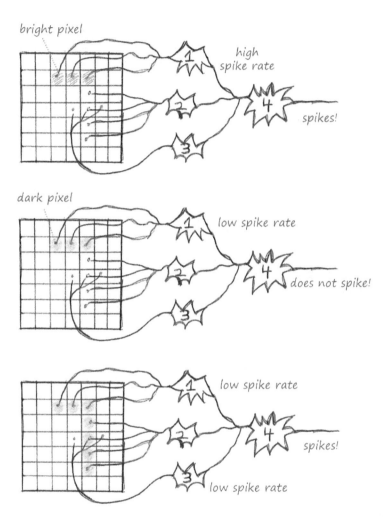

Figure 4.2: Another setting in which a single input neuron 1-3 that fires frequently can already result in a spiking neuron 4. If one of the input neurons fires only with a low firing rate, neuron 4 will not be excited. However, If two of the input neurons fire at a low firing rate, neuron 4 will be excited.

## 4.3 Neurons as temporal coincidence detectors

**Neurons can receive inputs from different sensor modalities.** In the previous example neuron 4 was able to detect a spatial pattern. But there is no need that the input connections to neuron 4 stem from a spatially connected region. Have a look at Fig. 4.3. Imagine you have never seen a coffee before! (What a nightmare!). Then someone shows you a picture of a coffee and tells you that this is a coffee. Let's say that the visual evidence of the coffee cup is encoded by the firing of neuron 1 (or a set of neurons, a neuron group 1) and the information that is given to you ("This is a coffee!") is encoded by the firing of neuron 4 (or a set of neurons, a neuron group 4). So both neurons fire together and this could result in a strengthen of the synapse (or synapses) from neuron 1 to neuron 4. Let's say that this synapse is strong enough to excite neuron 4 if neuron 1 fires (the visual evidence is enough to recognize that there is a coffee).

Figure 4.3: Neuron 4 integrates sensoric information from three different sensor modalities. In order to be sure that there is a coffee, it could mean that we need to detect the simultaneous firing of neurons 1-3, which corresponds to the evidence for the coffee concept from visual, smell and haptic modalities.

**Associative learning.** Now some days later you stand up in the morning, arrive in the kitchen and for the first time your wife made a coffee for you. You see it, but you can also smell it and you can even touch the warm coffee cup with your hands. The visual evidence excites neuron 4 and due to the fact that neuron 2 (encoding the smell) and neuron 3 (encoding some haptic information) fire at the same time, *associative learning* happens! The connection between neuron 2 and neuron 4 will be strengthened and also the connection between neuron 3 and neuron 4 due to the synaptic plasticity learn curve discussed before. Imagine you come to the breakfast the next morning and you do not see where the coffee cup is standing. It might be that the synaptic strength between neuron 2 and neuron 4 is already large enough to excite neuron 4: You can not see the coffee, you do not hold it in your hands, but already the smell is enough to associate it with the concept of a coffee (neuron 4).

**This is a simplistic example.** Please note that this is a highly simplistic description using only 4 neurons. Most neuroscience researchers will probably agree that the visual information that encodes a coffee cup, the information that encodes the smell and the sensation of holding a coffee cup in the hands and the concept of a coffee cup will not be encoded by just the firing of a single neuron each. The hypothetical cell that would fire if only one specific object (person, face, etc.) is perceived are called *grandmother cells*. Most neuroscientists believe that such cells do not exist. Instead *cell assemblies* (*neural ensembles*) are supposed to encode these concepts using many neurons, while their characteristic firing pattern is called a *population code*.

**Temporal detection.** However, the weights between neuron 1-3 to neuron 4 could also be set in another way, such that neuron 4 only fires if neuron 1-3 fire at the same time. In this case, the evidences stemming from the three different sensor modalities all need to be there, in order to conclude that there is a coffee cup. This means that neuron 4 would act a temporal coincidence detector.

## 4.4 Perceptron neuron model

**One of the most important neuron models.** The probably most widely used neuron model is the *Perceptron*. It is actually not only the name for a neuron model, but also the name of a first neuro-computer, that was build by *Frank Rosenblatt* already in 1958. Components of the Perceptron model are illustrated in Fig. 4.4.

**Firing rate.** The model makes an important simplification compared to the biological neuron model which is a strong assumption: It does not model at which point in time a neuron spikes, but only how often it spikes within some time frame, i.e., it "only" models the firing rate of a neuron. The firing rate is modeled by the help of a

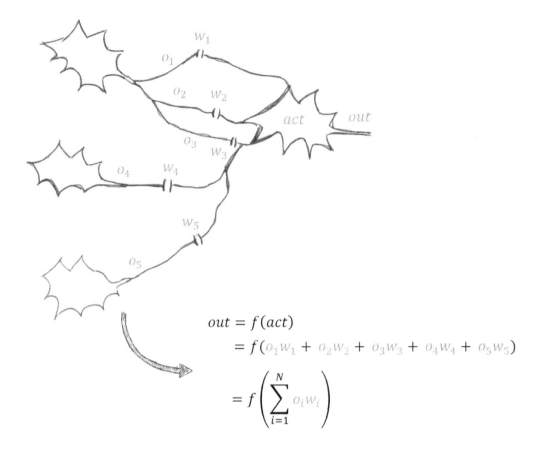

$$out = f(act)$$
$$= f(o_1 w_1 + o_2 w_2 + o_3 w_3 + o_4 w_4 + o_5 w_5)$$
$$= f\left(\sum_{i=1}^{N} o_i w_i\right)$$

Figure 4.4: The perceptron neuron model.

real number *out*.

**Synaptic weights.** Further, the model abstracts from geometric features of the neuron: there is no modeling where a synapse is located or how long dendrites and axons are. Only the synaptic transmission strength is modeled using the help of weights $w_i$. Since the strength of an EPSP or an IPSP are not only the result of the synaptic transmission strength, but also depend on the firing rate of the presynaptic neuron, the influence on the membrane potential *act* by an individual presynaptic neuron is modeled by $o_i * w_i$, i.e., the higher the firing rate of the presynaptic neuron and the higher the synaptic weight, the larger is the influence onto the membrane potential of the postsynaptic neuron. Note, that synaptic weights are modeled by real numbers and can therefore be negative as well, corresponding to inhibitory synapses. The value *act* is the model for the current value of the membrane potential. Since in real neurons the membrane potential results by EPSP and IPSP signals induced from several different presynaptic neurons, *act* is computed by the weighted sum of the firing rates of all sending neurons: $act = \sum_{i=1}^{N} o_i w_i$.

**Transfer function.** But why do we need this function $f$ that takes the activation value *act* as an argument? The transfer function is used to model actually two different aspects of the biological role model. First, the fact that real neurons do not fire until the threshold potential is reached. Second, the fact that real neurons cannot show negative or arbitrarily high firing rates. Remember that after a neuron has fired, there is a refractory period in which the resting potential is recovered and in which the neuron cannot fire. We said that due to the time a spike needs and due to the time of the refractory period, usually a maximum firing rate of about 300 spikes / second results. For this, Perceptrons are often used with firing rates limited to some interval $[0, max]$, which can be achieved by using some transfer function $f$ that maps the sum of the weighted inputs - the activation *act* - to exactly this interval, even for extreme large absolute values of *act*. Fig. 4.5 shows two transfer functions that take these considerations into account.

The *ramp transfer function* is defined by

$$out = f(x) = \begin{cases} 0 & , \ act < T1 \\ \frac{act-T1}{T2-T1} & , \ T1 \leq act \leq T2 \\ 1 & , \ act > T2 \end{cases} \qquad (4.1)$$

and realizes a ramp with the same slope everywhere on the ramp.

The *logistic transfer function* is defined by

$$out = f(x) = \frac{1}{1 + exp(-\gamma * act)} \qquad (4.2)$$

and realizes a soft version of the ramp function. The parameter $\gamma$ can be used to control how steep the ramp shall be. Making $\gamma$ larger will make the ramp steeper and steeper. For $\gamma \to \infty$ another transfer function results that is sometimes used as well:

It is called the *step function (Heaviside)* and is depicted in Fig. 4.6 and is defined by:

$$out = f(x) = \begin{cases} 0 & , \ act \leq T \\ 1 & , \ act > T \end{cases} \qquad (4.3)$$

Note that the usage of the step transfer function means that the output of a neuron is modeled by just a binary value. Either it fires (1) or it fires not (0).

## 4.5 Neurons as filters

**Similarity of the Perceptron neuron model with technical filters.** Modeling biological neurons using these components (weights, activation, transfer function) and computing the activation as the sum of weighted inputs unveils another face of neurons. The sum

$$act = \sum_{i=1}^{N} o_i w_i \tag{4.4}$$

can also be rewritten using linear algebra notation by

$$act = \mathbf{o} \cdot \mathbf{w} \tag{4.5}$$

where $\mathbf{o} = (o_1, o_2, ..., o_N)$ is the vector of the firing rates of the presynaptic neurons and $\mathbf{w} = (w_1, w_2, ..., w_N)$ is the vector of the corresponding weights. The operation $\cdot$ is called *dot product* or *scalar product* which takes two vectors of equal lengths (sequences of numbers) and maps it to single real number.

Now, this inner product is exactly what is computed as the basic operation in image processing if you want, e.g., to blur or sharpen an image or detect edges. The weights are then written in a two-dimensional arrangement and are called a *kernel*, *filter kernel* or *convolution matrix* $K$. The pixel values of the image region that is currently processed are also written in a two-dimensional arrangement $I$. Again, the result of this so called *convolution* is a real number which is then used as a new pixel value. For this it is also reasonable to compare the function of a neuron with a technical filter, see Fig.4.8.

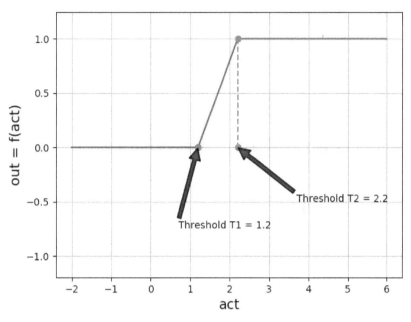

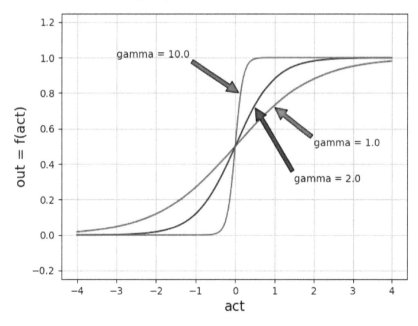

Figure 4.5: Two transfer functions that make sure, that 1. the activation *act* of a neuron is never mapped to a negative firing rate and 2. the firing rate is limited to some maximum value.

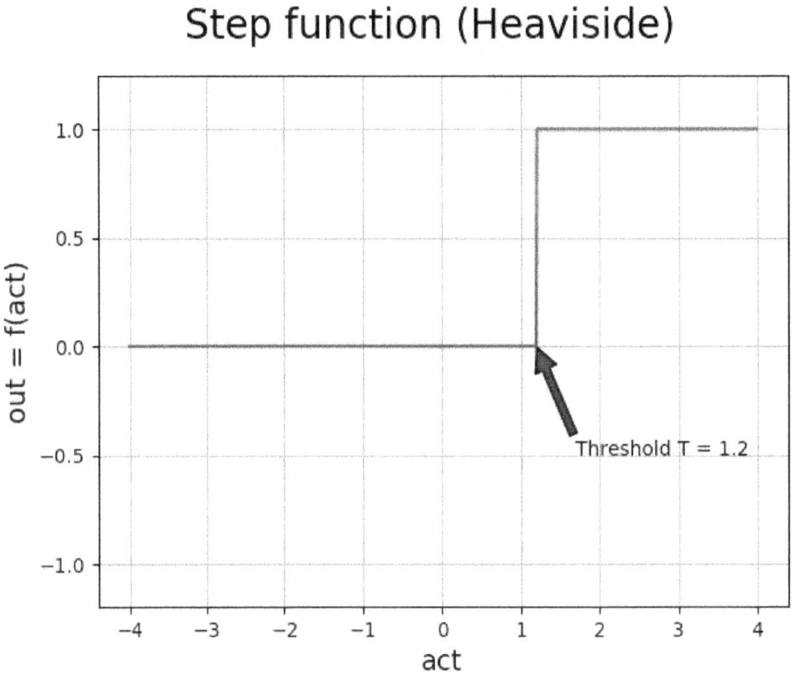

## Step function (Heaviside)

Figure 4.6: The step function maps all activations *act* of a neuron either to a zero firing rate or a firing rate of 1.

```
1   # ---
2   # Python code to generate the logistic transfer function plot
3   # ---
4
5   import numpy as np
6   import matplotlib.pyplot as plt
7
8   # Define the logistic transfer function
9   def f(x,gamma):
10      return 1.0 / (1.0 + np.exp(-gamma*x))
11
12  # Prepare a vector of x-values
13  x = np.arange(-4.0, 4.0, 0.01)
14
15  # Set title of the plot
16  fig = plt.figure()
17  fig.suptitle('Logistic transfer function', fontsize=20)
18
19  # Set y-range to display, use a grid, set label for axes
20  plt.ylim(-0.25, 1.25)
21  plt.grid(True)
22  plt.xlabel('act', fontsize=14)
23  plt.ylabel('out = f(act)', fontsize=14)
24
25  # Plot 3 versions of the logistic transfer function
26  # using different values for gamma
27  plt.plot(x, [f(b,1.0)  for b in x], 'r')
28  plt.plot(x, [f(b,2.0)  for b in x], 'b')
29  plt.plot(x, [f(b,10.0) for b in x], 'g')
30
31  # Show arrows with annotation text which gamma value
32  # was used for which graph
33  plt.annotate('gamma = 1.0', xy=(1, 0.72), xytext=(2, 0.5),
34  arrowprops=dict(facecolor='red', shrink=0.01))
35
36  plt.annotate('gamma = 2.0', xy=(0.5, 0.72), xytext=(1.5, 0.3),
37  arrowprops=dict(facecolor='blue', shrink=0.01))
38
39  plt.annotate('gamma = 10.0', xy=(0.1, 0.8), xytext=(-3, 1.0),
40  arrowprops=dict(facecolor='green', shrink=0.01))
41
42  # Generate image file
43  fig.savefig('tf_logistic.png')
44
45  # Show the plot also on the screen
46  plt.show()
47
```

Figure 4.7: Python code I used to generate the plot of the logistic transfer function.

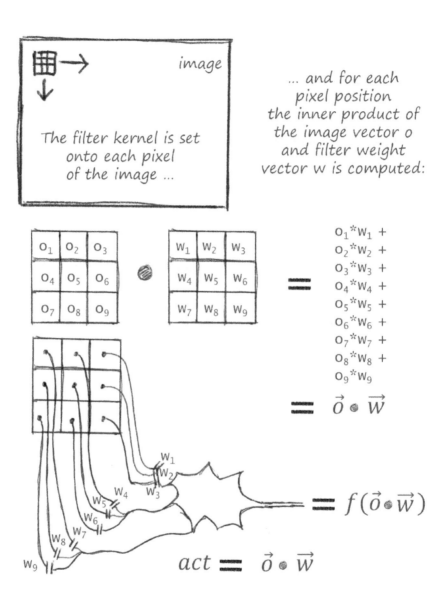

Figure 4.8: A neuron can also be considered as performing a filtering operation known from image processing. In this view, the synaptic weights correspond to the values of the filter kernel matrix while the firing rates of the sending neurons correspond to the pixel values of the image region that is filtered.

## 4.6 Other neuron models

**How to classify neuron models?** While in the field of DL, the Perceptron model is dominant, there are a lot more of different neuron models, which are used in Neuroscience. These different neuron models can be categorized according to their granularity at which processes and properties of biological neurons are modeled.

**Non-spiking neuron models / Firing rate models.** On this spectrum, the Perceptron neuron model can be considered as a very abstract model. It is a so called *non-spiking neuron model* or *firing rate model*: not the time points are simulated at which a neuron spikes, but its average spike rate within some time window, which is called its *firing rate*. However, the Perceptron neuron model is not the only non-spiking neuron model. As you will see in a later chapter, a simple neural network model which is called the *Self-Organizing Map* does not use Perceptrons, but "neurons", which can compute a distance between its inputs (input vector) and a stored vector.

**Spiking neuron models.** If also time points are modeled at which neurons spike, we are in the domain of the so called *spiking neurons*. However, the models in this domain further differ regarding the question whether neurons are simply modeled as points or whether geometrical aspects (size, detailed 2D or 3D structure of dendrites and axon) are modeled as well. In the first case, we are talking about *point based models* or *single compartment models*. These models ignore the *morphological structure* of neurons. In the second case, we are talking about *multi-compartment models* which are considered as one of the most detailed set of models for biological neurons.

**Different complexity of spiking neuron models.** The *Hodgkin - Huxely neuron model* is probably the most prominent spiking neuron model and stems from Alan Hodgkin and Andrew Huxely from 1952. In their experimental research they used the squid giant axon which has a large diameter of up to 1mm and approximately 0.5mm in average. They investigated the voltage dependence of ion channels and came up with a model that models the behavior of the ion channels through a set of four differential equations. The parameters to be set for this model stem directly from their experimental research. Since the model is computationally demanding, other researchers tried to simplify this model. Examples are the *Hindmarsh-Rose-Modell* with three differential equations or the *FithHugh-Nagumo neuron model* and the *Izhikevich neuron model* with two differential equations.

**Leaky Integrate-And-Fire (LIAF) neurons.** An even simpler spiking neuron model is the *Leaky Integrate-and-Fire neuron model*. While in the spiking models mentioned above, a biological plausible form of the action potential is achieved automatically with the help of a set of differential equations, the form of an action potential cannot be simulated with this model. Instead, if the threshold potential is reached, a "spike" is said to happen and the simulated membrane potential is reset to the resting potential and the summation of incoming signals starts again from this reseted resting potential.

## 4.7 Neural Coding

**Rate coding.** In 1926 Ed Adrian and Yngve Zotterman did an important experiment. Different weights were attached to a muscle and the number of spikes within a time interval (spike frequency, or firing rate) in sensory nerves innervating the muscle were observed while the weight was increased. They observed that the frequency of spikes increased as the weight was increased. For this, it seems that the firing rate encodes the weight. This is the idea of *rate coding*.

**Temporal coding.** In contrast, the *temporal coding* idea suggests that the exact time points or at least the time between subsequent action potentials - the *Inter-Spike Interval (ISI)* or *Inter-Pulse Interval (IPI)* - is not a result of irregularities, but important and encodes information as well! So according to temporal coding the two spike trains $T1 = 1000111001$ and $T2 = 0101101100$ (1=spike, 0=no spike) would encode a different information, while according to rate coding it would mean the same information since both spike trains show a firing rate of 5 spikes / interval, i.e., the same firing rate.

**Which code is used?** Since in motor neurons, e.g., the strength at which an innervated muscle is flexed depends solely on the firing rate, we can say that rate codes are used in the brain. But are used temporal codes as well? Yes! E.g., flies have so called H1 neurons which are located in the visual cortex. These neurons respond to horizontal motions in the visual field of the fly and help to stabilize their flight by initiating motor corrections. Interestingly, it was possible to reconstruct the movements seen by the fly using measurements of just the inter-spike intervals. This can be seen as proof that temporal coding is used in brains as well.

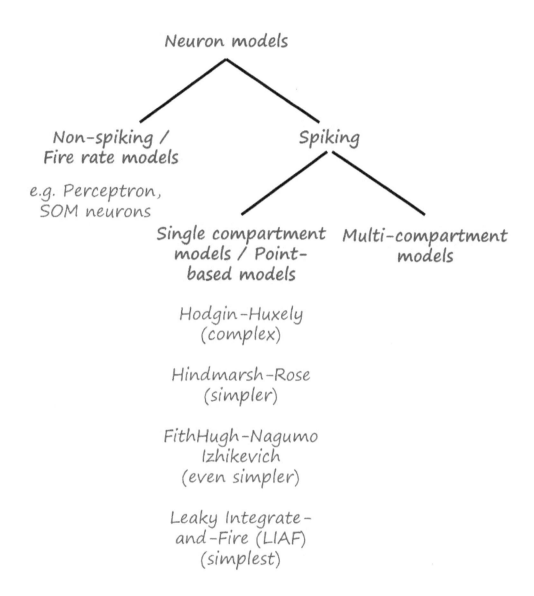

Figure 4.9: While in Deep Learning mainly Perceptron neuron models are used, many more neuron models are used in neuroscience which are also biologically more plausible. However, this "more" of plausibility comes with higher simulation costs due to the higher complexity of the models.

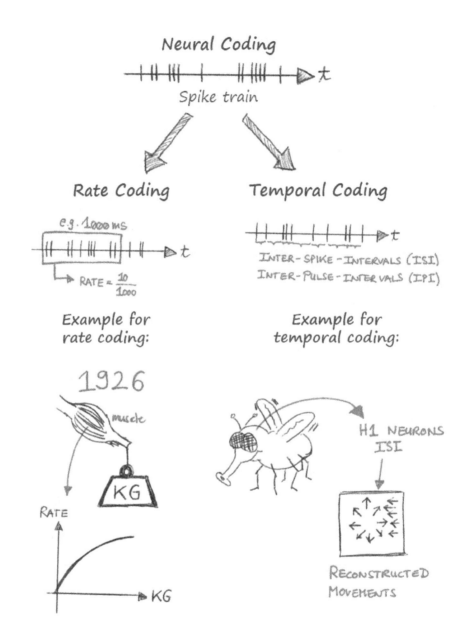

Figure 4.10: Information is encoded by neurons using rate codes and temporal codes.

# 5

# The Perceptron

## 5.1 The Perceptron neuro-computer

**An early neuro computer.** The perceptron is a neuron model. However, it was also a first neurocomputer invented by the American psychologist Frank Rosenblatt (1928-1971). Rosenblatt obtained his Ph.D. in 1956 from Cornell University and then went to Cornell Aeronautical Laboratory in Buffalo (New York). Here he invented the Perceptron learning algorithm which was firstly tested on a IBM 704 computer and only later implemented in hardware, the "Mark 1 Perceptron" neuro computer. The hardware was intended to do image recognition. As input sensors 400 photocells were used, which were arranged in a 20x20 grid (= only 400 pixel input image!). The photocells were connected to association units", which responded to certain features in the 20x20 input image. The wiring from the photocells to these association units ("features") was manually established and allowed to experiment with different input features. The association units were connected to "response units" which encoded the class that was detected. The weights from the association units to the response units were adjustable and could be learned. However, the "Mark 1 Perceptron" was an electro-mechanical computer: the weights were not stored in memory cells, but encoded by the position of potentiometers (resistors where the resistance can be changed by mechanical operations)!

Mark I Perceptron neurocomputer (1957)

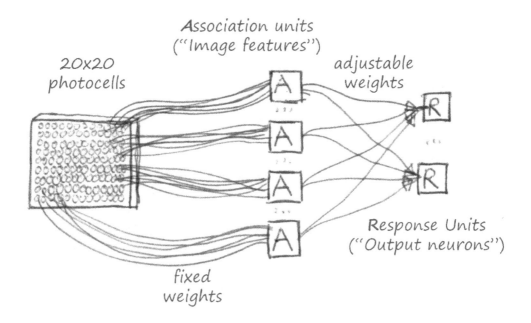

Figure 5.1: The "Mark 1 Perceptron" was a first neuro computer that was able to classify images of 26 different letters of different typefaces with a correct classification rate of 79% (see [15], p.1-3). And this already at the end of the 1950s! The "Mark 1 Perceptron" contained 512 association units and 8 response units, which allowed for $2^8 = 256$ different output patterns.

**Neuron model corresponding to the "Mark 1 Perceptron".** In an article about his neurocomputer that Frank Rosenblatt wrote in 1960 for the "Digital Computer Newsletter" of the Office of Naval Research / Mathematical Science Division, he wrote:

> *The response units are two state-devices which emit one output if their inputs is positive and a different output if their input is negative. [15]*

So the corresponding neuron model for the "Response units" corresponds to a neuron that computes its activity as the weighted sum of its inputs and then maps this activity to a binary output using the ramp transfer function:

$$act = \sum_{i=1}^{N} o_i w_i \quad \text{and} \quad out = f(act) = \begin{cases} 0 & , \; act \leq 0 \\ 1 & , \; act > 0 \end{cases} \tag{5.1}$$

However, instead of taking $act = 0$ as the threshold, where the output of the neuron jumps from 0 to 1, we can generalize this model to a model with an arbitrary threshold $T$:

$$act = \sum_{i=1}^{N} o_i w_i \quad \text{and} \quad out = f(act) = \begin{cases} 0 & , \; act \leq T \\ 1 & , \; act > T \end{cases} \tag{5.2}$$

Now comes a little trick. We want a learning algorithm not only to adjust the weights $w_i$ automatically, but also the threshold $T$. For this, we reformulate the last equations to:

$$act = \sum_{i=1}^{N} o_i w_i - T \quad \text{and} \quad out = f(act) = \begin{cases} 0 & , \; act \leq 0 \\ 1 & , \; act > 0 \end{cases} \tag{5.3}$$

and then establish a new input $o_0$ called "bias", which has always (!) the value 1 and consider the threshold T as another weight $w_0$ which can be learned as well.

$$act = \sum_{i=1}^{N} o_i w_i + o_0 w_0 = \sum_{i=0}^{N} o_i w_i \quad \text{and} \quad out = f(act) = \begin{cases} 0 & , \; act \leq 0 \\ 1 & , \; act > 0 \end{cases} \tag{5.4}$$

## 5.2 Perceptron learning

**The perceptron learning algorithm** Initially Rosenblatt experimented with the task to classify images each showing one of the 26 letters of the alphabet. Now the question was: how to adjust the weights? The basic idea behind the learning algorithm Rosenblatt found was extremely simple: Given an input pattern (20x20 input image), let the Perceptron compute its outputs ("Response units") and then let us compare what we have at each output value and what we wanted. Let us denote the actual output by *out* and the desired output by $t$ (also called a "teacher signal"). The difference *error* = $t - out$ is called an *error signal*.

**Case 1: Output is correct.** If *out* = 1 and $t = 1$ (or *out* = 0 and $t = 0$), the weights seem to be ok. So we should make sure, that the weights are not changed.

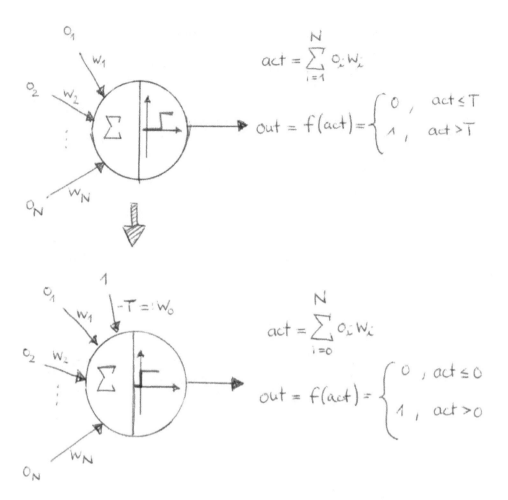

Figure 5.2: The "bias trick". In order to let a learning algorithm not only learn the weights $w_i$, but also learn the threshold T of the ramp function, we establish a new input weight $w_0$ and a new input $o_0$ which is always 1. This new input is called a "bias".

**Case 2: Output is wrong.** If $out = 0$ and $t = 1$ we should increase the weights coming from <u>active</u> inputs since weights are too small. We cannot blame weights $w_i$ to be incorrectly if the corresponding input $o_i$ is "quite", i.e., $o_i = 0$. For this, we should only correct a weight $w_i$ if $o_i \neq 0$. If $out = 1$ and $t = 0$ we should decrease the weights coming from <u>active</u> inputs since weights are too large.

We can therefore use the following weight update formula to update each weight by

$w_i = w_i + \Delta w_i$ with:

$$\Delta w_i = \alpha(t - out)o_i \tag{5.5}$$

Note, that if $o_i = 0$ no weight change will happen as desired. If the output *out* is too small compared to $t$, i.e., $t - out > 0$, the weights will be increased. If the output *out* is too large compared to $t$, i.e., $t - out < 0$, the weights will be decreased. $\alpha$ is called a *learning rate* and $\alpha \ll 1$ (e.g. $\alpha = 0.01$) makes sure that we do not change the weights too quickly. Let's say that for one input pattern the weight $w_i$ is too small. Then we increase the weight $w_i$. Then for the next input pattern the weight $w_i$ is to large. Then we decrease this weight $w_i$. $\alpha \ll 1$ makes sure, we do not forget everything we have learned before since we update the weights only slightly.

## 5.3 Perceptron in Python

**MNIST dataset.** "The MNIST database of handwritten digits" is an old benchmark for image recognition systems. It consists of 60.000 training images and 10.000 test images of the digits 0-9, where each 28x28 pixel image has pixel values between 0.0 and 1.0. It is widely used in the machine learning community for training, testing and comparing the performance of different machine learning algorithms. The smallest error reported so far is an error rate of 0.21% using a committee of 5 six-layer CNNs. Due to this small error rate, the low resolution of the images and the small number of classes (only 10 classes) of this benchmark, it can be said, that the benchmark has lost its popularity. However, it is now widely used in didactics on machine learning due to its simple structure.

**Fast code walk-through.** The code below starts with reading in the MNIST data using the functionality of TensorFlow. It then displays some of the MNIST 784 long input vectors by reshaping them to 2D matrices of size 28x28. The actual generation and learning of the Perceptron can be found in the function `generate_and_train_perceptron_classifier`.

Here a 2D matrix of size 785x10 is generated. Why 785x10? The 28x28 input images considered as 1D input vectors have actually length 784. But remember, that we need an additional bias input which is always "1". For this, the input vectors have length 785. The 10 is the number of output vectors. We use one output vector to encode each of the 10 classes (digits "0"-"9") that are present in this classification problem. Can you find the actual computation of the output values of these 10 neurons? It can be found in line 139 and 140. Line 139 computes the activity for each of the 10 neurons. Then in line 140 the activations are mapped using the ramp transfer functions.

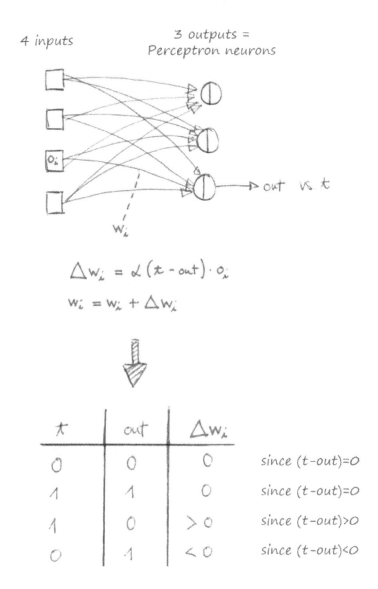

Figure 5.3: The Perceptron learning rule is a straightforward approach to adjust the weights into the correct direction by comparing the desired output $t$ with the actual output *out*. Note that the inputs $o_i$ are assumed to be positive.

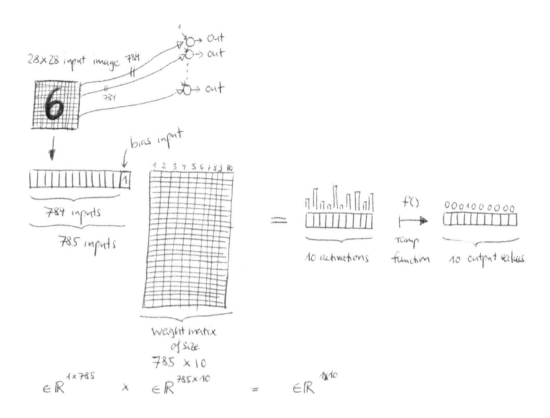

Figure 5.4: The computations in a Perceptron can be modeled using a matrix multiplication of the input and weight matrix and applying a transfer function f element wise on the resulting activation vector.

```
1  # The MNIST dataset http://yann.lecun.com/exdb/mnist/
2  # consists of 28x28 pixel images:
3  #    - 55.000 training images
4  #    - 10.000 test images
5
6  # for random numbers
7  from random import randint
8
9  # we will use OpenCV to display the data
10 import cv2
11
12 # we will use TensorFlow to access the MNIST data
13 from tensorflow.examples.tutorials.mnist import input_data
14
15 # for working with N-dimensional arrays
```

```
16  import numpy as np
17
18
19  '''
20  The ramp transfer function
21  '''
22  def f(x):
23      if (x<=0):
24          return 0
25      else:
26          return 1
27
28  f = np.vectorize(f)
29
30
31  '''
32  Donwload & unpack the MNIST data
33  Also prepare direct access to data matrices:
34  x_train, y_train, x_test, y_test
35  '''
36  def read_mnist_data():
37
38      # 1. download and read data
39      mnist = input_data.read_data_sets("MNIST_data/", one_hot=True)
40
41      # 2. show data type of the mnist object
42      print("type of mnist is ", type(mnist))
43
44      # 3. show number of training and test examples
45      print("There are ", mnist.train.num_examples,
46            " training examples available.")
47      print("There are ", mnist.test.num_examples,
48            " test examples available.")
49
50      # 4. prepare matrices (numpy.ndarrays) to
51      #    access the training / test images and labels
52      x_train = mnist.train.images
53      y_train = mnist.train.labels
54      x_test = mnist.test.images
55      y_test = mnist.test.labels
56      print("type of x_train is", type(x_train))
57      print("x_train: ", x_train.shape)
58      print("y_train: ", y_train.shape)
59      print("x_test: ", x_test.shape)
60      print("y_test: ", y_test.shape)
61
62      return x_train,y_train,x_test,y_test
63
64
65
```

```python
66  '''
67  This function will show n random example
68  images from the training set, visualized using
69  OpenCVs imshow() function
70  '''
71  def show_some_mnist_images(n, x_train, y_train):
72
73      nr_train_examples = x_train.shape[0]
74
75      for i in range(0,n):
76
77          # 1. guess a random number between 0 and 55.000-1
78          rnd_number = randint(0, nr_train_examples)
79
80          # 2. get corresponding output vector
81          correc_out_vec = y_train[rnd_number,:]
82          print("Here is example MNIST image #",i,
83                " It is a: ", np.argmax(correc_out_vec))
84
85          # 3. get first row of 28x28 pixels = 784 values
86          row_vec = x_train[rnd_number, :]
87          print("type of row_vec is ", type(row_vec))
88          print("shape of row_vec is ", row_vec.shape)
89
90          # 4. reshape 784 dimensional vector to 28x28
91          #    pixel matrix M
92          M = row_vec.reshape(28, 28)
93
94          # 5. resize image
95          M = cv2.resize(M, None, fx=10, fy=10,
96                         interpolation=cv2.INTER_CUBIC)
97
98          # 6. show that matrix using OpenCV
99          cv2.imshow('image', M)
100
101         # wait for a key
102         c = cv2.waitKey(0)
103
104         cv2.destroyAllWindows()
105
106
107 '''
108 Generate a weight matrix of dimension
109 (nr-of-inputs, nr-of-outputs)
110 and train the weights according to the
111 Perceptron learning rule using random sample
112 patterns <input,desired output> from the MNIST
113 training dataset
114 '''
115 def generate_and_train_perceptron_classifier\
```

```
116                          (nr_train_steps,x_train,y_train):
117
118        nr_train_examples = x_train.shape[0]
119
120        # 1. generate Perceptron with random weights
121        weights = np.random.rand(785, 10)
122
123        # 2. do the desired number of training steps
124        for train_step in range(0, nr_train_steps):
125
126            # 2.1 show that we are alive from time to time ...
127            if (train_step % 100 == 0):
128                print("train_step = ", train_step)
129
130            # 2.2 choose a random image
131            rnd_number = randint(0, nr_train_examples)
132            input_vec = x_train[rnd_number, :]
133            # add bias input "1"
134            input_vec = np.append(input_vec, [1])
135            input_vec = input_vec.reshape(1, 785)
136
137            # 2.3 compute Perceptron output.
138            #     Should have dimensions 1x10
139            act = np.matmul(input_vec, weights)
140            out_mat = f(act)
141
142            # 2.4 compute difference vector
143            teacher_out_mat = y_train[rnd_number, :]
144            teacher_out_mat = teacher_out_mat.reshape(1, 10)
145            diff_mat = teacher_out_mat - out_mat
146
147            # 2.5 correct weights
148            learn_rate = 0.01
149            for neuron_nr in range(0, 10):
150
151                # 2.5.1 get neuron error
152                neuron_error = diff_mat[0, neuron_nr]
153
154                # 2.5.2 for all weights to the current
155                #       neuron <neuron_nr>
156                for weight_nr in range(0, 785):
157
158                    # get input_value x_i
159                    x_i = input_vec[0, weight_nr]
160
161                    # compute weight change
162                    delta_w_i = learn_rate * neuron_error * x_i
163
164                    # add weight change to current weight
165                    weights[weight_nr, neuron_nr] += delta_w_i
```

```python
166
167
168        # 3. learning has finished.
169        #    Return the result: the 785x10 weight matrix
170        return weights
171
172
173
174 '''
175 Now test how good the Perceptron can classify
176 on data never seen before, i.e., the test data
177 '''
178 def test_perceptron(weights, x_test, y_test):
179
180     nr_test_examples = x_test.shape[0]
181
182     # 1. initialize counters
183     nr_correct = 0
184     nr_wrong = 0
185
186     # 2. forward all test patterns,
187     #    then compare predicted label with ground
188     #    truth label and check whether the prediction
189     #    is right or not
190     for test_vec_nr in range(0, nr_test_examples):
191
192         # 2.1 get the test vector
193         input_vec = x_test[test_vec_nr, :]
194         # add bias input "1"
195         input_vec = np.append(input_vec, [1])
196         input_vec = input_vec.reshape(1, 785)
197
198         # 2.2 get the desired output vector
199         teacher_out_mat = y_test[test_vec_nr, :]
200         teacher_out_mat = teacher_out_mat.reshape(1, 10)
201         teacher_class = np.argmax(teacher_out_mat)
202
203         # 2.3 compute the actual output of the Perceptron
204         act = np.matmul(input_vec, weights)
205         out_mat = f(act)
206         actual_class = np.argmax(out_mat)
207
208         # 2.4 is desired class and actual class the same?
209         if (teacher_class == actual_class):
210             nr_correct += 1
211         else:
212             nr_wrong += 1
213
214     # 3. return the test results
215     correct_rate =\
```

```
216          float(nr_correct) / float(nr_correct+nr_wrong)
217      return correct_rate, nr_correct, nr_wrong
218
219
220
221 def main():
222
223      print("\n1. Get the data")
224      x_train,y_train,x_test,y_test = read_mnist_data()
225
226      print("\n2. Show the data")
227      show_some_mnist_images(3, x_train, y_train)
228
229      print("\n3. Train Perceptron")
230      weights = \
231          generate_and_train_perceptron_classifier(1000, x_train,y_train)
232
233      print("\n4. Final test of Perceptron")
234      correct_rate, nr_correct, nr_wrong = \
235          test_perceptron(weights, x_test,y_test)
236      print(correct_rate*100.0,"% of the test patterns "
237                              "were correctly classified.")
238      print("correctly classified: ", nr_correct)
239      print("wrongly classified: ", nr_wrong)
240
241      print("Program end.")
242
243
244 main()
```

## 5.4 Limitations of the Perceptron

### Representing a straight line

Remember from math, that there are different possibilities to represent a straight line. The *general form* or *standard form* of a straight line is

$$y = mx + b \qquad (5.6)$$

and it represents a straight line with the help of a *slope m* and the *y-intercept b*. $x$ and $y$ are the free variables here, while $m$ and $b$ are the line parameters.

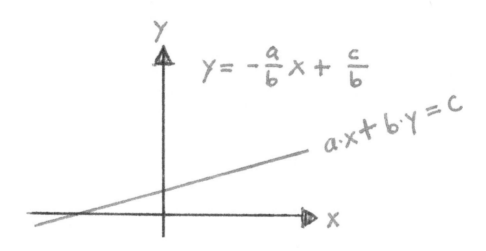

Figure 5.5: The coordinate form of a straight line uses three parameters to describe the line. It can be transformed into the well-known standard form of a straight line which describes a line using a slope and a y-intercept.

The *coordinate form* of a straight line uses three parameters:

$$ax + by = c \qquad (5.7)$$

where $a, b, c$ are the line parameters, where $a$ and $b$ cannot be both zero and $x, y$ are the free variables. The straight line is here defined by all points $(x, y)$ that satisfy this equation.

Assume that $b \neq 0$. Then we can transform the coordinate form into the standard form:

$$
\begin{aligned}
ax + by &= c \\
\Leftrightarrow \quad by &= -ax + c \\
\Leftrightarrow \quad y &= -\frac{a}{b}x + \frac{c}{b}
\end{aligned}
\tag{5.8}
$$

Thus we get the general form from the coordinate form with a slope corresponding to $-\frac{a}{b}$ and the y-intercept corresponding to $\frac{c}{b}$.

## Linearly separable sets

We will see in the following that we can expect a Perceptron to learn a two-class classification task perfectly only if the two sets fulfill a certain condition. For this we need to introduce the concept of *linear separability*.

Definition: Two sets $A, B \subset \mathbb{R}^n$ are called *linearly separable* if $n + 1$ numbers $w_1$, $w_2$, ..., $w_{n+1}$ exist, such that for all $\mathbf{a} = (a_1, ..., a_n) \in A$ and all $\mathbf{b} = (b_1, ..., b_n) \in B$ the following inequalities hold:

$$
\sum_{i=1}^{n} a_i w_i \leq w_{n+1}
\tag{5.9}
$$

$$
\sum_{i=1}^{n} b_i w_i > w_{n+1}
\tag{5.10}
$$

The set of all points $\mathbf{x} = (x_1, ..., x_n) \in \mathbb{R}^n$ for which the equation

$$
\sum_{i=1}^{n} x_i w_i = w_{n+1}
\tag{5.11}
$$

holds is called a *separating hyperplane*.

In 2D two sets $A, B$ are linearly separable if we can draw a line between the points of the two sets, such that all points of $A$ are on one side of the line and all points from $B$ are on the other side. In math, the two sides are called "half-spaces". Each hyperplane divides the corresponding space into two half-spaces.

## Perceptrons as classificators for linearly separable sets

Perceptrons can only be used as classifiers for linearly separable sets. What does this all have to do with Perceptrons? Consider Fig. 5.7. Here I have depicted a Perceptron

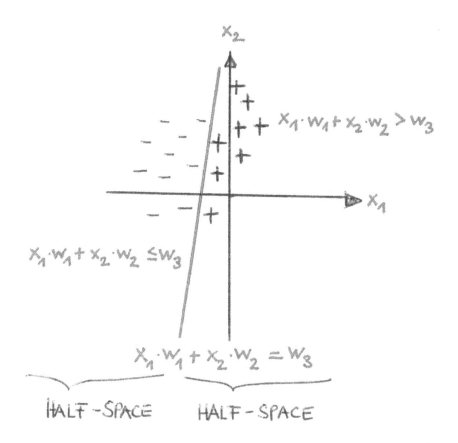

Figure 5.6: Two sets of points (set with "-" points and set with "+" points) that can be linearly separated using a straight line. The straight line is described here in coordinate form.

with only two inputs $o_1$ and $o_2$. The Perceptron computes its activation *act* and then compares the activation with the threshold $T$:

$$act = o_1 w_1 + o_2 w_2 > T? \ \rightarrow \ \begin{cases} \text{no} & \Rightarrow \text{out} = 0 \\ \text{yes} & \Rightarrow \text{out} = 1 \end{cases} \tag{5.12}$$

So the decision boundary of a perceptron corresponds to the coordinate form of a straight line - or according to the terminology above to a hyperplane. This means, every such Perceptron with two inputs will output a 0 for all points $(o_1, o_2) \in \mathbb{R}^2$ with $act = o_1 w_1 + o_2 w_2 \leq T$ and will output a 1 for all points with $act = o_1 w_1 + o_2 w_2 > T$. So it will always classify points with $act \leq T$ to belong to "class 0" and points with $act > T$ to belong to "class 1". And therefore it depends on the distribution of the

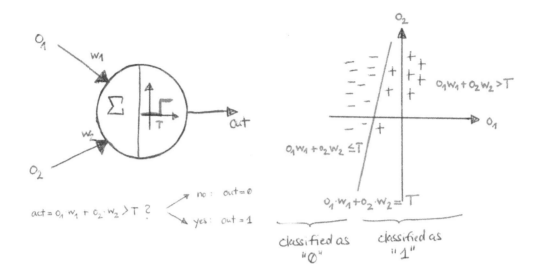

Figure 5.7: A Perceptron with two inputs can only classify two sets of 2D points if they are linearly separable!

points which we want to classify whether we have a chance to learn to classify them with a Perceptron or not. If they are not linearly separable, we have no chance to find weights $w_1, w_2$ and $w_3 := T$, that will produce the right classification outputs.

In their famous book *"Perceptrons: An Introduction to Computational Geometry"* [32] from 1969 Marvin Minsky and Seymour Papert showed that a Perceptron was not able to learn weights such that it could classify a dataset correctly that shows a XOR-pattern like distribution of the data points. See Fig. 5.8.

## A Multi-Layer Perceptron for the XOR function

While the XOR-pattern like datasets are a fundamental problem for Perceptrons, using an additional layer of Perceptron neurons already can solve the problem as is depicted in Fig. 5.9. Note how neuron with output $out_1$ and neuron with output $out_2$ divide the input space into half-spaces each and that neuron with output $out_3$ combines their outputs similar to an AND gate.

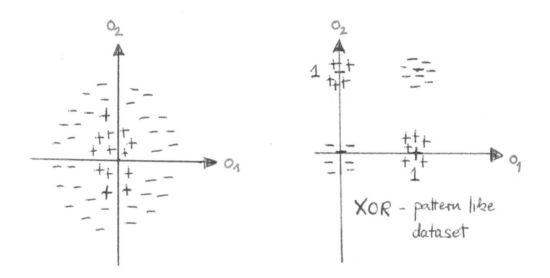

Figure 5.8: Try to find a straight line in each diagram that separates the "+"s and "-"s or accept that theses are examples of non-linearly separable sets.

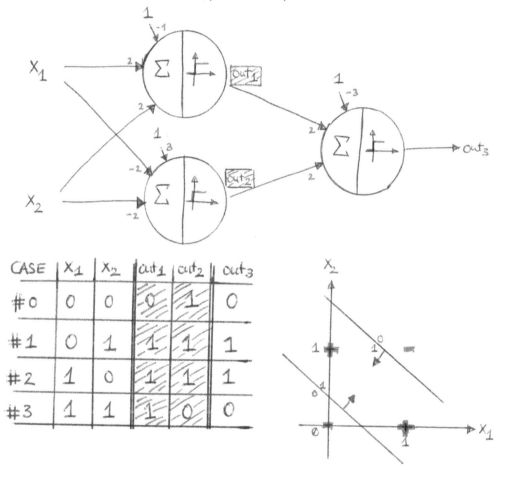

Figure 5.9: A Perceptron cannot represent the XOR function since it can only represent linearly separable datasets correctly. However, with using an additional layer of Perceptron neurons ("hidden" neurons), we can find weights, such that all inputs $x1, x2$ are correctly classified by this Multi-Layer Perceptron: $out3 = x1 \oplus x2$

# 6

# Self-Organizing Maps

The Perceptron learning algorithm realizes a form of learning which is called *error-correction learning* and falls into the category of supervised learning. We will now consider another neural network model which falls into the category of unsupervised learning and reveals another possible form of learning, namely *competitive learning*.

The Finish professor Teuvo Kohonen invented the Self-Organizing-Map (SOM) in 1982 [22]. My diploma thesis supervisor once was sitting in a session with Teuvo Kohonen. Kohonen said: "Please do not call it 'Kohonen map'! Call it 'Self-Organizing Map'". For this, we will avoid the name "Kohonen map" in the following.

## 6.1   The SOM neural network model

**A SOM learns unsupervised** To train a Perceptron we need for each input vector a desired output vector. This is different for SOMs! In order to train a SOM, we just need input vectors. This may sound strange at a first glance, since you should then ask yourself: What the hell does this thing learn then? However, there is a whole bunch of methods in machine learning which learn in this way. These methods fall into the category of *unsupervised learning*, since we provide no desired target or output vector for each input vector.

**What can we do with a SOM? Clustering!** Even if we just have input vectors we can learn a lot of useful things from this data. One important goal is, e.g., to identify clusters within the data: Where in the input space can we find accumulations / agglomerations of input vectors? And how many of such agglomeration areas (called *clusters*) are there? There are hundreds of different *clustering algorithms* available and a SOM is an important neural network model to perform clustering. Identifying clusters in your input data, describing them using cluster centers (also called *centroids*) and their spatial extension in the input space allows you to get another view onto your data.

**An example for a clustering application.** One application of clustering is e.g. *anomaly detection*. Imagine you can describe each input image that stems from a camera using a feature vector. Now you mount your camera oriented to a street, collect a lot of camera images, compute the corresponding feature features and cluster them. The cluster centers then represent "typical images" that were recorded in this training phase. In an application phase you can then test whether a new camera image (feature vector) fits to an already existing cluster by computing the distance to the nearest cluster center. This can give you a measure how normal or abnormal the new image is and can be used for detecting anomalies in your data.

**Simple neural structure.** The Perceptron was introduced first in this book since it is the most simple neural network structure we can think of: one layer of neurons which work independently from each other. The SOM has a similar simple structure. However, the neurons are here not independent from each other. Each neuron has some *neighbored neurons* with which it is connected. These connections are usually chosen in some regular form. Mostly, a 2D neighborhood relationship is chosen. So a neuron is connected with its neighbors, but not connected with all other neurons. However, each neuron is connected to the input vector (see Fig. 6.1).

**Neuron model used in a SOM.** The neuron model used in a SOM is very differently from the Perceptron neuron model. As said before, each neuron is connected to the input vector $\mathbf{v}$. A SOM neuron stores a weight vector $\mathbf{w}$. If a new input vector is present, each SOM neuron will compute the distance between its weight vector $\mathbf{w}$ and the input vector $\mathbf{v}$. Usually the Euclidean distance measure is used:

$$d(\mathbf{v}, \mathbf{w}) = \|\mathbf{v} - \mathbf{w}\|_2 = \sqrt{\sum_{i=1}^{N} (v_i - w_i)^2} \tag{6.1}$$

This distance is the output value of the SOM neuron.

**Only the Best Matching Unit and its neighbors adapt.** For a given input vector and all the computed neuron output values, the neuron which has the smallest distance / output value is called the *Best Matching Unit (BMU)*. This neuron is allowed to adapt slightly into the direction of the input vector. And now comes the neighborhood relationship into play. It is not only the BMU, but also its neighbors that are allowed to adapt slightly into the direction of the input vector, while all other neurons will keep their current weight vectors.

**Learning formula.** We can formulate this adaptation scheme into a formula. Let us assume the index of the BMU neuron is $a$. Then the weight $w_b$ for each neuron with index $b$ in the SOM network is adapted according to the following formula:

$$w_b^{t+1} = w_b^t + \alpha(t) * N(a, b, t) * (v^t - w_b^t) \tag{6.2}$$

where $t$ is the time index, $\alpha(t)$ is a learn rate that varies over time, $N(a, b, t)$ is a neighborhood relationship function and $v^t$ is the current input vector. The neighborhood relationship function $N(a, b, t)$ can be a binary function, but also a real-valued function. Often the Gaussian function is used for $N$.

**Why do we need a neighborhood relationship?** Imagine the 2D case and that there are no neighbors. What would happen if we start with all SOM neuron weight vectors near to zero vectors $(0, 0)$ and then enter input vectors $v^1, v^2, v^3, \dots$ into the SOM which stem from a region that is far away from $(0, 0)$? In the first step, the neuron with the smallest distance to $v_1$ would "win", i.e., be chosen to be the BMU and it would adapt into the direction of this region. With a high probability it would therefore become the winner in the following steps as well. So only one neuron would adapt to the input vectors, all other neurons would never change their weight vectors. In contrast, with adapting neighbors, not only the BMU but also some "nearby" neurons adapt into the direction of the region where the input vectors come from and get a chance to become the BMU for following vectors. The result of such a process can be seen in Fig. 6.2: The neurons distribute themselves automatically over the areas of the input space where the input vectors come from and thereby help to build a "map of the input data". Since there is no central control in this network to distribute these neurons into the regions where the input vectors come from, this process is called *self-organization*. It is an emerging behavior that is the result of the neighborhood relationship and the fact that not only the BMU but also its neighbors adapt.

**SOM can be used for supervised learning as well.** Typically SOMs are presented as a purely unsupervised machine learning algorithm. But we can augment the SOM neurons with class information as well. Imagine we have not only the input vectors, but for each input vector we have some class information, e.g.: this input vector encodes a horse (a cat / a dog). Then we can augment the SOM neuron model by class counter vectors and do not only adapt the BMU into the direction of the input vector, but also increment the counter value of the current class in the BMU class counter vector. Then after the learning we do not only have a map of the input data, but also the information encoded in the class counter vectors of each neuron, which class it corresponds to most likely. If a new input vector is presented, we can compute the BMU and look up which class it most likely stands for, i.e., perform classification.

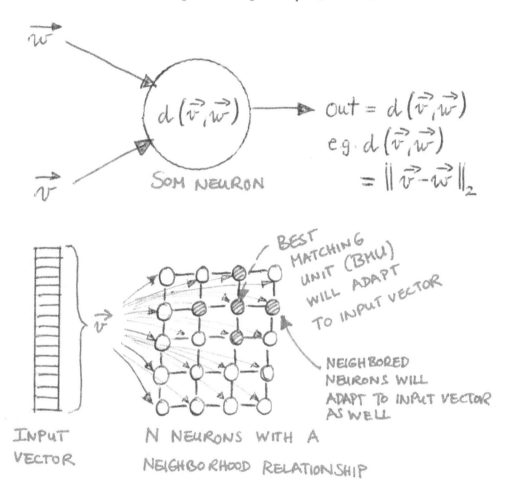

Figure 6.1: A Self-Organizing Map (SOM) consists of a set of neurons with a neighborhood relationship that defines whether two neurons are neighbored or not. The SOM is trained unsupervised: input vectors are presented, then the Best Matching Unit (BMU) is determined. The BMU and its neighbors adapt a little bit into the direction of the input vector.

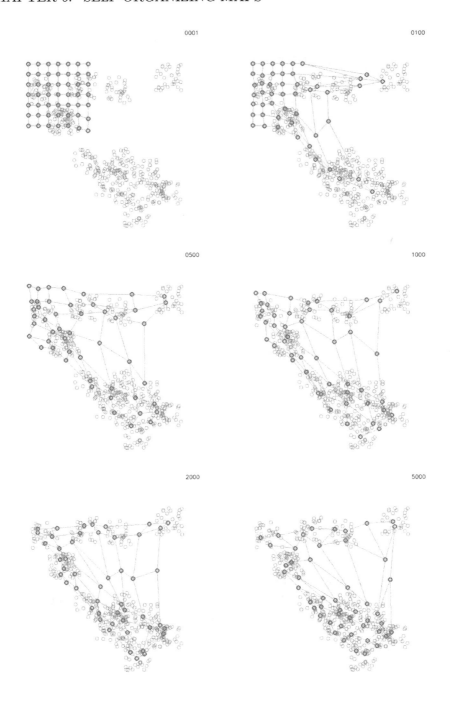

Figure 6.2: A Self-Organizing Map (SOM) unfolds to data. The map is shown after adaptation steps 1,100,500,1000,2000,5000. In this example the map consists of 7x7=49 neurons (fat circles) with a 2D topology depicted by the lines. The thin circles represent data samples. In each iteration one sample is drawn from the set of samples and the SOM adapts to this new (here: 2D) input vector.

## 6.2 A SOM in Python

In the following I will present the complete code for a SOM written by myself in Python. It needs some pages. However, my opinion is that it its good to have a source that gives you the possibility to understand all the details. A concrete implementation should in principle always be able to answer all questions. It consists of four files:

- `som_test.py`: Data samples are generated here and a SOM. The SOM is then fed in each step by a new data sample and adapts to the input data.

- `som.py`: Defines the SOM class. The most important methods here are `get_neighbors()` which defines a 2D topology / neighborhood relationship between the SOM neurons and `train()` which adapts the Best Matching Unit (BMU) and its neighbors into the direction of the input vector.

- `som_neuron.py`: The SOM neuron class for generating single SOM neuron instances. The method `compute_output()` defines how the output of a SOM neuron is computed given its current weight vector and an input vector. The method `adapt_to_vector()` implements the adaptation of the neuron's weight vector into the direction of the input vector.

- `data_generator.py`: The data generator class is a helper class to produce some samples. For this it assumes a certain number of clusters and generates some samples around each cluster. The samples are then returned as a list.

## The SOM test code

Listing 6.1: som_test.py

```python
'''
File: som_test.py

Data samples are generated, then a Self-Organizing Map (SOM).
The SOM is updated in each step with a randomly chosen data
sample.
Positions of samples, the "positions" (= weights) of the SOM
neurons and the 2D topology is visualized after each step.
'''

import sys
import cv2
import numpy as np
from data_generator import data_generator
from som import som

# SOM parameters
INPUT_DIM = 2
# square root of NR_NEURONS should be an integer!
NR_NEURONS = 7*7
LEARN_RATE = 0.2
adapt_neighbors = True

# visualization parameters
HEIGHT = 600
WIDTH  = 600
COLOR_SAMPLE        = (128,128,128)
COLOR_NEURON        = (0,0,255)
COLOR_NEIGHBORHOOD = (0,128,255)
RADIUS_SAMPLES = 5
RADIUS_NEURONS = 5

# set this to a higher value to
# speed up training dramatically!
VISUALIZE_EACH_N_STEPS = 1



print("Your Python version is: " + sys.version)
print("Your OpenCV version is: " + cv2.__version__)


print("************")
print("* SOM Test *")
print("************")
print("Press 's' to generate new samples.")
print("Press 'i' to initialize neurons to grid.")
```

```
48 print("Press 'j' to initialize neurons to (0,0).")
49 print("Press 'a' to swith on/off neighbor adaptation.")
50
51
52
53 # 1. generate samples
54 my_dg = data_generator(WIDTH, HEIGHT)
55 NR_CLUSTERS = 15
56 NR_SAMPLES_PER_CLUSTER = 30
57 data_samples = my_dg.generate_samples_near_to_clusters(
58     NR_CLUSTERS, NR_SAMPLES_PER_CLUSTER)
59 nr_samples = len(data_samples)
60 print("Type of data_samples is ", type(data_samples))
61 print("There are ", nr_samples, "samples in the list.")
62
63
64 # 2. generate a SOM
65 my_som = som(INPUT_DIM, NR_NEURONS)
66 my_som.initialize_neuron_weights_to_grid([100, 100, 200,200])
67
68
69 # 3. SOM training
70 while (True):
71
72     # 3.1 retrieve randomly a sample vector
73     rnd_vec_id = np.random.randint(nr_samples)
74     vec = data_samples[rnd_vec_id]
75
76
77     # 3.2 train the SOM with this vector
78     my_som.train( vec, LEARN_RATE, adapt_neighbors )
79
80
81     # 3.3 start visualization section?
82     if (my_som.nr_steps_trained % VISUALIZE_EACH_N_STEPS != 0):
83         continue
84
85     # 3.4 generate empty image for visualization
86     img = np.ones((HEIGHT, WIDTH, 3), np.uint8) * 255
87
88
89     # 3.5 visualize positions of samples
90     for i in range(nr_samples):
91
92         # get the next sample vector (it is an NumPy array)
93         # convert it to a tuple (which is need as coordinates
94         # for the circle draw command)
95         sample_coord = tuple(data_samples[i])
96         cv2.circle(img, sample_coord,
97                     RADIUS_SAMPLES, COLOR_SAMPLE)
```

```
 98
 99
100     # 3.6 visualize positions of neurons
101     for i in range(NR_NEURONS):
102
103         # get the neurons weight vector and
104         # convert it to a tuple
105         neuron_coord =\
106             tuple( (my_som.list_neurons[i].weight_vec).
107                     astype(int) )
108         cv2.circle(img, neuron_coord,
109                     RADIUS_NEURONS, COLOR_NEURON, 2)
110
111
112     # 3.7 visualize neighborhood relationship of neurons
113     #    by drawing a line between each two neighbored
114     #    neurons
115     for i in range(NR_NEURONS):
116
117         # prepare the neuron's coordinates as a tuple
118         # (for drawing coords)
119         neuron_i_coord =\
120             tuple((my_som.list_neurons[i].weight_vec).
121                     astype(int))
122
123         # now get a list of all neighbors of this neuron
124         neighbors = my_som.get_neighbors(i)
125         # print("Neighbors of neuron ",i," are: ", neighbors)
126
127         # for all neighbors of this neuron:
128         for j in neighbors:
129
130             # prepare the neuron's coordinates as a tuple
131             neuron_j_coord = \
132                 tuple((my_som.list_neurons[j].weight_vec).
133                         astype(int))
134
135             # draw a line between neuron i and
136             # its neighbored neuron j
137             cv2.line(img, neuron_i_coord, neuron_j_coord,
138                     COLOR_NEIGHBORHOOD, 1)
139
140     # 3.8 show how many steps we have already trained
141     font = cv2.FONT_HERSHEY_SIMPLEX
142     cv2.putText(img,
143                 str(my_som.nr_steps_trained).zfill(4),
144                 (WIDTH-50, 20), font, 0.5, (0,0,0), 1,
145                 cv2.LINE_AA)
146
147
```

```
148    # 3.9 show visualization of samples, neuron locations
149    #    and neuron neighborhood relations
150    cv2.imshow('img', img)
151
152
153    # 3.10 wait for a key
154    c = cv2.waitKey(1)
155
156
157    # 3.11 generate new sample distribution?
158    #      interesting to see, how an existing SOM adapts
159    #      to new input data!
160    if c!=-1:
161
162        # start with new samples?
163        if chr(c)=='s':
164            print("Generating new samples")
165            data_samples = \
166                my_dg.generate_samples_near_to_clusters\
167            (NR_CLUSTERS, NR_SAMPLES_PER_CLUSTER)
168
169        # reinitialize neuron weights to grid?
170        if chr(c)=='i':
171            print("Reinitialization of neuron weightsto grid")
172            my_som.initialize_neuron_weights_to_grid(
173                    [100, 100, WIDTH - 200, HEIGHT - 200])
174
175        # reinitialize neuron weights to (0,0)?
176        if chr(c) == 'j':
177            print("Reinitialization of neuron weights to (0,0)")
178            my_som.initialize_neuron_weights_to_origin()
179
180        # switch on/off neighbor adaptation
181        if chr(c)=='a':
182            adapt_neighbors = not adapt_neighbors
183            print("Adapt neighbors? --> ", adapt_neighbors )
184
185
186    # save image?
187    if False:
188        if (my_som.nr_steps_trained == 1 or
189            my_som.nr_steps_trained % 100 == 0):
190            cv2.imwrite("V:/tmp/" +
191                str(my_som.nr_steps_trained).zfill(4) + ".png", img)
```

## The SOM class

Listing 6.2: som.py

```python
"""
File: som.py

Here we define a class that implements the
Self-Organizing Map (SOM) neural network model.

A SOM is an unsupervised learning algorithm that
allows to distribute N prototype vectors ("neurons")
automatically in the input space.

It can be used for dimensionality reduction and
clustering.
"""

import numpy as np

from som_neuron import som_neuron

class som:

    list_neurons = []
    nr_neurons = 0
    nr_steps_trained = 0

    """
    Create a new Self-Organizing Map
    with the desired number of neurons.

    Each neuron will store input_dim many
    weights.
    """
    def __init__(self, input_dim, nr_neurons):

        # store number of neurons
        self.nr_neurons = nr_neurons

        # create the desired number of neurons
        for i in range(nr_neurons):

            # neurogenesis: create a new neuron
            neuron = som_neuron(input_dim)

            # store the new neuron in a list
            self.list_neurons.append( neuron )

        # prepare matrix for 2D neighborhood
        # topology
```

```python
     S = int(np.sqrt(nr_neurons))
     self.neighborhood = \
         np.arange(nr_neurons).reshape(S,S)

     print("Neuron neighborhood:\n", self.neighborhood)


 """
 Initializes the neuron positions to
 the specified rectangle
 """
 def initialize_neuron_weights_to_grid(self, rectangle):

     S = int(np.sqrt(self.nr_neurons))

     orig_x = rectangle[0]
     orig_y = rectangle[1]
     width  = rectangle[2]
     height = rectangle[3]

     for id in range(self.nr_neurons):

         # get the next neuron
         neuron = self.list_neurons[id]

         # compute a 2D coordinate in input space
         # to initialize the weight vector with this
         # 2D coordinate
         grid_y = int(id / S)
         grid_x = id % S
         ispace_x = orig_x + grid_x * (width  / S)
         ispace_y = orig_y + grid_y * (height / S)

         # store that coordinates
         neuron.weight_vec[0] = ispace_x
         neuron.weight_vec[1] = ispace_y


 """
 Initializes the neuron positions to origin
 """
 def initialize_neuron_weights_to_origin(self):

     for id in range(self.nr_neurons):

         # get the next neuron
         neuron = self.list_neurons[id]

         # store that coordinates
         neuron.weight_vec[0] = 0
```

```
 98                     neuron.weight_vec[1] = 0
 99
100
101         """
102         Returns all the neighbors of a given neuron
103         Example:
104         2D Neuron neighborhood of 49 neurons arranged in a 7x7 grid:
105             [[ 0  1  2  3  4  5  6]
106              [ 7  8  9 10 11 12 13]
107              [14 15 16 17 18 19 20]
108              [21 22 23 24 25 26 27]
109              [28 29 30 31 32 33 34]
110              [35 36 37 38 39 40 41]
111              [42 43 44 45 46 47 48]]
112         """
113         def get_neighbors(self, id):
114
115             N = self.nr_neurons
116             S = int(np.sqrt(N))
117
118             # case #1: corner?
119
120             # top left corner
121             if id==0:
122                 return [1,S]
123
124             # top right corner
125             if id==S-1:
126                 return [S-2,2*S-1]
127
128             # bottom left corner:
129             if id==N-S:
130                 return [N-S-S, N-S+1]
131
132             # bottom right corner:
133             if id==N-1:
134                 return [N-1-S, N-1-1]
135
136
137             # case #2: border?
138             y = int(id / S)
139             x = id % S
140
141             # top border
142             if (y==0):
143                 return [id-1,id+1,id+S]
144
145             # bottom border
146             if (y==S-1):
147                 return [id-1,id+1,id-S]
```

```
148
149        # left border
150        if (x==0):
151            return [id-S,id+S,id+1]
152
153        # right border
154        if (x==S-1):
155            return [id-S,id+S,id-1]
156
157
158        # case #3: normal cell?
159        return [id-S,id-1,id+1,id+S]
160
161
162
163
164    """
165    Train the SOM with one more training vector,
166    i.e.,
167    - determine the Best Matching Unit (BMU)
168    - adapt the BMU and its neighbored neurons
169      into the direction of the input vector
170    """
171    def train(self, input_vec, learn_rate, adapt_neighbors):
172
173        self.nr_steps_trained += 1
174
175        if (self.nr_steps_trained % 1000 == 0):
176            print("SOM has been trained for",
177                  self.nr_steps_trained, "steps.")
178
179        # 1. let all neurons comput their output values
180        for neuron_nr in range(self.nr_neurons):
181
182            # get the next neuron
183            neuron = self.list_neurons[neuron_nr]
184
185            # compute new output value of neuron
186            neuron.compute_output(input_vec)
187
188
189        # 2. now determine the Best Matching Unit (BMU),
190        #    i.e., the neuron with the smallest output
191        #    value (each neuron computes the distance of
192        #    its weight vector to the input vector)
193        BMU_nr = 0
194        minimum_dist = self.list_neurons[0].output
195        for neuron_nr in range(1,self.nr_neurons):
196
197            if (self.list_neurons[neuron_nr].output < minimum_dist):
```

```
198            minimum_dist = self.list_neurons[neuron_nr].output
199            BMU_nr = neuron_nr
200
201       #print("The BMU is neuron #", BMU_nr,
202       #      "and the distance is", minimum_dist)
203
204
205       # 3. now move the BMU a little bit into the direction
206       #    of the input vector
207       BMU_neuron = self.list_neurons[BMU_nr]
208       BMU_neuron.adapt_to_vector(input_vec, learn_rate)
209
210
211       # 4. now get the list of all neighbors of the BMU
212       #    and move the neighbors a little bit into the
213       #    direction of the input vector as well
214       if (adapt_neighbors):
215
216           neighbors = self.get_neighbors(BMU_nr)
217
218           # for all neighbors of this neuron:
219           for j in neighbors:
220
221               # get that neuron
222               neighbored_neuron = self.list_neurons[j]
223
224               # adapt the neighbored neuron to input vector
225               # as well
226               neighbored_neuron.adapt_to_vector(input_vec, learn_rate
      /2.0)
```

## The SOM neuron class

Listing 6.3: som_neuron.py

```python
"""
File: som_neuron.py

A SOM neuron is a special type of neuron.
It stores a prototype vector in its weights.
Given an input vector, it computes some "distance"
between its input vector and its stored prototype vector.
"""

import numpy as np

class som_neuron:

    output = 0.0

    def __init__(self, nr_weights):

        self.weight_vec = np.zeros(nr_weights)


    def compute_output(self, input_vec):

        # this will compute the Euclidean distance between
        # the weight vector and the input vector
        self.output = np.linalg.norm(self.weight_vec-input_vec)


    """
    This will adapt the neuron's weight vector
    'a little bit' into the direction of the
    specified <adapt_vec>.
    """
    def adapt_to_vector(self, adapt_vec, learn_rate):

        delta_w = learn_rate * (adapt_vec - self.weight_vec)
        self.weight_vec += delta_w
```

## The data generator class

Listing 6.4: data_generator.py

```python
"""
File: data_generator.py

In this file a class data_generator is defined that
allows to generate data sample distributions of different
forms.

It is meant to be a helper class for the SOM test.
We want to test and see how the SOM adapts to different
sample distributions.
"""

import numpy as np


class data_generator:

    img_width  = 0
    img_height = 0

    def __init__(self, width, height):
        print("A new data generator object has been created.")
        self.img_width  = width
        self.img_height = height


    def generate_samples_near_to_clusters(self, nr_clusters,
    nr_samples_per_cluster):

        SPACE = 100
        CLUSTER_RADIUS = 75


        # 1. create <nr_clusters> random 2D cluster centers
        #    with <nr_samples_per_cluster> random samples per cluster
        data_samples = []
        for i in range(nr_clusters):

            # generate random cluster center
            center_x = SPACE + np.random.randint(self.img_width-2*SPACE)
            center_y = SPACE + np.random.randint(self.img_height-2*SPACE)

            for j in range(nr_samples_per_cluster):

                # compute random offset vector to cluster center
                rnd_offset_x = np.random.randint(CLUSTER_RADIUS)
                rnd_offset_y = np.random.randint(CLUSTER_RADIUS)
```

```
47
48          # compute final 2D sample coordinates
49          x = center_x + rnd_offset_x
50          y = center_y + rnd_offset_y
51
52          # is the sample within the image dimension?
53          if (x<0): x=0
54          if (y<0): y=0
55          if (x>self.img_width) : x = self.img_width
56          if (y>self.img_height): y = self.img_height
57
58          # store the sample coordinate in the list
59          data_samples.append( np.array([x,y]) )
60
61      return data_samples
```

## 6.3   SOM and the Cortex

### Interesting observation 1: Cortical homunculi

**Sensory homunculi.** The *primary somatosensory cortex* is a region of the cortex that receives tactile information from the whole body. The information comes from sensors in the skin (exteroception) but also from sensoric receptors located in the inner of the body (proprioception). Two interesting observations can be made if we label each part of this somatosensory cortex with the name of the body region where the information is sent from: First, the amount of cortex devoted to a specific body part is not proportional to the size of the corresponding body part, but to the density of tactile receptors present in this body part. Second, neighbored body parts are mapped to neighbored areas on the primary somatosensory cortex, i.e., the neighborhood relationship is maintained. The somatosensory cortex is said to show a *somatotopic arrangement.* If we draw a small man directly onto the surface of the primary somatosensory cortex where we draw the size of the body parts proportionally to the size of the cortex that deals with the corresponding body part, we end up with a distorted strange man (or woman) that is called the *sensory homonculus.* Note that tactile information coming from the left side of the body is processed in the right hemisphere and information coming from the right side of the body is processed in the left hemisphere. So there are actually two *sensory homunculi.*

**Motor homunculi.** Directly beside the primary somatosensory cortex we can find the *primary motor cortex* which works together with other motor areas in order to plan and execute movements. Similar to the primary somatosencoric cortex we can find a distorted somatotopic map for body parts where the amount of cortex which is devoted to a body part is not proportional to the absolute size of this part, but to the density of cutaneous receptors on the body part. Cutaneous receptors allow to measure, e.g., how much the skin is stretched (Ruffini's end organ), changes in texture (Meissner's corpuscle), pain (nociceptors) and temperature (thermoceptors). The density of these receptors is an indicator how precisely movements are required for that body part. E.g., the human hands and the face have a much larger representation than the legs. So beside two sensory homonculi we can find two *motor homonculi*.

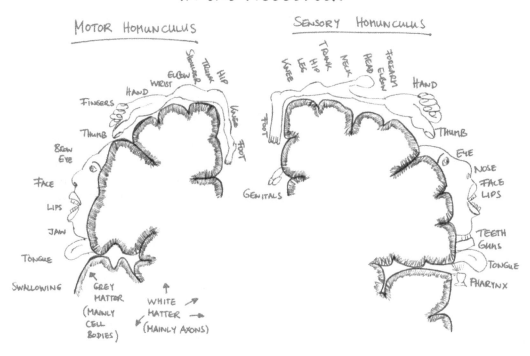

Figure 6.3: In the primary sensory motor cortex tactile information is processed such that neighbored body regions are processed in neighbored cortex areas as well. However, the areas of such a region responsible for a certain body part does not correspond to the size of the body part, but is proportional to the density of tactile receptors present in this body part.

## Interesting observation 2: Cortical plasticity

**Phantom lib sensations and broken arms.** Another fascinating observation regarding the cortex is its plasticity. The sensoric and motoric maps of the body that are described above are not static, but highly plastic. If a body part of a patient has to be amputated the sensoric input coming from that body part will be missing. What can be observed then is that neighbored body parts will use this "dormant" cortical areas for their representation, i.e., the neighbored body parts of the homunculus "grow" into these regions. This often leads to the phenomenon of *phantom limb sensation* which means that a person continues to feel pain or sensation within a part of their body that has been amputated. It occurs in ca. 60–80% of all amputation cases. A possible explanation of these phantom limb sensations is that an misinterpretation of the activity in the area of the cortex that formerly was responsible for the amputated limb happens. Even if a body part is no amputated, immobilization of a body part (e.g. due to a broken hand or arm) already leads to reduction of the cortical size in the motor cortex areas related to that body parts after two weeks [25].

**Changes of cortical maps due to training.** Many experiments show that training of specific body parts can change the form of the sensoric and motoric homunculi. E.g. it was shown that a daily piano practice for the fingers for 2 hours will already result in a perceptible change of the motoric homunculi. Similarly, a golf training for 40 hours [2] or a juggle training for three months increases the gray matter involved in task relevant cortical areas [8].

## Neocortex

**A layered structure.** The *neocortex* (also called *isocortex*) is a 2-4mm thick part of the brain that is involved in "higher" cognitive functions such as perception, cognition and generation of motor commands. It is widely accepted that it can be divided into six layers, which are labeled with roman numbers from I to VI, where I is the outermost and VI is the innermost layer. Interestingly it has a smooth surface in rodent brains, whereas in primates the surface reminds of a walnut with deep grooves (called *sulci*) and ridges (called *gyri*). A popular hypothesis is that the reason for this wavy surface is that it allows the surface of the neocortex to be increased. How can we say that it consists of six layers? The layers can visually be discriminated due to different neuronal cell types and different connection patterns. However, there are some exceptions from this typical six layer structure. E.g., in the primary sensory cortex layer V is very small or even not present. There is a regular connection pattern: e.g., neurons in layer IV receive the majority of their inputs from outside the cortex, namely mostly the *thalamus* - a brain region that is said to play an important role in deciding which information will be sent to the cortex. Neurons in layer IV then send their outputs to neurons in other layers. Pyramidal neurons in the "upper layers" II and III project to other areas of the neocortex, while neurons from layers V and VI mostly project out of the cortex to brain structures as the thalamus, the brain stem and the spinal cord.

**Neocortex vs. Cortex.** Note that the terms *neocortex* and *(cerebral) cortex* do not exactly mean the same. The neocortex is the "newest" part of the cortex from an evolutionary view point, while the other older parts of the cortex are called *allocortex*.

**Cortical minicolumns.** The layered structure and the regular connection pattern found in the neocortex is a highly interesting observation since it rises the question: What is the fundamental algorithm or information flow that happens in this important brain structure? This question has not yet been answered. However, another important observation has been made: the cortex is structured into *minicolumns* and *macrocolumns*. A cortical minicolumn (or *cortical microcolumn*) is a vertical column of ca. 80-120 neurons (some authors estimate the number of neurons to 50-100) with a diameter of the column of ca. 50 $\mu m$. About 200.000.000 minicolumns can be found in the human brain. Vernon Mountcastle described it for the first time and suggested that it could be an elementary unit of information processing [33].

**Cortical macrocolumns.** It can further be observed that several minicolumns group to a larger structure called macrocolumn (also called *hypercolumn* in the visual cortex) in the following sense: Neurons within a minicolumn have all the same receptive field and encode similar features. Minicolumns that group to a macrocolumn have all the same receptive fields but encode different features. A macrocolumn has a diameter of ca. 500 $\mu m$ and consists of 50-100 minicolumns. The number of macrocolumns in the human brain is about 1-2 millions.

**Connectivity pattern for minicolumns.** There can be found lateral connections between minicolumns with exciting connections to neighbored minicolumns and inhibiting connections to minicolumns that are far away.

**An open discussion.** It is still unclear whether the cortical columns are just a by-product or whether they have a function regarding the information processing. On the one hand, some others do not see the necessity that the columnar structures that can be found serve a purpose. In their paper *"The cortical column: a structure without a function"* by Horton and Adams [17] the authors say:

> "Equally dubious is the concept that minicolumns are basic modular units of the adult cortex, rather than simply remnants of fetal development."

On the other hand, other authors have developed theories of Neocortical information processing around these columnar organization. E.g. Rinkus [39] suggests in his paper *"A cortical sparse distributed coding model linking mini- and macrocolumn-scale functionality"* that

> "(a) a macrocolumn's function is to store sparse distributed representations of its inputs and to be a recognizer of those inputs; and (b) the generic function of the minicolumn is to enforce macrocolumnar code sparseness."

Another prominent example of a theory built around the idea of columnar organization is the *Hierarchical Temporal Memory* model by Jeff Hawkins which allows to store, infer and recall sequences in an unsupervised fashion, i.e., using unlabeled data.

## SOM as a coarse model of the Neocortex

**Similarities.** So what is the connection between SOMs and the Neocortex? Summarizing the findings above, we know i) that the Neocortex builds somatotopic maps of inputs signals. This is also true for SOMs! It builds maps of input signals where neighbored neurons represent similar patterns (according to the distance metric used). We also know ii) that if suddenly inputs signals are missing from a body part the neocortical homunculus will change. This is also true for SOMs! If input signals from some part of the input space are omitted, the corresponding neurons move to other input regions. We further know iii) that there are minicolumns in the Neocortex with exciting connections to neighbored minicolumns and inhibiting connections to minicolumns far away. This idea is also used in SOMs! The BMU can be said to "excite" also the neighbored SOM neurons such that these can adapt as well. In sum, the SOM can be understood as a (very) rough model of the function of the Neocortex, where temporal aspects are not modeled In this sense the biological counterpart of a SOM neuron is not a Neocortical neuron, but rather a complete minicolumn of the Neocortex and the complete SOM corresponds to a macrocolumn.

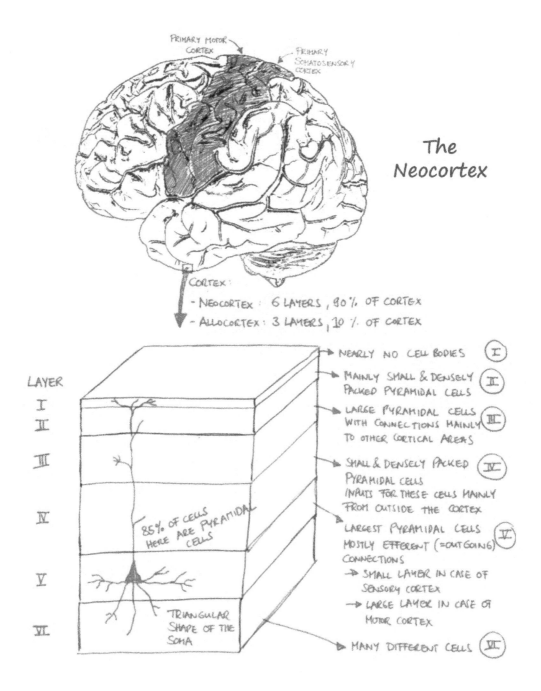

Figure 6.4: The Neocortex is a six-layered neuronal structure with a relatively stable pattern of layer thickness, neurons found in these layers and connections between neurons.

# Cortical minicolumns and macrocolumns

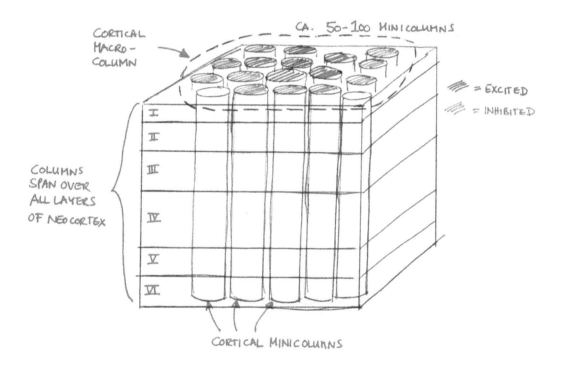

Figure 6.5: It seems that the Neocortex is not only structured into six layers but also structured into minicolumns where neurons encode the same feature and macrocolumns consisting of 50-100 minicolumns where each minicolumn has the same receptive field but represents another feature.

7

# Multi Layer Perceptrons

## 7.1 The goal

**Computation layer by layer.** A Multi Layer Perceptron (MLP) - as depicted in Fig. 1.1 - is composed of several layers of Perceptron neurons. An input vector is fed into the MLP by setting the outputs of the input neurons. Then each neuron in the first layer computes its output value. Afterwards neurons in the second layer compute their outputs and so forth till the last layer, the output layer is reached. This process is called *feedforward*. The result is that the MLP has mapped an input vector $\mathbf{x} \in \mathbb{R}^n$ to some output vector $\mathbf{y} \in \mathbb{R}^m$. For this we can say, that a MLP represents a function $f : \mathbb{R}^n \to \mathbb{R}^m$.

**Generalization is the goal.** Assume that we have a lot of training examples

$$D = \{p_i = (\mathbf{x}, \mathbf{t})_i : \mathbf{x} \in \mathbb{R}^n, \mathbf{t} \in \mathbb{R}^m, i = 1, \ldots, d\} \tag{7.1}$$

from some underlying function $f : \mathbb{R}^n \to \mathbb{R}^m$.

We want the MLP to map each training vector $\mathbf{x}$ to the corresponding output vector $\mathbf{t}$ (also called *teacher vector*. But actually we want more. We also want the MLP to *generalize*, such that a new - never seen before - input vector $\mathbf{x}$ is mapped to the output vector $\mathbf{y}$ if $f(\mathbf{x}) = \mathbf{y}$.

Note that this desired generalization behavior will not be formulated directly into the learning problem! For this, we can just hope, that the MLP trained with some input/output-examples will generalize for new input vectors. Later we will discuss some *regularization techniques* that indeed guide the learning process such that generalization is promoted and not memorization.

**Definition of an error function.** For realizing a learning process, an error for individual training samples and for the whole training dataset is defined. The error of an individual training pattern $\mathbf{p_i} = (\mathbf{x}, \mathbf{t})$ is defined as the sum of squared differences between the desired output vector values $\mathbf{t}_m^i$ and the actual output values $\mathbf{y}_m^i$ of the MLP that has processed the input vector with the current set of weights $W$. The index $b$ denotes the b-th output neuron and index $i$ stands for the i-th training pattern. This error is defined as:

$$E = E(W, \mathbf{p_i}) = \frac{1}{2} \sum_{b=1}^{B} (t_b^i - y_b^i)^2 \tag{7.2}$$

where $B$ is the number of output neurons. Why the $\frac{1}{2}$? You will see in the following that it is just introduced for convenience reasons to compensate for a factor of 2 when we will compute derivatives of this error function.

Now we can also define an error for a given weight configuration $W$ and a whole dataset $D$:

$$E_D = E(W, D) = \frac{1}{d} \sum_{i=1}^{d} E(W, \mathbf{p_i}) \tag{7.3}$$

## 7.2 Basic idea is gradient descent

**The problem.** In chapter 5 we have seen a learning rule for the single layer Perceptron weights that was somewhat straightforward: The actual output value is too high? Ok, let's turn the weights down. The actual output value is too small? Ok, let's turn the weights up. The error signal that we had defined was defined for each output neuron. However, now in a MLP there can be weights to hidden neurons but we have no desired target values for these weights to hidden neurons. So how shall we update these weights?

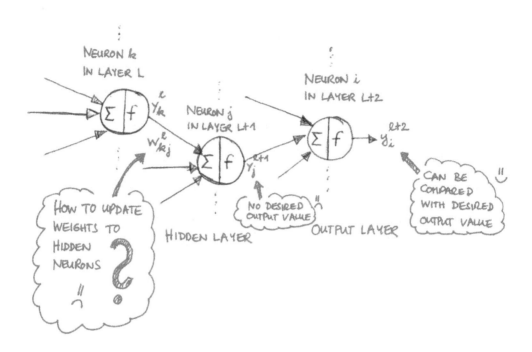

Figure 7.1: For a single layer Perceptron there are only output neurons and no hidden neurons. So we can compute an error signal for each neuron. In a Multi Layer Perceptron there are output neurons and hidden neurons. How shall we define an error for a hidden neuron? And if we cannot define an error for hidden neurons how should we change the weights to these neurons?

**The basic idea: walk on the error surface into directions of smaller errors.** Consider Fig. 7.2. Given a very small neural network with just two weights $w_0$ and $w_1$ the error $E$ for an individual input vector depends on just these two weights. The resulting error value can be plotted as a function $E(w_0, w_1)$ of these two weights. Now to reduce the error, the idea of gradient descent is to compute the gradient of E at the position on this error surface corresponding to the current weight values $(w_0, w_1)$. The gradient of the error is defined as the vector of partial derivatives:

$$grad(E) = \nabla E = \begin{pmatrix} \dfrac{\partial E}{w_0} \\ \dfrac{\partial E}{w_1} \end{pmatrix} \tag{7.4}$$

Since the gradient points into the direction of steepest ascent, we will use the negative gradient to "do a step" into the steepest descent. With this approach we will change the weights such that error is reduced. Problem: it might happen that we get stuck in a local minimum of the error surface.

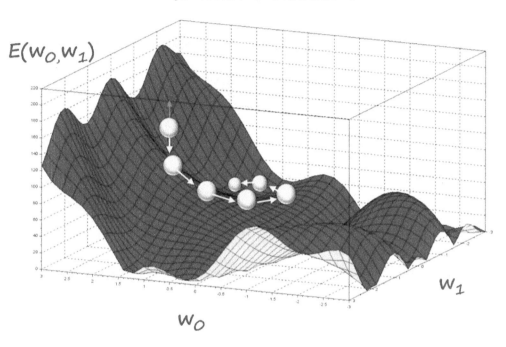

Figure 7.2: Idea of gradient descent. In order to minimize the error $E$ that depends in this example on two parameters $w_0$ and $w_1$ we compute the gradient at the current values of $w_0$ and $w_1$. This results in the vector pointing upwards. However, this vector points into the direction of the steepest ascent. Since we want to minimize $E$ and not maximize $E$, we go into the opposite direction which is visualized by the other vectors.

## 7.3   Splitting the weight change formula into three parts

**Each weight is changed.** The learning algorithm for the weights we will derive now is called *Backpropagation* and sometimes *Backpropagation of error*. It will compute a weight change $\Delta w_{kj}$ in each step for each weight $w_{kj}$ from neuron $k$ to neuron $j$. More precisely, in order to realize gradient descent we will change the weight into the opposite direction of the derivative of the error with respect to the weight:

$$\Delta w_{kj} = -\alpha \frac{\partial E}{\partial w_{kj}} \tag{7.5}$$

where $\alpha$ is the gradient descent step width and can be called a learn rate.

**We start with applying the chain rule.** The key step in deriving the Backpropagation learning formulas is to apply the chain rule of differential calculus:

$$\Delta w_{kj} = -\alpha \underbrace{\frac{\partial E}{\partial y_j}}_{3} \underbrace{\frac{\partial y_j}{\partial act_j}}_{2} \underbrace{\frac{\partial act_j}{\partial w_{kj}}}_{1} \tag{7.6}$$

The application of the chain rule allows to follow a *divide-and-conquer* strategy. The large problem which is to compute $\Delta w_{kj}$ has been split into three smaller problems, namely to compute the factors 1,2 and 3.

**Definition of an error signal.** The product of the two terms 3 and 2 together with the minus sign is called the *error term* or *error signal* in the context of MLPs. Thus the error signal is:

$$\delta_j := -\underbrace{\frac{\partial E}{\partial y_j}}_{3} \underbrace{\frac{\partial y_j}{\partial act_j}}_{2} \tag{7.7}$$

and therefore the weight change formula can be rewritten to:

$$\Delta w_{kj} = \alpha \delta_j \frac{\partial act_j}{\partial w_{kj}} \tag{7.8}$$

## 7.4  Computing the first part

**It's the easiest part.** In order to derive the first part $\frac{\partial act_j}{\partial w_{kj}}$ we remember that the activity of a neuron is just the weighted sum of its inputs. Therefore:

$$\underbrace{\frac{\partial act_j}{\partial w_{kj}}}_{1} = \frac{\partial \sum\limits_{a=1}^{A} w_{aj} y_a^l}{\partial w_{kj}} = y_k \tag{7.9}$$

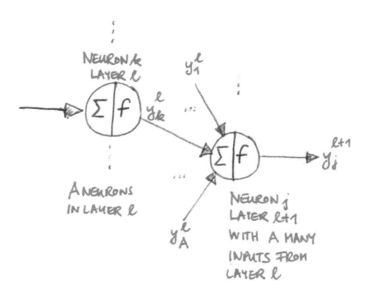

So the derivative is just $y_k$! Why? If we derive the function in the numerator with respect to the denominator $w_{kj}$ all the other variables in the sum can be regarded as constants regarding the derivation process. So we have to derive $w_{kj}y_k$ with respect to $w_{kj}$. The derivative of this function is $y_k$.

## 7.5 Computing the second part

**It's not much more difficult.** In order to derive the second part $\frac{\partial y_j}{\partial act_j}$ we remember that $y_j$ is the output of neuron $j$. This output $y_j$ depends on the transfer function $f$ which is used and the activity of the neuron which is $y_j = f(act_j)$. For this:

$$\underbrace{\frac{\partial y_j}{\partial act_j}}_{2} = \frac{\partial f(act_j)}{\partial act_j} = f'(act_j) \tag{7.10}$$

## 7.6 Computing the third part

For computing the third part $\frac{\partial E}{\partial y_j}$ we will differ between two cases depending on whether we consider an output neuron or a hidden neuron. The easier part is the case if we consider an output neuron. So let's start with this case.

### First case: neuron $j$ is an output neuron

If neuron $j$ is an output neuron there is a desired output value $t_j$ for that neuron. Using the definition of the error function $E$ we have for a fixed training pattern (we omit the training pattern index $i$ in the following):

$$\frac{\partial E}{\partial y_j} = \frac{\partial \frac{1}{2} \sum_{b=1}^{B} (t_b - y_b)^2}{\partial y_j} = \frac{\partial \frac{1}{2}(t_j - y_j)^2}{\partial y_j} = \frac{1}{2}2(t_j - y_j) * (0 - 1) = y_j - t_j \qquad (7.11)$$

Great! So for the case of output neurons we have already computed all the three parts and can make up a final weight change formula for output neurons by gluing the results together:

$$\Delta w_{kj} = -\alpha \underbrace{\frac{\partial E}{\partial y_j}}_{3} \underbrace{\frac{\partial y_j}{\partial act_j}}_{2} \underbrace{\frac{\partial act_j}{\partial w_{kj}}}_{1} = -\alpha \underbrace{(y_j - t_j)}_{3} \underbrace{f'(act_j)}_{2} \underbrace{y_k}_{1} \qquad (7.12)$$

### Second case: neuron $j$ is a hidden neuron

Now let's face the slightly more complicated case, which is the case where neuron $j$ is not an output neuron. In order to derive also the third part in such a case, we will need the *multivariate chain rule (MCR)* for n-dimensional functions. First let us consider the MCR for 2-dimensional functions.

**Multivariate chain rule for a 2D function f.** Suppose $f(x, y) = z$ is a 2D function, i.e., $f : \mathbb{R}^2 \to \mathbb{R}$ where the arguments $x$ and $y$ depend on one or more variables themselves. Then the MCR allows us to differentiate $f$ with respect to any of the variables being involved. To be more specific:

Let $x = x(t)$ and $y = y(t)$ be differentiable at $t$ and suppose that $z = f(x, y)$ is differentiable at the 2D point $(x(t), y(t))$. Then $f$ is also differentiable at $t$ and the derivative can be computed as follows:

$$\frac{\partial z}{\partial t} = \frac{\partial z}{\partial x}\frac{\partial x}{\partial t} + \frac{\partial z}{\partial y}\frac{\partial y}{\partial t} \qquad (7.13)$$

MULTIVARIATE CHAIN RULE

FOR A 2D FUNCTION $f(x,y)=z$ :

DEPEND ON ONE
OR MORE VARIABLES
THEMSELVES

$$\frac{\partial z}{\partial t} = \frac{\partial z}{\partial x}\frac{\partial x}{\partial t} + \frac{\partial z}{\partial y}\frac{\partial y}{\partial t}$$

EXAMPLE.

$$z = f(x,y) = x^2 y - y^2 \quad \text{WITH} \quad x = t^2$$
$$y = 2t$$

THEN :

$$\frac{\partial z}{\partial t} = \frac{\partial z}{\partial x}\frac{\partial x}{\partial t} + \frac{\partial z}{\partial y}\frac{\partial y}{\partial t}$$

$$= (2xy)(2t) + (x^2 - 2y)(2)$$

$$= (2(t^2)(2t))(2t) + ((t^2)^2 - 2(2t))(2)$$

$x = t^2$
$y = 2t$

$$= 8t^4 + 2t^4 - 8t$$

$$= 10t^4 - 8t$$

**Multivariate chain rule for a n-dimensional function f.** Now suppose $f : \mathbb{R}^m \rightarrow$

$\mathbb{R}$ and $g : \mathbb{R}^n \to \mathbb{R}^m$ with

$$z = f(\mathbf{u}) = f(u_1, u_2, \ldots, u_m) = f(g_1(\mathbf{x}), \ldots, g_m(\mathbf{x})) \tag{7.14}$$

Then the derivative of $f$ with respect to a variable $x_i$ can be computed as follows:

$$\frac{\partial z}{\partial x_i} = \sum_{l=1}^{m} \frac{\partial z}{\partial u_l} \frac{\partial u_l}{\partial x_i} \tag{7.15}$$

Note that in the 2D case of the MCR described above $m$ was 2 with $u_1 = x(t)$ and $u_2 = y(t)$.

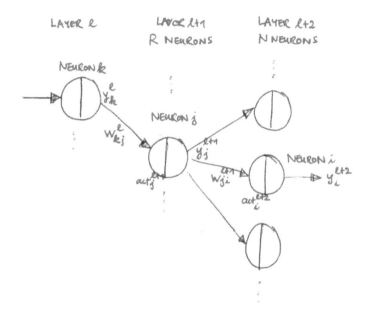

**Using the MCR to compute the third part for hidden neurons.** Now given the MCR we can compute the third part for neuron $j$ living in layer $l + 1$ as follows with the help of all the error signals from the following neurons $i$ living in layer $l + 2$:

$$\frac{\partial E}{\partial y_j} = \frac{\partial E}{\partial y_j^{l+1}} = \sum_{i=1}^{N} \frac{\partial E}{\partial y_i^{l+2}} \frac{\partial y_i^{l+2}}{\partial y_i^{l+1}} \tag{7.16}$$

So how can this be interpreted? We want to compute how the error $E$ changes if we change the output of the neuron $j$ in layer $l + 1$. For this we applied the MCR and compute instead how the error $E$ changes if we change the output of neurons $i$ in the next layer $l + 2$ *and* how their outputs $y_i^{l+2}$ change if we change the output of neuron $j$ in layer $l + 1$, i.e., $y_j^{l+1}$.

Now we can continue with the normal chain rule:

$$\sum_{i=1}^{N} \frac{\partial E}{\partial y_i^{l+2}} \frac{\partial y_i^{l+2}}{\partial y_i^{l+1}} = \sum_{i=1}^{N} \underbrace{\frac{\partial E}{\partial y_i^{l+2}} \frac{\partial y_i^{l+2}}{\partial act_i^{l+2}}}_{=-\delta_i^{l+2}} \frac{\partial act_i^{l+2}}{\partial y_j^{l+1}} \qquad (7.17)$$

$$= -\sum_{i=1}^{N} \delta_i^{l+2} \frac{\partial act_i^{l+2}}{\partial y_j^{l+1}} \qquad (7.18)$$

$$= -\sum_{i=1}^{N} \delta_i^{l+2} \frac{\partial \sum_{r=1}^{R} w_{ri}^{l+1} y_r^{l+1}}{\partial y_j^{l+1}} \qquad (7.19)$$

$$= -\sum_{i=1}^{N} \delta_i^{l+2} w_{ji}^{l+1} \qquad (7.20)$$

The battle of induces is over! Now let us also glue together the three parts that we have computed for the case of a hidden neuron:

$$\Delta w_{kj} = -\alpha \underbrace{\frac{\partial E}{\partial y_j}}_{3} \underbrace{\frac{\partial y_j}{\partial act_j}}_{2} \underbrace{\frac{\partial act_j}{\partial w_{kj}}}_{1} = -\alpha \underbrace{\left(-\sum_{i=1}^{N} \delta_i^{l+2} w_{ji}^{l+1}\right)}_{3} \underbrace{f'(act_j^{l+1})}_{2} \underbrace{y_k^l}_{1} \qquad (7.21)$$

So the difference regarding the weight update formula between output neurons and non-output neurons is only the error signal! The rest is the same. The error signal for neuron $j$ refers to the $N$ error signals from the neurons $i$ in the following layer which have to be computed first.

**Why the name *Backpropagation*?** It are the error signals $\delta_i$ that are propagated back through the network neurons in previous layers and which gave this learning algorithm its name *Backpropagation of error signals*. Since we need the error signals from layer $l+2$ if we want to compute the error for a neuron in layer $l+1$ we first need to compute the error signals for the output neurons, then we can compute the error signals for neurons in the previous layer and so forth. So the layer wise update scheme during the error signal computation phase is the opposite direction compared to the feedforward step: we start at the last layer and move towards the input layer.

## 7.7 Backpropagation pseudo code

**Stochastic Gradient Descent (SGD) with one sample.** The following pseudo-code shows how the Backpropagation algorithm uses the derived weight change formulas in order to adapt the weights of a given MLP. Note that the approach presented here is called *Stochastic Gradient Descent (SGD)* with one training sample: one training sample is feedforwarded, the weight changes are computed for all weights and directly applied. This means that the gradient descent steps are based on the evaluation of just one training sample from the dataset $D$.

**Batch Gradient Descent (BGD).** The alternative is to accumulate the weight changes first for all training samples of the dataset $D$ and then update the weights based on the accumulated changes. Since we use the whole batch of samples to update the weight changes, this version of gradient descent is also called *Batch Gradient Descent* (sometimes also called *Vanilla Gradient Descent*, since it is the standard version of GD). The problem of BGD is that in the case of very large datasets BGD needs a long time to compute just a single weight update: the larger the training set, the slower our algorithm will update the weights.

**SGD and BGD walk different paths.** SGD and BGD will take different paths to a local minimum of the error surface. Due to its stochastic nature, SGD will often walk "zig-zag" paths towards a local minimum, while the path chosen by BGD is more "smooth" and direct towards a local minimum. The term "stochastic" goes back to the fact that the error gradient based on a single training sample that is used in SGD can be considered a "stochastic approximation" of the true error gradient that is computed by BGD. SGD works well in practice and only rarely BGD is used. One reason is probably that for error surfaces that have lots of local maxima and minima the noisier gradient calculated by SGD allows to escape a local minimum which BGD cannot.

**Mini-Batch Gradient Descent (MBGD).** *Mini-Batch Gradient descent* or *Stochastic Gradient Descent with a mini-batch of samples* is a compromise between SGD with one sample and BGD. The model (here: the MLP) is updated based on a smaller group of samples from the dataset $D$, e.g. just 100 samples. In the context of neural networks, MBGD is most often used to compute the gradient compared to SGD with just one sample and BGD.

Listing 7.1: Backpropagation algorithm

```
Backpropagation(MLP, training data D, nr_epochs)
{

for epoch=1...nr_epochs:

  shuffle training data D
  for each training pair p_i = (x, t_i) ∈ D:

```

```
 9    initialize output values of input neurons with x
10
11    # feedforward step
12    for all layers l = 1...L:
13      for all neurons j in layer l:
14        compute act_j (sum of weighted inputs) for neuron j
15        y_j := out_j := f(act_j)
16
17    # Backpropagation step 1: compute error signals
18    for all layers l = L...1:
19      for all neurons j in layer l:
20        if neuron j is output neuron:
21          δ_j := -(y_j - t_j) * f'(act_j)
22        else:
23          sumerrors := 0
24          for all N neurons i in next layer l+1:
25            sumerrors+ = w_ji * δ_i
26          δ_j := sumerrors * f'(act_j)
27
28    # Backpropagation step 2: adapt weights
29    for all layers l = L...1 (or layers l = 1...L, order irrelevant now):
30      for all neurons j in layer l:
31        for all inputs from neurons k in layer l-1:
32          Δw_kj := α * δ_j * y_k
33          w_kj := w_kj + Δw_kj
34 }
```

## 7.8  MLP in Python

Listing 7.2: test_mlp.py

```python
 1 import numpy as np
 2 from data_generator import data_generator
 3 from mlp import mlp
 4 from mlp import TF
 5 import cv2
 6
 7
 8 # test data parameters
 9 WINSIZE = 600
10 NR_CLUSTERS = 5
11 NR_SAMPLES_TO_GENERATE = 20000
12
13 # MLP parameters
14 NR_EPOCHS = 21
15 LEARN_RATE = 0.1
16
17 # visualization parameters
```

```
18  RADIUS_SAMPLE = 3
19  COLOR_CLASS0 = (255,0,0)
20  COLOR_CLASS1 = (0,0,255)
21  NR_TEST_SAMPLES = 10000
22
23  # for saving images
24  image_counter = 0
25
26
27  def visualize_decision_boundaries(the_mlp, epoch_nr):
28
29      global image_counter
30
31      # 1. generate empty white color image
32      img = np.ones((WINSIZE, WINSIZE, 3), np.uint8) * 255
33
34      for i in range(NR_TEST_SAMPLES):
35
36          # 2. generate random coordinate in [0,1) x [0,1)
37          rnd_x = np.random.rand()
38          rnd_y = np.random.rand()
39
40          # 3. prepare an input vector
41          input_vec = np.array( [rnd_x, rnd_y] )
42
43          # 4. now do a feedforward step with that
44          #    input vector, i.e., compute the output values
45          #    of the MLP for that input vector
46          the_mlp.feedforward( input_vec )
47
48          # 5. now get the predicted class from the output
49          #    vector
50          output_vec = the_mlp.get_output_vector()
51          class_label = 0 if output_vec[0]>output_vec[1] else 1
52
53          # 6. Map class label to a color
54          color = COLOR_CLASS0 if class_label == 0 else COLOR_CLASS1
55
56          # 7. Draw circle
57          sample_coord = (int(input_vec[0] * WINSIZE),
58                          int(input_vec[1] * WINSIZE))
59          cv2.circle(img, sample_coord, RADIUS_SAMPLE, color)
60
61      # 8. show image with decision boundaries
62      cv2.rectangle(img, (WINSIZE-120,0), (WINSIZE-1,20),
63                    (255,255,255), -1)
64      font = cv2.FONT_HERSHEY_SIMPLEX
65      cv2.putText(img,
66                  "epoch #"+str(epoch_nr).zfill(3),
67                  (WINSIZE - 110, 15), font, 0.5, (0, 0, 0), 1,
```

```
68                      cv2.LINE_AA)
69      cv2.imshow('Decision boundaries of trained MLP', img)
70      c = cv2.waitKey(1)
71
72      # 9. save that image?
73      if True:
74          filename = "V:/tmp/img_{0:0>4}".format(image_counter)
75          image_counter +=1
76          cv2.imwrite(filename + ".png", img)
77
78
79
80  # 1. create a new MLP
81  my_mlp = mlp()
82
83
84  # 2. build a MLP
85  my_mlp.add_layer(2,   TF.identity)
86  my_mlp.add_layer(10,  TF.sigmoid)
87  my_mlp.add_layer(6,   TF.sigmoid)
88  my_mlp.add_layer(2,   TF.identity)
89
90
91  # 3. generate training data
92  my_dg = data_generator()
93  data_samples = \
94      my_dg.generate_samples_two_class_problem(NR_CLUSTERS,
95                                     NR_SAMPLES_TO_GENERATE)
96  nr_samples = len(data_samples)
97
98
99  # 4. generate empty image for visualization
100 #    initialize image with white pixels (255,255,255)
101 img = np.ones((WINSIZE, WINSIZE, 3), np.uint8) * 255
102
103
104 # 5. visualize positions of samples
105 for i in range(nr_samples):
106
107     # 5.1 get the next data sample
108     next_sample = data_samples[i]
109
110     # 5.2 get input and output vector
111     #     (which are both NumPy arrays)
112     input_vec = next_sample[0]
113     output_vec = next_sample[1]
114
115     # 5.3 prepare a tupel from the NumPy input vector
116     sample_coord = (int(input_vec[0]*WINSIZE),
117                     int(input_vec[1]*WINSIZE))
```

```
118
119     # 5.4 get class label from output vector
120     if output_vec[0]>output_vec[1]:
121         class_label = 0
122     else:
123         class_label = 1
124     color = (0,0,0)
125     if class_label == 0:
126         color = COLOR_CLASS0
127     elif class_label == 1:
128         color = COLOR_CLASS1
129
130     # 5.5
131     cv2.circle(img, sample_coord, RADIUS_SAMPLE, color)
132
133
134 # 6. show visualization of samples
135 cv2.imshow('Training data', img)
136 c = cv2.waitKey(1)
137 cv2.imwrite("V:/tmp/training_data.png", img)
138 #cv2.destroyAllWindows()
139
140
141 # 7. now train the MLP
142 my_mlp.set_learn_rate( LEARN_RATE )
143 for epoch_nr in range(NR_EPOCHS):
144
145     print("Training epoch#", epoch_nr)
146
147     sample_indices = np.arange(nr_samples)
148     np.random.shuffle(sample_indices)
149
150     for train_sample_nr in range(nr_samples):
151
152         # get index of next training sample
153         index = sample_indices[train_sample_nr]
154
155         # get that training sample
156         next_sample = data_samples[index]
157
158         # get input and output vector
159         # (which are both NumPy arrays)
160         input_vec = next_sample[0]
161         output_vec = next_sample[1]
162
163         # train the MLP with that vector pair
164         my_mlp.train(input_vec, output_vec)
165
166     print("\nMLP state after training epoch #",epoch_nr,":")
167     my_mlp.show_weight_statistics()
```

```
168     my_mlp.show_neuron_states()
169     visualize_decision_boundaries(my_mlp, epoch_nr)
170     #input("Press Enter to train next epoch")
171
172 print("MLP test finished.")
```

Listing 7.3: mlp.py

```
1  import numpy as np
2  import math
3
4
5  def func_identity(x):
6      return x
7
8  def func_sigmoid(x):
9      return 1 / (1 + math.exp(-x))
10
11 def func_relu(x):
12     return x if x>0 else 0
13
14 def func_squared(x):
15     return x*x
16
17
18 def derivative_identity(x):
19     return 1
20
21
22
23 """
24 derivative of standard logistic function
25 f(x) is f'(x) = f(x)*(1-f(x))
26 see https://en.wikipedia.org/wiki/Logistic_function#Derivative
27 """
28 def derivative_sigmoid(x):
29     return func_sigmoid(x) * (1 - func_sigmoid(x))
30
31 def derivative_relu(x):
32     return 1 if x>0 else 0
33
34 def derivative_squared(x):
35     return 2*x
36
37
38 func_identity   = np.vectorize(func_identity)
39 func_sigmoid    = np.vectorize(func_sigmoid)
40 func_relu       = np.vectorize(func_relu)
41 func_skew_ramp  = np.vectorize(func_squared)
42 derivative_identity  = np.vectorize(derivative_identity)
```

```python
43  derivative_sigmoid    = np.vectorize(derivative_sigmoid)
44  derivative_relu       = np.vectorize(derivative_relu)
45  derivative_skew_ramp  = np.vectorize(derivative_squared)
46
47
48  class TF:
49      identity = 1
50      sigmoid  = 2
51      relu     = 3
52      squared  = 4
53
54
55
56
57  class mlp:
58
59      nr_layers            = 0
60      nr_neurons_per_layer = []
61      tf_per_layer         = []
62      weight_matrices      = []
63      neuron_act_vecs      = []
64      neuron_out_vecs      = []
65
66      learn_rate           = 0.01
67      neuron_err_vecs      = []
68
69      def __init__(self):
70          print("Generated a new empty MLP")
71
72
73      """
74      Returns the output vector of the MLP
75      as a NumPy array
76      """
77      def get_output_vector(self):
78
79          return self.neuron_out_vecs[len(self.neuron_out_vecs)-1]
80
81
82
83      def show_architecture(self):
84
85          print("MLP architecture is now: ", end=" ")
86
87          for i in range(self.nr_layers):
88              print(str(self.nr_neurons_per_layer[i]), end=" ")
89
90          print("\n")
91
92
```

```
 93      """
 94      Adds a new layer of neurons
 95      """
 96      def add_layer(self, nr_neurons, transfer_function):
 97
 98          # 1. store number of neurons of this new layer
 99          #    and type of transfer function to use
100          self.nr_neurons_per_layer.append( nr_neurons )
101          self.tf_per_layer.append( transfer_function )
102
103          # 2. generate a weight matrix?
104          if self.nr_layers>=1:
105
106              # 2.1 how many neurons are there in the
107              #     previous layer?
108              nr_neurons_before =\
109                  self.nr_neurons_per_layer[self.nr_layers-1]
110
111              # 2.2 initialize weight matrix with random
112              #     values from (0,1)
113              #     Do not forget the BIAS input for each
114              #     neuron! For this: nr_neurons_before + 1
115              W = np.random.uniform(low=-1.0, high=1.0,
116                                    size=(nr_neurons_before+1,nr_neurons))
117
118              # 2.3 store the new weight matrix
119              self.weight_matrices.append(W)
120
121              # 2.4 output some information about the
122              #     weight matrix just generated
123              print("Generated a new weight matrix W. Shape is",
124                    W.shape)
125              size = W.nbytes/1024.0
126              print("Size of weight matrix in KB"
127                    " is {0:.2f}".format(size))
128
129
130          # 3. generate a new neuron activity and
131          # #  neuron output vector
132          act_vec = np.zeros(nr_neurons)
133          out_vec = np.zeros(nr_neurons)
134          err_vec = np.zeros(nr_neurons)
135          self.neuron_act_vecs.append( act_vec )
136          self.neuron_out_vecs.append( out_vec )
137          self.neuron_err_vecs.append( err_vec )
138
139          # 4. update number of layers
140          self.nr_layers += 1
141
142          # 5. show current MLP architecture
```

```
143         self.show_architecture()
144
145
146     """
147     Given an input vector, we compute
148     the output of all the neurons layer by layer
149     into the direction of the output layer
150     """
151     def feedforward(self, input_vec):
152
153         # 1. set output of neurons from first layer
154         #     to input vector values
155         N = len(input_vec)
156         self.neuron_out_vecs[0] = input_vec
157
158         # 2. now compute neuron outputs layer by layer
159         for layer_nr in range(1,self.nr_layers):
160
161             # 2.1 get output vector previously computed
162             o = self.neuron_out_vecs[layer_nr-1]
163
164             # 2.2 add bias input
165             o = np.append([1], o)
166
167             # 2.3 vectors are one-dimensional
168             #     but for matrix*matrix multiplication we need
169             #     a matrix in the following
170             N = len(o)
171             o_mat = o.reshape(1,N)
172
173             # 2.4 now get the right weight matrix
174             W = self.weight_matrices[layer_nr-1]
175
176             # 2.5 compute the product of the output (vector)
177             #     and the weight matrix to get the output values
178             #     of neurons in the current layer
179             act_mat_this_layer = np.matmul(o_mat,W)
180
181             # 2.6 apply transfer function
182             if self.tf_per_layer[layer_nr]==TF.sigmoid:
183                 out_mat_this_layer =\
184                     func_sigmoid(act_mat_this_layer)
185             elif self.tf_per_layer[layer_nr]==TF.identity:
186                 out_mat_this_layer =\
187                     func_identity(act_mat_this_layer)
188             elif self.tf_per_layer[layer_nr]==TF.relu:
189                 out_mat_this_layer = \
190                     func_relu(act_mat_this_layer)
191             elif self.tf_per_layer[layer_nr]==TF.squared:
192                 out_mat_this_layer = \
```

```
193                         func_squared(act_mat_this_layer)
194
195                 # 2.7 store activity and output of neurons
196                 self.neuron_act_vecs[layer_nr] = \
197                     act_mat_this_layer.flatten()
198                 self.neuron_out_vecs[layer_nr] = \
199                     out_mat_this_layer.flatten()
200
201
202
203         """
204         Show output values of all neurons
205         in the specified layer
206         """
207         def show_output(self, layer):
208
209             print("output values of neuron in layer",layer,":",
210                 self.neuron_out_vecs[layer])
211
212
213         """
214         Shows some statistics about the weights,
215         e.g. what is the maximum and the minimum weight in
216         each weight matrix
217         """
218         def show_weight_statistics(self):
219
220             for layer_nr in range(0,self.nr_layers-1):
221                 W = self.weight_matrices[layer_nr]
222                 print("Weight matrix for weights from"
223                     "layer #",layer_nr,"to layer #",
224                     layer_nr+1, ":")
225                 print("\t shape:", W.shape)
226                 print("\t min value: ", np.amin(W))
227                 print("\t max value: ", np.amax(W))
228                 print("\t W", W)
229             print("\n")
230
231
232         """
233         Show state of neurons (activity and output values)
234         """
235         def show_neuron_states(self):
236
237             for layer_nr in range(0, self.nr_layers):
238                 print("Layer #", layer_nr)
239                 print("\t act:", self.neuron_act_vecs[layer_nr])
240                 print("\t out:", self.neuron_out_vecs[layer_nr])
241             print("\n")
242
```

```
243
244        """
245        Set a new learn rate which is used in the
246        weight update step
247        """
248        def set_learn_rate(self, new_learn_rate):
249            self.learn_rate = new_learn_rate
250
251
252        """
253        Given a pair (input_vec, teacher_vec) we adapt
254        the weights of the MLP such that the desired output vector
255        (which is the teacher vector)
256        is more likely to be generated the next time if the
257        input vector is presented as input
258
259        Note: this is the Backpropagation learning algorithm!
260        """
261        def train(self, input_vec, teacher_vec):
262
263            # 1. first do a feedfoward step with the input vector
264            self.feedforward(input_vec)
265
266            # 2. first compute the error signals for the output
267            #    neurons
268            tf_type    = self.tf_per_layer[self.nr_layers-1]
269            nr_neurons = self.nr_neurons_per_layer[self.nr_layers-1]
270            act_vec    = self.neuron_act_vecs[self.nr_layers-1]
271            out_vec    = self.neuron_out_vecs[self.nr_layers-1]
272            err_vec    = -(out_vec-teacher_vec)
273            if tf_type==TF.sigmoid:
274                err_vec *= derivative_sigmoid(act_vec)
275            elif tf_type==TF.identity:
276                err_vec *= derivative_identity(act_vec)
277            elif tf_type==TF.relu:
278                err_vec *= derivative_relu(act_vec)
279            elif tf_type==TF.squared:
280                err_vec *= derivative_squared(act_vec)
281            self.neuron_err_vecs[self.nr_layers-1] = err_vec
282
283            # 3. now go from layer N-1 to layer 2 and
284            #    compute for each hidden layer the
285            #    error signals for each neuron
286
287            # going layer for layer backwards ...
288            for layer_nr in range(self.nr_layers-2, 0, -1):
289
290                nr_neurons_this_layer = \
291                    self.nr_neurons_per_layer[layer_nr]
292                nr_neurons_next_layer = \
```

```
293                    self.nr_neurons_per_layer[layer_nr+1]
294            W       = self.weight_matrices[layer_nr]
295            act_vec = self.neuron_act_vecs[layer_nr]
296            tf_type = self.tf_per_layer[layer_nr]
297
298            # run over all neurons in this layer ...
299            for neuron_nr in range(0,nr_neurons_this_layer):
300
301                # compute the sum of weighted error signals from
302                # neurons in the next layer
303                sum_of_weighted_error_signals = 0.0
304
305                # run over all neurons in next layer ...
306                for neuron_nr2 in range (0,nr_neurons_next_layer):
307
308                    # get error signal for neuron_nr2 in next layer
309                    err_vec = self.neuron_err_vecs[layer_nr+1]
310                    err_signal = err_vec[neuron_nr2]
311
312                    # get weight from
313                    # neuron_nr  in layer_nr to
314                    # neuron_nr2 in layer_nr+1
315                    #
316                    # Important:
317                    # at W[0][neuron_nr2] is the bias
318                    # weight to neuron_nr2
319                    # at W[1][neuron_nr2] is the first
320                    # "real" weight to neuron_nr2
321                    weight = W[neuron_nr+1][neuron_nr2]
322
323                    # update sum
324                    sum_of_weighted_error_signals +=\
325                        err_signal * weight
326
327                # compute and store error signal for
328                # neuron with id neuron_nr in this layer
329                err_signal = sum_of_weighted_error_signals
330                if tf_type == TF.sigmoid:
331                    err_signal *= \
332                        derivative_sigmoid(act_vec[neuron_nr])
333                elif tf_type == TF.identity:
334                    err_signal *= \
335                        derivative_identity(act_vec[neuron_nr])
336                elif tf_type == TF.relu:
337                    err_signal *= \
338                        derivative_relu(act_vec[neuron_nr])
339                elif tf_type == TF.squared:
340                    err_signal *= \
341                        derivative_squared(act_vec[neuron_nr])
342                self.neuron_err_vecs[layer_nr][neuron_nr] =\
```

```
343                          err_signal
344
345
346           # 4. now that we have the error signals for all
347           #    neurons (hidden and output neurons) in the net
348           #    computed, let's change the weights according to
349           #    the weight update formulas
350           for layer_nr in range(self.nr_layers - 1, 0, -1):
351
352               nr_neurons_this_layer = \
353                   self.nr_neurons_per_layer[layer_nr]
354               nr_neurons_prev_layer = \
355                   self.nr_neurons_per_layer[layer_nr-1]
356
357               for neuron_nr in range(0, nr_neurons_this_layer):
358
359                   # get error signal for this neuron
360                   err_signal = \
361                       self.neuron_err_vecs[layer_nr][neuron_nr]
362
363                   for weight_nr in range(0, nr_neurons_prev_layer+1):
364
365                       # get output value of sending neuron
366                       out_val_sending_neuron = 1
367                       if weight_nr>0:
368                           out_val_sending_neuron = \
369                               self.neuron_out_vecs[layer_nr-1][weight_nr-1]
370
371                       # compute weight change
372                       weight_change = \
373                           self.learn_rate * \
374                           err_signal * \
375                           out_val_sending_neuron
376
377                       self.weight_matrices[layer_nr-1][weight_nr][neuron_nr]
       += \
378                           weight_change
```

Listing 7.4: data_generator.py

```
1  import numpy as np
2
3  class data_generator:
4
5      def __init__(self):
6          print("A new data generator object has been created.")
7
8
9      def generate_samples_two_class_problem\
10         (self, nr_clusters, nr_samples_to_generate):
```

```
np.random.seed(4)
CLUSTER_RADIUS = 0.2

# 1. generate random cluster coordinates
clusters = []
for i in range(nr_samples_to_generate):

    # 1.1 generate random cluster center
    center_x = np.random.rand()
    center_y = np.random.rand()

    # 1.2 store that center
    clusters.append(  np.array([center_x,center_y])  )


# 2. generate random samples
data_samples = []
for i in range(nr_samples_to_generate):

    # 2.1 generate random coordinate
    rnd_x = np.random.rand()
    rnd_y = np.random.rand()
    rnd_coord = np.array( [rnd_x,rnd_y] )

    # 2.2 check whether that coordinate is
    #     near to a cluster
    #     if yes, we say it belongs to class 1
    #     if no,  we say it belongs to class 0
    class_label = 0
    for j in range(nr_clusters):

        # get cluster coordinates
        cluster_coords = clusters[j]

        # compute distance of sample (rnd_x,rnd_y) to
        # cluster coordinates (center_x,center_y)
        dist = np.linalg.norm( cluster_coords - rnd_coord )

        # is the sample near to that cluster
        if dist < CLUSTER_RADIUS:
            class_label = 1
            break

    # 2.3 store the sample
    input_vec = np.array([rnd_x, rnd_y])
    output_vec = np.array([1-class_label, class_label])
    data_samples.append( [input_vec,output_vec] )
```

```
61        # 3. return the generated samples
62        return data_samples
```

# Final Backpropagation weight update formulas

## For output neurons:

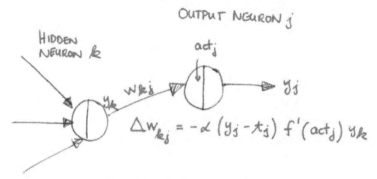

$$\Delta w_{kj} = -\alpha \left( y_j - t_j \right) f'(act_j) \, y_k$$

## For hidden neurons:

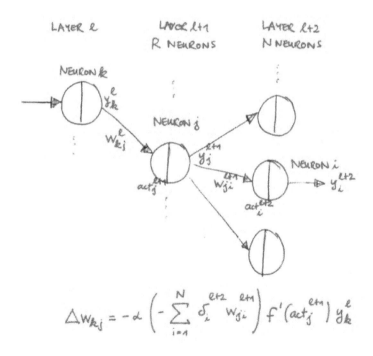

$$\Delta w_{kj} = -\alpha \left( -\sum_{i=1}^{N} \delta_i^{\ell+2} \, w_{ji}^{\ell+1} \right) f'\left(act_j^{\ell+1}\right) y_k^{\ell}$$

Figure 7.3: These are the final weight update formulas for the Backpropagation learning algorithm.

## 7.9   Visualization of decision boundaries

**Visualizing the classifier.** In the Python code example shown in the previous section a simple idea is used to visualize the classification behavior of the learned MLP. The training data of a two class classification problem is generated by using five clusters: If a randomly generated 2D sample $(x, y)$ is within some radius of one of these five clusters it is defined to belong to class 1 and class 0 else. For visualizing how the intermediate MLPs and the final MLP classify patterns according to their weights, 10.000 randomly generated samples $(x, y)$ are fed into the MLP and the classification result is read from the two output neurons by determining which one has the highest output value. Samples that are classified into class 1 are visualized by circle type 1 and samples that are classified by the MLP into class 0 are visualized by circle type 2. This allows us to visualize and see the *decision boundaries* of the MLP. Fig. 7.5 (logistic transfer function) and Fig. 7.6 (ReLU transfer function) show the decision boundaries of the MLP models during training after each epoch.

**Two further transfer functions.** Fig. 7.4 shows the graphs of two further transfer functions which are now often used. Note that they are not biologically plausible since they are unbounded. However, the advantage of both is that there is no need to compute the exponential function which is computationally costly.

The *Rectified Linear Unit (ReLU)* is defined by:

$$f(x) = max(0, x) = \begin{cases} 0 & , x < 0 \\ x & , x \geq 0 \end{cases} \tag{7.22}$$

The *Leaky Rectified Linear Unit (LReLU)* is defined by:

$$f(x) = \begin{cases} 0.01x & , x < 0 \\ x & , x \geq 0 \end{cases} \tag{7.23}$$

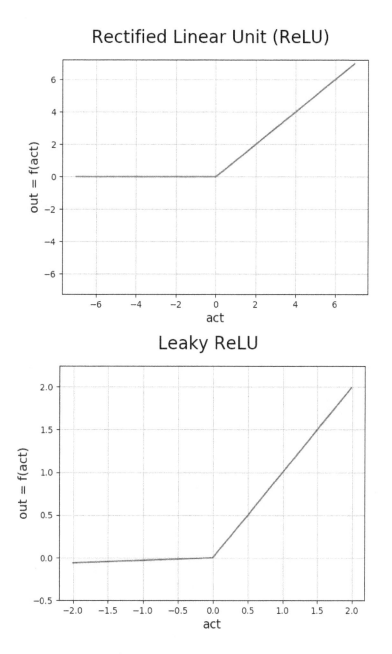

Figure 7.4: Two further transfer functions currently often used.

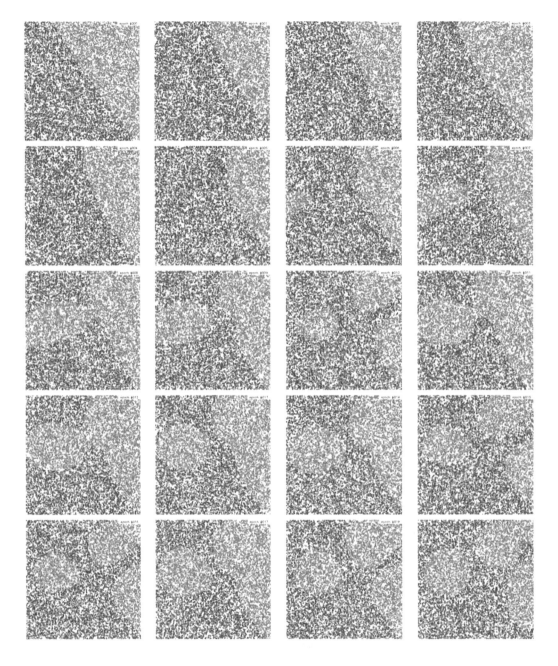

Figure 7.5: Decision boundaries of a MLP after epoch 0-18. The training data used is shown in the last image. The MLP is a 2id-10sig-6sig-2id network with 2 input neurons with the identity as transfer function, 10 neurons in the first hidden layer with sigmoid transfer functions, 6 neurons in the second hidden layer with sigmoid transfer functions and 2 output neurons with identity as transfer function.

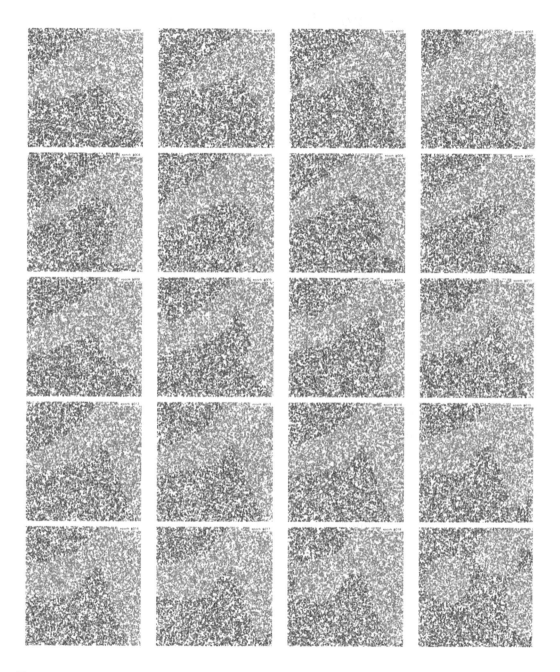

Figure 7.6: Decision boundaries of a MLP after epoch 0-18. The training data used is shown in the last image. The MLP is a 2id-10relu-6relu-2id network with the ReLU as transfer function in the hidden layers.

## 7.10 The need for non-linear transfer functions

**A MLP with identity transfer functions only.** Have a look at Fig. 7.7. Here I used a 2-10-6-2 MLP network with the identity as transfer function in all layers. Compare the resulting decision boundaries after epoch 18 with the decision boundaries from Fig. 7.5 and Fig. 7.6, where we used the logisitic function and the ReLU function respectively as transfer functions in the hidden layers. It can be seen that in the case of using identity transfer functions only the intermediate and the final decision boundaries are just a linear separation of the input space in two half-spaces. And there is a reason for this!

**No advantage of using several layers.** We have seen in section 5.4 that a single layer Perceptron can only separate the input space into two half-spaces. We could expect that this must not hold true for a MLP with several layers. However, we can easily show that even if we use several layers of neurons with identity transfer functions we still end up with a classifier that can only divide the input space into two half-spaces. Fig. 7.8 illustrates why. Each MLP with neurons that just use the identity as transfer function can be transformed successively into a single layer Perceptron which produces the same output. Since single layer Perceptrons are know to be just linear separators, this must hold true for a MLP with just linear transfer functions as well. This is the reason why we need *non-linear transfer functions* in the hidden layers.

**The need for non-linear transfer functions in biological neurons.** It is interesting to see that nature has developed some "non-linear transfer function" as well: if the sum of inputs of a neuron (the sum of IPSPs and EPSPs that change the membrane potential) is below the threshold potential no spikes will be generated. But if the threshold potential is reached the spike rate increases "nearly linearly" with the membrane potential. This is a non-linear mapping of the input activity of a neuron to its output value that resembles the ramp transfer function and the ReLU transfer function. However, the ReLU transfer function has an important difference to its biological counterpart: it is unbounded. So here is a research question: did anyone in the Deep Learning community try out whether a ramp transfer function (which is bounded and therefore more biologically plausible) has a drawback compared to the ReLU?

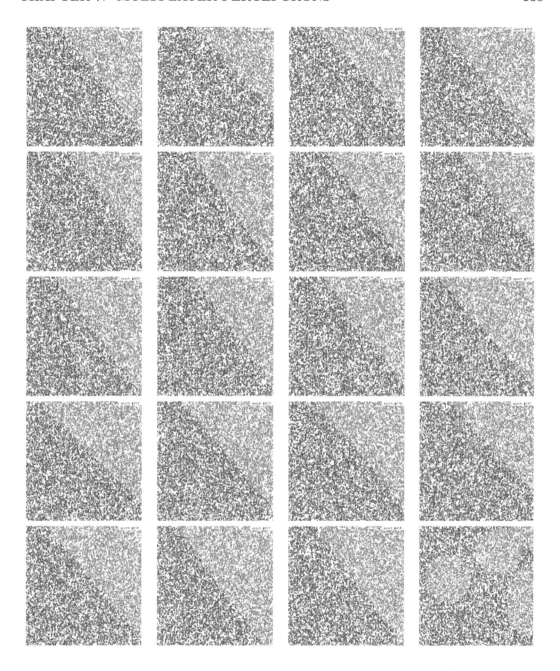

Figure 7.7: Decision boundaries of a MLP after epoch 0-18. The training data used is shown in the last image. The MLP is a 2id-10id-6id-2id network that uses only the identity as transfer function in all layers.

## A MLP with neurons that just use the identity as transfer function ...

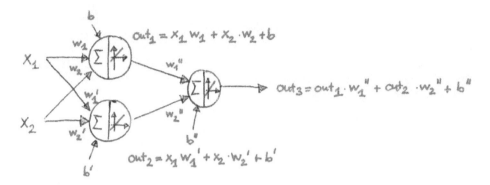

$$out_1 = x_1 w_1 + x_2 \cdot w_2 + b$$

$$out_3 = out_1 \cdot w_1'' + out_2 \cdot w_2'' + b''$$

$$out_2 = x_1 w_1' + x_2 \cdot w_2' + b'$$

## ... is equivalent to a single layer Perceptron:

$$\Rightarrow \quad out_3 = \underbrace{(x_1 w_1 + x_2 \cdot w_2 + b)}_{\hat{=}\, out_1} \cdot w_1'' + \underbrace{(x_1 w_1' + x_2 w_2' + b')}_{\hat{=}\, out_2} \cdot w_2'' + b''$$

$$= x_1 w_1 w_1'' + x_2 w_2 w_1'' + b w_1'' + x_1 w_1' w_2'' + x_2 w_2' w_2'' + b' w_2'' + b''$$

$$= x_1 \underbrace{\left[ w_1 w_1'' + w_1' w_2'' \right]}_{=:\, w_1'''} + x_2 \underbrace{\left[ w_2 w_1'' + w_2' w_2'' \right]}_{=:\, w_2'''} + \underbrace{b w_1'' + b' w_2'' + b}_{=:\, b'''}$$

$$out_3 = x_1 w_1''' + x_2 w_2''' + b'''$$

Figure 7.8: A MLP with hidden neurons that use just the transfer functions does not give us any advantage over using a single layer Perceptron since for each MLP we can find a single layer Perceptron (here: with weights $w_1'''$, $w_2'''$, $b'''$) that produces the same output. Since single layer Perceptrons are known to be limited to separating the input space by a hyperplane into two half spaces this also has to hold true for a MLP that uses just linear transfer functions.

*8*

# TensorFlow

## 8.1 Introduction

### Basic idea behind TensorFlow

The basic idea behind Google's Deep Learning library TensorFlow is to describe all computations as a graph. Nodes in this (directed) graph describe operations on the data and the data itself is packed into n-dimensional arrays. In the TensorFlow jargon these n-dimensional arrays are called *tensors*. Since the data is reached from one node to the other it is the data that "flows" through the graph. For this the name *Tensor-Flow*. Note that the tensors in a computation graph can have different shapes: E.g., there can be 0-dimensional tensors ("scalars"), 1-dimensional tensors ("vectors"), 2-dimensional tensors ("matrices"), 3-dimensional tensors ("cuboids of data"), etc.

### Version check

At the time of writing this text line (November 2017) the newest version of TensorFlow was 1.4.0. To quickly check which version you have installed, type in:

```
import tensorflow as tf
print("Your TF version is", tf.__version__)
```

`tf.__version__` is a string and in my case the result was:

```
Your TF version is 1.2.1
```

## TensorFlow graphs can run on different computing devices

A very interesting feature of TensorFlow is that it allows to distribute a computation graph across multiple devices. Note that if you plan to distribute the graphs also on GPUs you have to install the GPU version of TensorFlow. It is possible to retrieve the list of available computing devices from TensorFlow:

```
from tensorflow.python.client import device_lib
devices = [x.name for x in device_lib.list_local_devices()]
print(devices)
```

In my case the result was:

```
['/cpu:0']
```

But if you have a GPU available the result could also be:

```
['/cpu:0', '/gpu:0']
```

## Types of tensors

In TensorFlow there are three different types of tensors.

`tf.Variable` is a tensor that is used to store a parameter value, e.g., a single weight, a vector of weights or a whole weight matrix that will adapted during a training procedure:

```
a = tf.Variable(3, name='var1')
b = tf.Variable([1.0,2.0,3.0], name='var2')
c = tf.Variable([[1,0],[0,1]], name='var3')
print(a)
print(b)
```

```
6 print(c)
```

Output:

```
1 <tf.Variable 'var1:0' shape=() dtype=int32_ref>
2 <tf.Variable 'var2:0' shape=(3,) dtype=float32_ref>
3 <tf.Variable 'var3:0' shape=(2, 2) dtype=int32_ref>
```

Note that the `print()` calls does not output the value of the tensor, but type information. The name which we define in the variable is shown in the output and augmented by a ":0". What does this mean? It means that this variable "lives" in graph 0. TensorFlow allows us to construct several computations graphs.

`tf.constant` is another tensor type and used for storing constant values:

```
1 d = tf.constant(3.14159, name='pi')
```

Output:

```
1 Tensor("pi:0", shape=(), dtype=float32)
```

`tf.placeholder` is the third tensor type and used as a placeholder for data that will be filled in later, e.g., during training for an input image:

```
1 e = tf.placeholder(tf.float32, shape=[28, 28], name="myPlaceholder-input-
    image")
```

Output:

```
1 Tensor("myPlaceholder-input-image:0", shape=(28, 28), dtype=float32)
```

### Running a first computation

It is important to understand that a graph just defines a computation but it does not execute it. It also does not hold any values. In order to run a computation we need a session. Sessions allow to run a computation in a graph or a subset of nodes in the graph. Initializing a session means that TensorFlow will choose a device on which to compute your graph. If you installed the GPU version of TensorFlow, Tensorflow will automatically distribute the graph onto the GPU.

```
a = tf.Variable(3.0)
b = tf.Variable(4.0)
c = tf.multiply(a, b)
print(c)
with tf.Session() as my_session:
    my_session.run(tf.global_variables_initializer())
    resulting_tensor = my_session.run(c)
    print("resulting tensor=",resulting_tensor)
```

```
Tensor("Mul:0", shape=(), dtype=float32)
resulting tensor= 12.0
```

## A simple graph example with placeholders

```
a = tf.placeholder(tf.float32)
b = tf.placeholder(tf.float32)
adder_node = a + b  # shortcut for tf.add(a, b)
with tf.Session() as my_session:
    my_session.run(tf.global_variables_initializer())
    print(my_session.run(adder_node, {a:3, b:4} ))
    print(my_session.run(adder_node, {a: [1,2], b: [3,4]} ))
    print(my_session.run(adder_node, {a: [[1, 1],[1,1]], b: [[1, 1],[0,1]]}
    ))
```

```
7.0
[ 4.  6.]
[[ 2.  2.]
 [ 1.  2.]]
```

## TensorFlow only computes what is needed

When running an operator node - in the following example the node d - TensorFlow automatically determines which parts of the graph have to be computed as well. In the following it would conclude that operator node c has to be computed first in order to be able to evaluate node d.

```
a = tf.Variable(2)
b = tf.Variable(5)
c = tf.multiply(a,b)
d = tf.add(a,c)
print(d)
```

```
6  with tf.Session() as my_session:
7      my_session.run(tf.global_variables_initializer())
8      d_value = my_session.run(d)
9      print ("d_value=",d_value)
```

```
1  Tensor("Add:0", shape=(), dtype=int32)
2  d_value= 12
```

## Saving and restoring variables

We will use TensorFlow graphs in order to realize neural networks in the following. The `tf.Variables` will be used to represent the weights of the network. Training can last for a long time. So it makes sense to save learned weights. This can easily be done with TensorFlow.

Example that shows how to save all variables of a session:

```
1  a = tf.Variable(3)
2  b = tf.Variable(15, name="variable-b")
3  saver = tf.train.Saver()
4  print("type of save is ",type(saver))
5  with tf.Session() as my_session:
6      my_session.run(tf.global_variables_initializer())
7      print("a:", my_session.run(a))
8      print("b:", my_session.run(b))
```

```
1  type of save is  <class 'tensorflow.python.training.saver.Saver'>
2  a: 3
3  b: 15
```

Restoring variable values from a previously stored session:

```
1  a = tf.Variable(0)
2  b = tf.Variable(0, name="variable-b")
3  saver = tf.train.Saver()
4  print("type of save is ",type(saver))
5  with tf.Session() as my_session:
6      saver.restore(my_session, "V:/tmp/my_model.ckpt")
7      print("a:", my_session.run(a))
8      print("b:", my_session.run(b))
```

```
1  type of save is  <class 'tensorflow.python.training.saver.Saver'>
```

```
2 a: 3
3 b: 15
```

Note that it is important for restoring variables that we use the same computation graph. Let's see what happens if we just change the name of the second variable:

```
1 a = tf.Variable(0)
2 b = tf.Variable(0, name="variable-c")
3 saver = tf.train.Saver()
4 print("type of save is ",type(saver))
5 with tf.Session() as my_session:
6     saver.restore(my_session, "V:/tmp/my_model.ckpt")
7     print("a:", my_session.run(a))
8     print("b:", my_session.run(b))
```

```
1 NotFoundError (see above for traceback): Key variable-c not found in checkpoint
```

### Visualizing the graph using TensorBoard

Generating a visualization of the graph can be easily done by using `tf.summary.FileWriter()` and *TensorBoard*.

```
1 a = tf.Variable(3, name="var-a")
2 b = tf.Variable(4, name="var-b")
3 c = tf.Variable(5, name="var-c")
4 d = tf.multiply(a,b, name="op-multiply")
5 e = tf.add(c,d, name="op-add")
6 with tf.Session() as my_session:
7     my_session.run(tf.global_variables_initializer())
8     print (my_session.run(d))
9     fw = tf.summary.FileWriter("V:/tmp/summary", my_session.graph)
```

Then start TensorBoard using:

```
1 > tensorboard --logdir=V:\tmp\summary
2 Starting TensorBoard b'39' on port 6006
3 (You can navigate to http://192.168.126.1:6006)
```

Here is the final (interactive) visualization of the computation graph generated by TensorBoard:

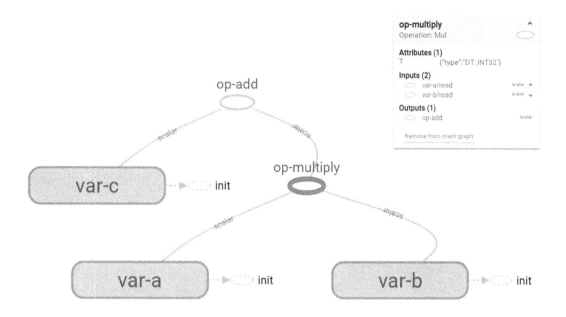

## Grouping nodes in the visualization

In order to achieve a better overview over complex models, nodes can be grouped via `tf.name_scope`. Note that scopes can be nested, i.e., a scope can contain sub-scopes.

```
with tf.name_scope("All_my_variables") as scope:
    a = tf.Variable(3, name="var-a")
    b = tf.Variable(4, name="var-b")
    c = tf.Variable(5, name="var-c")

with tf.name_scope("My_operations") as scope:

    with tf.name_scope("Some_additions") as scope:
        aplusb = tf.add(a, b, name="a-plus-b")
        bplusc = tf.add(b, c, name="b-plus-c")

    with tf.name_scope("Some_multiplications") as scope:
        asquared = tf.multiply(a, a, name="a-squared")
        csquared = tf.multiply(c, c, name="c-squared")

    with tf.name_scope("Final_computation") as scope:
        compresult = tf.add(asquared,csquared, "final-add")

with tf.Session() as my_session:
    my_session.run(tf.global_variables_initializer())
    print(my_session.run(compresult))
    fw = tf.summary.FileWriter("V:/tmp/summary", my_session.graph)
```

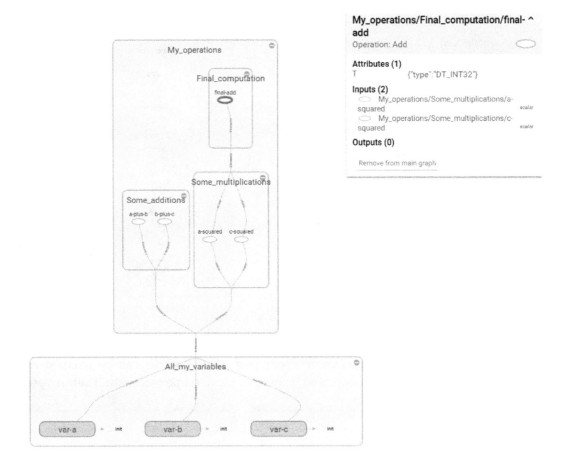

## Tracking a scalar value over time

We have seen how to visualize the computation graph. But we can also use the
`tf.summary` class in order to write summaries of variables that have scalar shape.
TensorBoard allows to plot these summaries then as graphs as the following example
shows:

```python
import random

# the value of a will be incremented by some
# placeholder value
a = tf.Variable(42, name="var-a")
rndnumber_placeholder = \
    tf.placeholder(tf.int32, shape=[], name="rndnumber_placeholder")
update_node = tf.assign(a,tf.add(a, rndnumber_placeholder))

# create a summary to track value of a
```

```
11  tf.summary.scalar("Value-of-a", a)
12
13  # in case we want to track multiple summaries
14  # merge all summaries into a single operation
15  summary_op = tf.summary.merge_all()
16
17  with tf.Session() as my_session:
18      my_session.run(tf.global_variables_initializer())
19      fw = tf.summary.FileWriter("V:/tmp/summary", my_session.graph)
20
21      # generate random numbers that are used
22      # as values for the placeholder
23      for step in range(500):
24
25          rndnum = int(-10 + random.random() * 20)
26          new_value_of_a = \
27              my_session.run(update_node,
28                  feed_dict={rndnumber_placeholder: rndnum})
29
30          print("new_value_of_a=", new_value_of_a)
31
32          # compute summary
33          summary = my_session.run(summary_op)
34
35          # add merged summaries to filewriter,
36          # this will save the data to the file
37          fw.add_summary(summary, step)
```

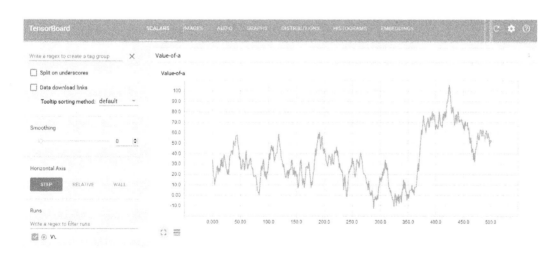

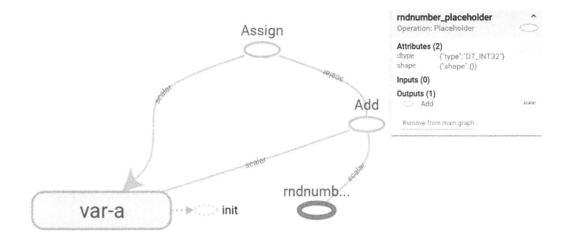

## 8.2   Training a linear model with TensorFlow

```
 1  # A first simple TensorFlow learner
 2  #
 3  # Given some random samples of 2D data points (x,y),
 4  # the following TF script tries to find a line
 5  # that best describes the data points in terms of
 6  # a minimal sum of squared errors (SSE)
 7
 8  import tensorflow as tf
 9  import numpy as np
10
11  # 1.1 create 1D array with 100 random numbers drawn uniformly from [0,1)
12  x_data = np.random.rand(100)
13  print("\nx_data:", x_data)
14  print("data type:", type(x_data))
15
16  # 1.2 now compute the y-points
17  y_data = x_data * 1.2345 + 0.6789
18
19  # so now we have ground truth samples (x,y)
20  # and the TF learner will have to estimate the line parameters
21  # y=W*x+b with W=1.2345 and b=0.6789
22  #
23  # These parameters are called variables in TF.
24
25
26  # 2. We initialize them with a random W and b=0
27  W = tf.Variable(tf.random_uniform([1], -1.0, 1.0))
28  b = tf.Variable(tf.zeros([1]))
29  y = tf.add(tf.multiply(W,x_data), b)
```

```
30
31  # 3.1 Now define what to optimize at all:
32  #     here we want to minimize the SSE.
33  #     This is our "loss" of a certain line model
34  #     Note: this is just another node in the
35  #     computation graph that computes something
36  loss_func = tf.reduce_mean(tf.square(y - y_data))
37
38  # 3.2 We can use different optimizers in TF for model learning
39  my_optimizer = tf.train.GradientDescentOptimizer(0.5)
40
41  # 3.3 Tell the optimizer object to minimize the loss function
42  train = my_optimizer.minimize(loss_func)
43
44  with tf.Session() as my_session:
45
46      my_session.run(tf.global_variables_initializer())
47
48      # 4. Print inial value of W and b
49      print("\n")
50      print("initial W", my_session.run(W))
51      print("initial b", my_session.run(b))
52
53      # 5. Do 201 gradient descent steps...
54      print("\n")
55      for step in range(201):
56
57          # Do another gradient descent step to come to a better
58          # W and b
59          my_session.run(train)
60
61          # From time to time, print the current value of W and b
62          if step % 10 == 0:
63              print(step, my_session.run(W), my_session.run(b))
```

```
1   initial W [ 0.28849196]
2   initial b [ 0.]
3
4
5   0 [ 0.87854469] [ 1.10748446]
6   10 [ 1.0283134] [ 0.78003669]
7   20 [ 1.14134669] [ 0.72459263]
8   30 [ 1.19241428] [ 0.69954348]
9   40 [ 1.21548605] [ 0.68822652]
10  50 [ 1.22590971] [ 0.68311363]
11  60 [ 1.23061907] [ 0.68080366]
12  70 [ 1.2327466] [ 0.67976004]
13  80 [ 1.2337079] [ 0.67928857]
14  90 [ 1.23414207] [ 0.67907554]
15  100 [ 1.23433828] [ 0.67897934]
```

```
16  110 [ 1.23442698] [ 0.67893583]
17  120 [ 1.23446703] [ 0.67891616]
18  130 [ 1.23448491] [ 0.67890739]
19  140 [ 1.23449326] [ 0.67890334]
20  150 [ 1.23449683] [ 0.67890155]
21  160 [ 1.2344985] [ 0.67890072]
22  170 [ 1.23449934] [ 0.6789003]
23  180 [ 1.23449957] [ 0.67890018]
24  190 [ 1.23449957] [ 0.67890018]
25  200 [ 1.23449957] [ 0.67890018]
```

## 8.3  A MLP with TensorFlow

```python
1  '''
2  Minimalistic exmaple of a MLP in TensorFlow
3  '''
4
5  import numpy as np
6  from data_generator import data_generator
7  import tensorflow as tf
8  import cv2
9  from timeit import default_timer as timer
10
11
12  # test data parameters
13  WINSIZE = 600
14  NR_CLUSTERS = 5
15  NR_SAMPLES_TO_GENERATE = 10000
16
17  # MLP parameters
18  NR_EPOCHS = 2000
19
20  # for RELU transfer function use smaller learn rate
21  # than for logistic transfer function
22  # Also use more hidden neurons! (e.g. 2-30-12-2)
23  #LEARN_RATE = 0.1
24
25  # for logistic transfer function
26  LEARN_RATE = 0.5
27
28  MINI_BATCH_SIZE = 100
29  NR_NEURONS_INPUT   = 2
30  NR_NEURONS_HIDDEN1 = 10  # nr of neurons in 1st hidden layer
31  NR_NEURONS_HIDDEN2 = 6   # nr of neurons in 2nd hidden layer
32  NR_NEURONS_OUTPUT  = 2
33
34  # store 2D weight matrices & 1D bias vectors for all
```

```
35  # neuron layers in two dictionaries
36  weights = {
37      'h1': tf.Variable(tf.random_normal(
38          [NR_NEURONS_INPUT, NR_NEURONS_HIDDEN1])),
39      'h2': tf.Variable(tf.random_normal(
40          [NR_NEURONS_HIDDEN1, NR_NEURONS_HIDDEN2])),
41      'out': tf.Variable(tf.random_normal(
42          [NR_NEURONS_HIDDEN2, NR_NEURONS_OUTPUT]))
43  }
44  biases = {
45      'b1': tf.Variable(tf.random_normal(
46          [NR_NEURONS_HIDDEN1])),
47      'b2': tf.Variable(tf.random_normal(
48          [NR_NEURONS_HIDDEN2])),
49      'out': tf.Variable(tf.random_normal(
50          [NR_NEURONS_OUTPUT]))
51  }
52
53
54  # visualization parameters
55  RADIUS_SAMPLE = 3
56  COLOR_CLASS0 = (255,0,0)
57  COLOR_CLASS1 = (0,0,255)
58  NR_TEST_SAMPLES = 10000
59
60  # for saving images
61  image_counter = 0
62
63
64  '''
65  helper function to create a 4 layer MLP
66  input-layer -->
67    hidden layer #1 -->
68      hidden layer #2 -->
69        output layer
70  '''
71  def multilayer_perceptron(x, weights, biases):
72
73      # hidden layer #1 with RELU
74      layer_1 = tf.add(tf.matmul(x, weights['h1']),
75                      biases['b1'])
76      #layer_1 = tf.nn.relu(layer_1)
77      layer_1 = tf.nn.sigmoid(layer_1)
78
79      # hidden layer #2 with RELU
80      layer_2 = tf.add(tf.matmul(layer_1, weights['h2']),
81                      biases['b2'])
82      #layer_2 = tf.nn.relu(layer_2)
83      layer_2 = tf.nn.sigmoid(layer_2)
84
```

```
85      # output layer with linear activation (no RELUs!)
86      out_layer = tf.matmul(layer_2, weights['out'])\
87                  + biases['out']
88
89      # return the MLP model
90      return out_layer
91
92
93
94  def generate_and_show_training_data():
95
96      #  1. generate training data
97      my_dg = data_generator()
98      data_samples = \
99          my_dg.generate_samples_two_class_problem(
100             NR_CLUSTERS,
101             NR_SAMPLES_TO_GENERATE)
102     nr_samples = len(data_samples)
103
104     # 2. generate empty image for visualization
105     #    initialize image with white pixels (255,255,255)
106     img = np.ones((WINSIZE, WINSIZE, 3), np.uint8) * 255
107
108     # 3. visualize positions of samples
109     for i in range(nr_samples):
110
111         # 3.1 get the next data sample
112         next_sample = data_samples[i]
113
114         # 3.2 get input and output vector
115         #     (which are both NumPy arrays)
116         input_vec = next_sample[0]
117         output_vec = next_sample[1]
118
119         # 3.3 prepare a tupel from the NumPy input vector
120         sample_coord = (int(input_vec[0] * WINSIZE),
121                         int(input_vec[1] * WINSIZE))
122
123         # 3.4 get class label from output vector
124         if output_vec[0] > output_vec[1]:
125             class_label = 0
126         else:
127             class_label = 1
128         color = (0, 0, 0)
129         if class_label == 0:
130             color = COLOR_CLASS0
131         elif class_label == 1:
132             color = COLOR_CLASS1
133
134         # 3.4
```

```
135          cv2.circle(img, sample_coord, RADIUS_SAMPLE, color)
136
137      # 4. show visualization of samples
138      cv2.imshow('Training data', img)
139      c = cv2.waitKey(1)
140      cv2.imwrite("V:/tmp/training_data.png", img)
141
142      return data_samples
143
144
145  def visualize_decision_boundaries(
146          the_session, epoch_nr, x_in, mlp_output_vec):
147
148      global image_counter
149
150      NR_TEST_SAMPLES = 10000
151
152      # 1. prepare a large input matrix
153      input_mat = np.zeros((NR_TEST_SAMPLES,NR_NEURONS_INPUT))
154      for i in range(NR_TEST_SAMPLES):
155
156          # generate random coordinate in [0,1) x [0,1)
157          rnd_x = np.random.rand()
158          rnd_y = np.random.rand()
159
160          # prepare an input vector
161          input_vec = np.array([rnd_x, rnd_y])
162
163          # set corresponding line in input matrix
164          input_mat[i,:] = input_vec
165
166
167      # 2. do a feedforward step for all test vectors
168      #    in the input matrix
169      res = the_session.run(mlp_output_vec,
170                            feed_dict={x_in: input_mat})
171
172
173      # 3. draw each sample in predicted class color
174
175      # generate empty white color image
176      img = np.ones((WINSIZE, WINSIZE, 3), np.uint8) * 255
177      #print(res)
178      for i in range(NR_TEST_SAMPLES):
179
180          # get the input vector back from matrix
181          input_vec = input_mat[i,:]
182
183          # get the output vector from result tensor
184          output_vec = res[i,:]
```

```
185
186          # now get the predicted class from the output
187          # vector
188          class_label = 0 if output_vec[0] > output_vec[1] else 1
189
190          # map class label to a color
191          color = COLOR_CLASS0 if class_label == 0 else COLOR_CLASS1
192
193          # draw circle
194          sample_coord = (int(input_vec[0] * WINSIZE),
195                          int(input_vec[1] * WINSIZE))
196          cv2.circle(img, sample_coord, RADIUS_SAMPLE, color)
197
198
199
200      # 4. finaly show the image
201      cv2.rectangle(img, (WINSIZE - 120, 0), (WINSIZE - 1, 20),
202                    (255, 255, 255), -1)
203      font = cv2.FONT_HERSHEY_SIMPLEX
204      cv2.putText(img,
205                  "epoch #" + str(epoch_nr).zfill(3),
206                  (WINSIZE - 110, 15), font, 0.5, (0, 0, 0), 1,
207                  cv2.LINE_AA)
208      cv2.imshow('Decision boundaries of trained MLP', img)
209      c = cv2.waitKey(1)
210
211      # 5. save that image?
212      if False:
213          filename = "V:/tmp/img_{0:0>4}".format(image_counter)
214          image_counter +=1
215          cv2.imwrite(filename + ".png", img)
216
217
218 def build_TF_graph():
219
220      # 1. prepare placeholders for the input and output values
221
222      # the input is a 2D matrix:
223      # in each row we store one input vector
224      x_in = tf.placeholder("float")
225
226      # the output is a 2D matrix:
227      # in each row we store one output vector
228      y_out = tf.placeholder("float")
229
230      # 2. now the use helper function defined before to
231      #    generate a MLP
232      mlp_output_vec = multilayer_perceptron(x_in, weights, biases)
233
234      # 3. define a loss function
```

```
235    # loss = tf.reduce_mean(tf.nn.softmax_cross_entropy_with_logits(my_mlp,
       y))
236    loss = \
237        tf.reduce_mean(tf.squared_difference(mlp_output_vec, y_out))
238
239    # 4. add an optimizer to the graph
240    # optimizer = tf.train.AdamOptimizer(learning_rate=learn_rate).minimize
       (cost)
241    optimizer =\
242        tf.train.GradientDescentOptimizer(LEARN_RATE).minimize(loss)
243
244    # 5. create a summary to track current
245    #     value of loss function
246    tf.summary.scalar("Value-of-loss", loss)
247
248    # 6. in case we want to track multiple summaries
249    #     merge all summaries into a single operation
250    summary_op = tf.summary.merge_all()
251
252    return optimizer, mlp_output_vec, loss, x_in, y_out
253
254
255
256 def MLP_training(data_samples, optimizer, mlp_output_vec,
257                  loss, x_in, y_out):
258
259    NR_SAMPLES = len(data_samples)
260
261    with tf.Session() as my_session:
262
263        # initialize all variables
264        my_session.run(tf.global_variables_initializer())
265        fw = tf.summary.FileWriter("V:/tmp/summary", my_session.graph)
266
267        # how many mini batches do we have to process?
268        nr_batches_to_process = \
269            int(NR_SAMPLES / MINI_BATCH_SIZE)
270
271        # in each epoch all training samples will be presented
272        for epoch_nr in range(0, NR_EPOCHS):
273
274            print("Training MLP. Epoch nr #", epoch_nr)
275
276            # in each mini batch some of the training samples
277            # will be feed-forwarded, the weight changes for a
278            # single sample will be computed and all weight changes
279            # be accumulated for all samples in the mini-batch.
280            # Then the weights will be updated.
281            start = timer()
282            for mini_batch_nr in range(0, nr_batches_to_process):
```

```
283
284            # a) generate list of indices
285            sample_indices = np.arange(0, NR_SAMPLES)
286
287            # b) shuffle the indices list
288            sample_indices = np.random.shuffle(sample_indices)
289
290            # c) now prepare a matrix
291            #    with one sample input vector in each row and
292            #    another matrix with the corresponding desired
293            #    output vector in each row
294            input_matrix =\
295                np.zeros((MINI_BATCH_SIZE, NR_NEURONS_INPUT))
296            output_matrix =\
297                np.zeros((MINI_BATCH_SIZE, NR_NEURONS_OUTPUT))
298            startpos = mini_batch_nr * MINI_BATCH_SIZE
299            row_counter = 0
300            for next_sample_id in \
301                    range(startpos, startpos + MINI_BATCH_SIZE):
302                # get next training sample from dataset class
303                # the dataset is a list of lists
304                # in each list entry there are two vectors:
305                # the input vector and the output vector
306                next_sample = data_samples[next_sample_id]
307
308                # get input and output vector
309                # (which are both NumPy arrays)
310                input_vec = next_sample[0]
311                output_vec = next_sample[1]
312
313                # copy input vector to respective
314                # row in input matrix
315                input_matrix[row_counter, :] = input_vec
316
317                # copy output vector respective
318                # row in output matrix
319                output_matrix[row_counter, :] = output_vec
320
321                row_counter += 1
322
323            # d) run the optimizer node --> training will happen
324            #    now the actual feed-forward step and the
325            #    computations will happen!
326            _, curr_loss = my_session.run(
327                [optimizer, loss],
328                feed_dict={x_in: input_matrix,
329                           y_out: output_matrix})
330
331            # print("current loss for mini-batch=", curr_loss)
332
```

```
333            # after each epoch:
334            # visualize the decision boundaries of the MLP
335            # trained so far
336            end = timer()
337            print("Time needed to train one epoch: ",
338                    end - start, "sec")
339
340            print("Now testing the MLP...")
341            visualize_decision_boundaries(my_session,
342                                          epoch_nr,
343                                          x_in,
344                                          mlp_output_vec)
345
346
347 def main():
348
349     data_samples = generate_and_show_training_data()
350
351     optimizer, mlp_output_vec, loss, x_in, y_out = build_TF_graph()
352
353     MLP_training(data_samples, optimizer, mlp_output_vec, loss,
354                  x_in, y_out)
355
356     print("End of MLP TensorFlow test.")
357
358 main()
```

# 9

# Convolutional Neural Networks

## 9.1 Introduction

We are now ready to talk about the most important Deep Learning model: the Convolutional Neural Network (CNN).

**Some recent history: AlexNet.** The breakthrough of the CNN model started with a paper in 2012. In their paper "ImageNet Classification with Deep Convolutional Neural Networks" by Alex Krizhevsky, Ilya Sutskever and Geoffrey Hinton [24], the authors used a CNN and reached a never seen before performance on the ImageNet Large Scale Visual Recognition Challenge of the year 2012 (ILSVRC 2012). They trained their 8 layer model which has 60 million parameters and consists of 650.000 neurons on two GPUs which took six days for the 1,2 million training images of the competition. The test data set consisted of 150.000 photographs which had to be classified into one of 1000 possible classes. The authors achieved a top-5 error rate of 15.3%, compared to an error rate of 26.2% of a "classical approach" which used SIFT features described by Fisher Vectors (FV). For this, the new model was considered a quantum leap for image classification tasks and the model is now simply known as the *AlexNet.*

**Structure of a CNN: the input side.** Let's walk through a CNN in order to get to know its structure (see Fig. 9.1). On the input side there is the input image. If it is a color image, it is typically represented as a 3 channel matrix. In TensorFlow's terminology it is just a 3D tensor of dimension width × height × nr-of-channels. If it is a gray image? It would be a 3D tensor as well with dimension width × height × 1.

**Convolutional Layers.** In section 4.5 we have argued that neurons can be considered as filters since the activity of a neuron is just the inner product of the input vector and its weights. In the context of CNNs we can now talk about neurons or directly call them filters. In a convolutional layer there are a lof of these filters used. But compared to a MLP there are two important differences. First, the filters do not get their input from all the output values from the previous layer, but from just a small region, which is called *receptive field (RF)*. This idea was stolen from the biological role model! And it is important to know that in a convolutional layer, there are used many different filters for the same receptive field. In the illustration there are e.g. 16 different filters used for each RF. Second, the filters within one depth slice, also called *feature map* share their weights! And this idea is of high importance.

**The concept of weight sharing.** The reason for introducing weight sharing is that for learning local feature detectors it is not important where the features are in the image. We want to be able to detect vertical lines also in the right bottom corner even if we have seen such a image structure only in the top left corner during training. So weight sharing reduces the amount of training data we need to see. We do not need a training data set where each image structure is shown in each receptive field. And this in turn reduces training time. Another important reason is that weight sharing dramatically reduces the number of parameters of the model (= of the CNN) that we have to adapt.

**How RFs and weight sharing help: A sample calculation.** Imagine we would use a fully connected approach without weight sharing. Each of the 200x200x16=640.000 neurons in the first conv layer in Fig. 9.1 would get input from 200x200x3=120.000 input values, i.e., there would be 76.800.000.000 weights already in the first layer! Now compare it to the approach of using RFs and weight sharing. There are 16 filters in the first conv layer. Each filter gets its input from a small RF of size 5x5x3=75. So there are only 75*16=1200 weights.

**Intuition: What does a conv layer?** As we said in section 4.2 neurons cannot only be considered as filters, but can also be regarded as feature detectors. So the

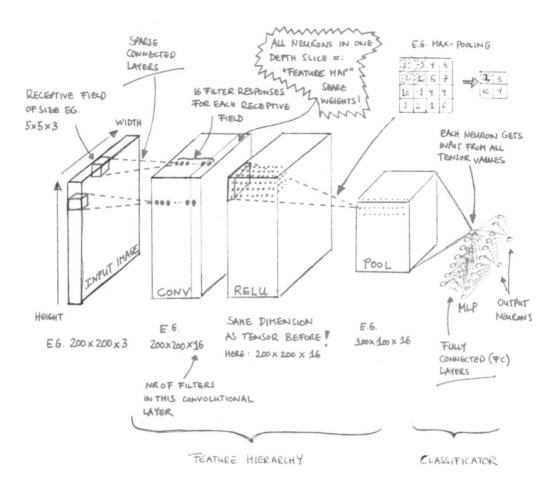

Figure 9.1: Structure of a Convolutional Neural Network (CNN). The CNN takes an input tensor, e.g., an input image of dimension 200x200 with 3 color channels and detects local features using filters in convolutional layers (CONV). The ReLU layer maps the filter responses (neuron activities) non-linearly to neuron output values. Pooling layers are inserted into the processing pipeline in order to reduce the dimensionality of the tensors and help to detect patterns invariant to translations and rotations. Finally a classifier, e.g., a MLP, is used to map high-level features to output values.

neurons in a conv layer analyze the spatial input in a small region of the image and their activation value (= filter response value) represents a measure of similarity between the feature the neuron represents and the input values that are currently present.

**ReLU layer.** In section 7.10 we have seen that a MLP with just linear transfer functions in all hidden layers cannot be used to classify non-linearly separable datasets. The same problem would occur in a CNN. For this, it is important to use a non-linear transfer function in a CNN as well. This is the task of the next layer, the ReLU layer. Very good results have been presented for CNNs with the ReLU transfer function and since it is also fast to compute, most often the ReLU is used as transfer function for the neuron activities computed in the conv layer. Note that often the (ReLU) transfer function computation is considered as a part of the conv layer as well. Also note that the ReLU layer does not change the dimensions of the input tensor. If the input tensor has dimension W × H × D, then the output tensor produced by the ReLU layer has the same dimensions.

**Pooling layers.** While the ReLU layers do not change the dimensions of a tensor, the task of the *Pooling layer* is to reduce the spatial dimensions of it. An operation called *max pooling* is applied to small receptive fields (normally of size 2x2) on every depth slice of the input tensor. This does not only reduce compute time since the input tensor for the next conv layers is smaller, but also allows the CNN to analyze larger and larger image areas while the RF size in the conv layer is kept constant. The effect of the max pooling operation is depicted in the top right corner of Fig. 9.1. Since a single max pooling operation means that we do not care where a certain strong feature response was within a 2x2 area and since normally many pooling layers are inserted from time to time within the processing pipeline in a CNN, we can achieve to some aspect translational and rotational invariant pattern recognition.

**Repeating CONV-ReLU-POOL layers.** A sequence of many conv, ReLU and pool layers is used to extract image information, gradually increasing rotational and translational invariance as we go up from lower towards higher layers. Note that the pooling layer is a structure which is dedicated directly in order to achieve translational and rotational invariance. However, there are other invariance properties that we often wish to achieve. E.g., we want to detect objects invariant to their size or to different lighting situations. These invariance properties of the CNN can be achieved by learning different feature detectors. E.g., a feature detector for small faces, a feature detector for middle size faces and a feature detector for large faces.

**Feature hierarchy vs. classificator.** The sequence of conv, ReLU and pool layers establishes as feature hierarchy. At the end of the feature hierarchy a classifiers can be used to exploit the nice high-level features which are invariant to many variances present in the input data. Note, that we are not forced to use a MLP as classifier here. And indeed, other classifiers have been used successfully in combination with the feature hierarchy, e.g., Support Vector Machines (SVM) [41].

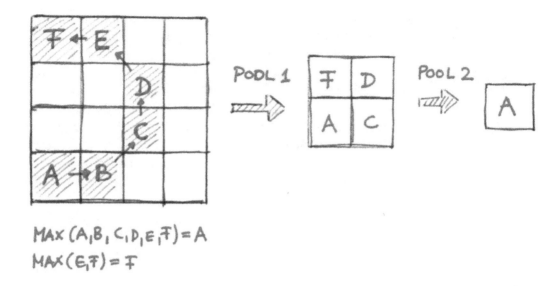

Figure 9.2: How a CNN realizes rotational invariance. Imagine the strongest feature response in a 4x4 area is A (and F>E). Then it does not matter where the A is on the shaded fields. After two max pooling steps it will always be chosen as the final value. In this example we assume that all values depicted in the 2x2 areas are larger than the values not depicted in each 2x2 area (in the white non-shaded fields). Note, that A will always be chosen as the final value, even if it stood in one of the white non-shaded fields! So this 4x4 translational invariance goes hand in hand with the rotational invariance depicted.

## 9.2 Some history about the CNN model

Was the CNN model invented in the 2012 paper by Krizhevsky et al. [24]? No! Interestingly, the CNN model was invented many years before.

**1975: The Cognitron model.** A first step towards the CNN model were the works by the Japanese researcher Kunihiko Fukushima. Fukushima experimented with neural network models that were trained using unsupervised learning rules, i.e., the synaptic weights were changed just based on input data. E.g., in his 1975 paper "Cognitron: A self-organizing multilayered neural network" [13] Fukushima tried out a simple idea for the adaptation of synapses between neurons:

> "The synapse from neuron $x$ to neuron $y$ is reinforced when $x$ fires provided that no neuron in the vicinity of $y$ is firing stronger than $y$"

In this study Fukushima came to the result that the neurons organize themselves such that they will selectively respond to different input patterns after training:

> "In a cognitron, similarly to the animal's brain, synaptic connections between neurons are plastically modified so as to match the nature of its experience. The neurons become selectively responsive to the features which have been frequently presented."

However, Fukushima already understood in 1975 that another part was missing, namely a classifier that works on top of the features learned by the cognitron:

> "The cognitron discussed in this paper is not intended to be a complete system for pattern recognition: if we want to make a pattern recognizer with a cognitron, some other functions must be added to it. For instance, a feature extractor with a function of normalization of position, size, etc. would be necessary to be added in front of the cognitron, and a decision circuit should be cascaded after the last layer of the cognitron."

**1980: The Neocognitron model.** Some years later in 1980 Fukushima published a new model, which was called "Neocognitron", since it was a new ("neo") version of the Cognitron model. The paper [14] was called:

"Neocognitron: A self-organizing neural network model for a mechanism of pattern recognition unaffected by shift in position"

The title already tells us a lot about the difference compared to the Cognitron model. The Cognitron model had the ability to respond with different neurons specifically to certain input patterns, but unfortunately its response was dependent upon the location of the pattern in the input image

> "That is, the same patterns which were presented at different positions were taken as different patterns by the conventional cognitron. In the Neocognitron proposed here, however, the response of the network is little affected by the position of the stimulus patterns."

How did Fukushima achieve this translation invariant pattern recognition? His Neocognitron architecture was inspired by the neuroscientific findings of Hubel and Wiesel:

> "After completion of self-organization, the network has a structure similar to the hierarchy model of the visual nervous system proposed by Hubel and Wiesel. The network consists of an input layer (photoreceptor array) followed by a cascade connection of a number of modular structures, each of

> *which is composed of two layers of cells connected in a cascade. The first*
> *layer of each module consists of "S-cells', which show characteristics simi-*
> *lar to simple cells or lower order hyper-complex cells, and the second layer*
> *consists of "C-cells" similar to complex cells or higher order hypercomplex*
> *cells."*

Hubel and Wiesel did a famous experiment in 1959. They inserted a microelectrode into the primary visual cortex of an anesthetized cat. Then rectangular patterns of light were projected onto a screen in front of the cat. By recording the firing rates of some neurons it could be observed that on the one hand some neurons only responded when the pattern was presented at a certain angle in a certain region in the visual field of the cat. These neurons were called "simple cells". On the other hand, neurons were observed which could detect lines independently of where they were presented in the visual field. These cells were named "complex cells". Fukushima directly build his work on top of these findings by using a cascade of alternating layers of S- and C-cells, where S-cells were used to detect features and C-cells were used to introduce translation invariance. Note, that the concept of weight sharing was already used in the Neocognitron model (!): neurons in a "cell plane" (today: "feature map") shared their weights.

**1990s: The LeNet model.** Fukushima's Cognitron and Neocognitron models used a feature hierarchy as the CNN models use today, but both were trained unsupervised However, there was also another model that established a hierarchy of features within a training phase and that was trained in a supervised fashion using Backpropagation: the LeNet model. The first model, LeNet1 was developed between 1988 and 1993 in the Adaptive System Research Department at Bell Labs. It was published in a paper by Yann LeCun (LeCun spoken with nasalized French "un") in 1989:

*"Backpropagation Applied to Handwritten Zip Code Recognition"* [27]

A demo of the LeNet1 model in action with a young Yann LeCun can be watched in the "Convolutional Network Demo from 1993" video at YouTube:

`https://www.youtube.com/watch?v=FwFduRA_L6Q`

This new model was very successful as Yann LeCun writes on YouTube:

> *Shortly after this demo was put together, we started working with a devel-*
> *opment group and a product group at NCR (then a subsidiary of AT&T).*
> *NCR soon deployed ATM machines that could read the numerical amounts*

> *on checks, initially in Europe and then in the US. The ConvNet was run-*
> *ning on the DSP32C card sitting in a PC inside the ATM. Later, NCR*
> *deployed a similar system in large check reading machines that banks use*
> *in their back offices. At some point in the late 90's these machines were*
> *processing 10 to 20% of all the checks in the US.*

Later, in 1998, LeNet5 was published in another paper by LeCun et al. [28]: A 7-layer Convolutional Neural Network that consists of convolutional and subsampling layers (which are today called: "pooling layers"). The authors write in their introduction:

> *The main message of this paper is that better pattern recognition systems*
> *can be built by relying more on automatic learning, and less on hand-*
> *designed heuristics. [...] Using character recognition as a case study, we*
> *show that hand-crafted feature extraction can be advantageously replaced by*
> *carefully designed learning machines that operate directly on pixel images.*
> *Using document understanding as a case study, we show that the traditional*
> *way of building recognition systems by manually integrating individually*
> *designed modules can be replaced by a unified and well-principled design*
> *paradigm, called Graph Transformer Networks, that allows training all the*
> *modules to optimize a global performance criterion.*

With this they underlined a very important change in the field of pattern recognition that now really is happening: the approach of hand-crafting features is vanishing more and more while learning good features (for the classification task or whatever the task is) from large amount of data is now the dominating approach. And the authors postulated this in 1998, while the change only started in 2012! Note, that TensorFlow with its computation graph approach could be called a Graph Transformer Network: We define a model or a processing pipeline where each transformation step is trainable in order to fulfill a global performance criterion.

## 9.3 Convolutional and pooling layers in TensorFlow

The following code shows how to implement a convolution and a pooling operation with TensorFlow:

- The example code first loads two test images in
  `load_two_test_images()`.

- These two test images are then put into one 4D tensor since both the convolution and the pooling operators in TensorFlow expect 4D tensors as input! Note, that each color image is already a 3D tensor, so we need one more (array-)dimension in order to store several images, hence a 4D tensor of shape: (nr-of-images, img-height, img-width, nr-img-channels).

- In the `conv2d_demo()` function the complete mini-batch will be convolved with a set of filters. For this, a 4D filter tensor `filters` has to be generated of shape (filter-height, filter-width, filter-depth, nr-of-filters). Then a TensorFlow graph is generated where X is a placeholder for a 4D tensor and will later be filled in a computation session with a mini-batch. The actual convolution operator is generated with

```
tf.nn.conv2d(X, filters, strides=[1,2,2,1],
             padding="SAME")
```

where X is the placeholder for the input tensor, `filters` is the 4D tensor of filters and strides describes the filter step size in each dimension. Here a new filter position is set for the two 5x5x3 filters by striding two pixels to the right or two pixels to the bottom respectively. The padding string has to be set to "SAME" or "VALID" and determines whether the border of the image shall be padded with zeros ("SAME") in order to realize that the output tensor has the same spatial dimensions or whether it is ok, when it has smaller spatial dimensions and no zero padding shall be used ("VALID"). We will explain this later in detail.

The actual computation of the convolutions can be started by running the convolution operator node `convop` using

```
convresult = my_session.run(convop,
                            feed_dict={X:minibatch})
```

Here we feed the placeholder 4D tensor X with the 4D minibatch tensor and thereby let TensorFlow convolve each of the two images with each of the two filters defined before in the 4D `filters` tensor. The resulting tensor is a 4D tensor as well, where the first dimension addresses the test image, the second and third dimension are the spatial dimensions and the fourth dimension is for the filter-nr ("feature map nr"). In the example code we retrieve the resulting two feature maps for the first image, normalize the resulting values to the interval [0,1] and then display the results using OpenCV's `imshow()` function. Why the normalization? The reason is, that OpenCV's `imshow()` function expects the values to be in [0,1] if the NumPy array values are float values.

- The `maxpool_demo()` function works similarly. However, there is no need to provide a filter tensor, since the max-pooling operation is already clearly defined. The only free parameters when generating a max-pooling operation are the filter size (here: 2x2), the filter stride (here: 2x2) and whether to use padding ("SAME") or not ("VALID").

Figure 9.3: Resulting feature maps after convolving a test image with two different pre-defined filters. Note that the filter responses in the left feature map are high (white pixels), if there is a vertical image structure while they are high in the right feature map if there are horizontal image structures.

Listing 9.1: conv2d_and_maxpool.py

```
1  '''
2  Code to show effect of TensorFlow's
3  - conv2d() operator
4  - max_pool() operator
5  '''
6
7  import numpy as np
8  import cv2
9  import tensorflow as tf
10
11
12 def load_two_test_images():
13
14     # load two test images and
15     # convert int values to float values in [0,1]
16     img0 = cv2.imread("test0.jpg")
17     img1 = cv2.imread("test1.jpg")
18     #print("max value of img0 is", img0.max())
19     img0 = img0.astype(np.float32)/255.0
20     img1 = img1.astype(np.float32)/255.0
21     cv2.imshow("img0", img0)
22     #cv2.imshow("img1", img1)
23     print("img0 has shape", img0.shape)
24     print("img1 has shape", img1.shape)
25     print("img0 has dtype", img0.dtype)
26
27     return img0,img1
28
29
30
31 def conv2d_demo(minibatch, height, width, channels):
32
33     # create a filter array with two filters:
34     # filter / kernel tensor has to have shape
35     # [filter_height, filter_width, in_channels, out_channels]
36     filters = np.ones(shape=(5,5,channels,2), dtype=np.float32) * -1.0/20.0
37     filters[:,2,:,0] = 1.0/5.0 # vertical line (in all 3 channels)
38     filters[2,:,:,1] = 1.0/5.0 # horizontal line (in all 3 channels)
39
40     # create TF graph
41     X = tf.placeholder(tf.float32, shape=(None,height,width,channels))
42     convop = tf.nn.conv2d(X,
43                           filters,
44                           strides=[1,2,2,1],
45                           padding="SAME")
46
47     # filter both images (mini batch)
48     # by running the convolution op in the graph
```

```
49    with tf.Session() as my_session:
50        convresult = my_session.run(convop, feed_dict={X:minibatch})
51
52    print("shape of convresult is", convresult.shape)
53
54    convres_img0_filt0 = convresult[0,:,:,0]
55    convres_img0_filt1 = convresult[0,:,:,1]
56
57    print("max/min value of convres_img0_filt0 is",
58          convres_img0_filt0.max(), convres_img0_filt0.min())
59
60    convres_img0_filt0 = convres_img0_filt0 / convres_img0_filt0.max()
61    convres_img0_filt1 = convres_img0_filt1 / convres_img0_filt1.max()
62
63    print("max/min value of convres_img0_filt0"
64          " after normalization is now",
65          convres_img0_filt0.max(), convres_img0_filt0.min())
66
67    cv2.imshow("conv result img0 filter0", convres_img0_filt0)
68    cv2.imshow("conv result img0 filter1", convres_img0_filt1)
69
70    cv2.imwrite("conv result img0 filter0.png", convres_img0_filt0)
71    cv2.imwrite("conv result img0 filter1.png", convres_img0_filt1)
72
73
74 def maxpool_demo(minibatch, height, width, channels):
75
76    # create TF graph
77    X = tf.placeholder(tf.float32, shape=(None, height, width, channels))
78    maxpool_op = tf.nn.max_pool(X,
79                                ksize=[1,2,2,1],
80                                strides=[1,2,2,1],
81                                padding="VALID")
82
83    # filter both images (mini batch)
84    # by running the convolution op in the graph
85    with tf.Session() as my_session:
86        maxpool_result = my_session.run(maxpool_op, feed_dict={X: minibatch
      })
87
88    print("shape of maxpool_result is", maxpool_result.shape)
89
90    poolres_img0_chan0 = maxpool_result[0, :, :, 0]
91
92    print("max/min value of poolres_img0_chan0 is",
93          poolres_img0_chan0.max(), poolres_img0_chan0.min())
94
95    poolres_img0_chan0 = poolres_img0_chan0 / poolres_img0_chan0.max()
96
97    print("max/min value of poolres_img0_chan0"
```

```
 98            " after normalization is now",
 99            poolres_img0_chan0.max(), poolres_img0_chan0.min())
100
101    cv2.imshow("poolres_img0_chan0", poolres_img0_chan0)
102
103    cv2.imshow("max_pooled image as color image", maxpool_result[0, :,:,:])
104
105
106 def main():
107
108    # 1. load two test images
109    img0, img1 = load_two_test_images()
110
111    # 2. put the two test images into a mini-batch
112    #     so the mini-batch is a 4D array of dimension:
113    #     (nr-of-images, img-height, img-width, nr-img-channels)
114    height = img0.shape[0]
115    width = img0.shape[1]
116    channels = img0.shape[2]
117    minibatch = np.zeros([2,height,width,channels], dtype=np.float32)
118    print("minibatch has shape",minibatch.shape)
119    minibatch[0,:,:,:] = img0
120    minibatch[1,:,:,:] = img1
121
122    # 3. filter each image in the mini-batch with
123    #     two different 3D filters
124    conv2d_demo(minibatch, height, width, channels)
125
126
127    # 4. now create a graph where we process the mini-batch
128    #     with the max pool operation
129    maxpool_demo(minibatch, height, width, channels)
130
131    # 5. the show is over. wait for a key press.
132    cv2.waitKey(0)
133    cv2.destroyAllWindows()
134
135 main()
```

## 9.4   Parameters to be defined for a convolution layer

**Parameters vs. Hyperparameters.** In Fig. 9.4 we depict three important parameters that are to be defined for a convolution layer. Weights are also parameters of our CNN model. However, the weights that define the filters in a convolution layer are learned and are set indirectly due to the training data. Parameters of a model that are set directly (manually) and that are not learned during training are called *hyperparameters.*

# Hyperparameters to be defined for a Convolution Layer

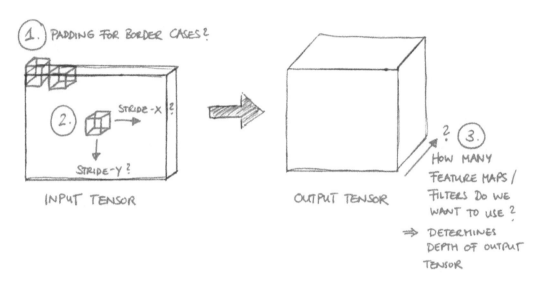

Figure 9.4: There are three hyperparameters to be defined for a convolution layer. 1.) Do we want to use padding? 2.) How to stride the receptive fields? 3.) How many feature maps do we want to learn?

**1.) Padding.** The first important question that we have to answer is whether we want to process the image information on the borders of the image as well if the next RF position does not fit completely into the image dimensions. The usual way to deal with such a case is to fill or to "pad" the missing entries for these border cases with zeros. In Fig. 9.5 I have illustrated the two different options "VALID" (do not use zero padding) and "SAME" (use zero padding), that can be specified when generating a convolution operator with `conv2d()`

**2.) Receptive field (RF) stride.** We have also to define where we want to put receptive fields into the input tensor. Some authors use overlapping receptive fields, where the filter stride is smaller than the filter width. If we set the stride equal to the filter width, we get non-overlapping receptive fields. However, we could also follow the approach of "sparse sampling", where we skip some of the input values and set the filter stride larger than the filter width. Note, that we could even use different filter widths and filter strides for the two spatial dimensions. In certain special applications where we want to encode e.g. the horizontal information in more detail compared to the vertical information it might be helpful to make use of this freedom. However, up to now, I have never seen a CNN that makes use of this freedom. What does nature do? We can find many studies that show that biological neurons often have overlapping receptive fields. E.g., retinal ganglion cells (RGC) show overlapping receptive fields.

**3.) Number of filters.** Another important question is how many filters do we want to use. Note that the number of filters is the same as the depth of the output tensor. Remember that for each filter the convolution layer will compute the response at each RF location. So the more filters we will use, the more computation time we will need for a feedforward step but also for the training step, since we need to adapt more filter weights.

**A thought experiment: Using only one feature map.** Currently there is no real theory that could guide the choice for the number of filters. However, let us assume we would use only 1 filter in a convolution layer and that the receptive field size is 5x5x3 (5 pixels in width, 5 pixels in height, 3 = number of color channels). There could be a lot of different spatial colored image structures in a 5x5x3 receptive field if there are 256 different values for each of the 5x5x3 entries. But with only 1 filter we can only analyze whether one typical colored image structure is present or not. Let's say the filter weights are set such that the filter "likes" vertical white structures (with "likes" I mean that it produces high filter response values for vertical white structures). In this case, it produces a high output and a low output if there is no vertical structure. So the feature map encodes the image from another viewpoint: How much "verticalness" is there in each RF? But that is all. With only one filter we could not distinguish other important (colored) image structures.

**A thought experiment: Using one million feature maps.** So we could come to the following idea: Why not use really many, let's say, 1 million filters? Let us first ignore the computation time and space problems that we would introduce by computing 1 million feature maps. In the 5x5x3 receptive field we could observe theoretically $256^{75} = ca.\,4.2 * 10^{180}$ different inputs which is much more than 1 million (different features). So we would already classify this extremely large amount of possible different inputs to a much smaller set of 1 million different features. However, since natural images will have a large tendency to show only a subset of these $4.2 * 10^{180}$ different inputs, we would make up probably thousands of different classes for vertical image structures. On the other hand we want to encode the image in such a way, that we *become invariant* to small changes in the input. It should not be important whether you write a "1" with a slightly rotated vertical line! For this, it makes sense not to use such a high number of filters, but to use a substantially smaller number of filters in order to put different inputs into the same equivalence class. Only by this means our output tensor becomes a new image representation that will be more robust against slight changes in the input data. For these reasons people typically choose the number of filters between 10-1000 in a convolution layer. Note, that we assume here when using a small set of features, that the features are not "similar". It will not help us neither if we only use 100 filters but all of the 100 filters describe minimal different variants of vertical structures. For this it is interesting to see that a CNN learns a set of features in each conv layer that are different while we do not directly foster this in the learning process by using Backpropagation.

**The question of how many features to use is an old one.** Actually this question is an old one which emerged in computer vision many decades before in the era where hand-crafted feature detectors and descriptor vectors like SIFT and SURF were used. Examples of these 64- and 128-dimensional descriptor vectors computed on basis of local keypoints sampled from natural images were often clustered to build up a *codebook* of N different feature prototypes (*codewords*) and during a classification step local image features found on a test image were mapped onto one of these codewords. And then you could learn how many codewords of each type you find if a certain object class is present (*bag of features, bag of words* approach). Again the question was here: How large should my codebook be, so how to choose N? A small codebook maps very different image structures to the same few codewords. It is very robust against changes in the input image structures, but shows only a poor discriminative performance. A large codebook maps different image structures to mostly different codewords. It shows a high discriminative performance, but only a poor robustness against minor changes of these image structures. So choosing a "good" codebook size N was always a trade-off between keeping discriminative image structure information on the one side and establishing invariance performance against changes in the input image structures. For this, similar to the question of how many feature maps to chose nowadays in convolution layers, authors chose codebook sizes of some ten to hundreds of codewords as a trade-off between these two goals (invariance vs. discriminative performance).

# Dealing with border cases:
## "To pad, or not to pad, that is the question!"

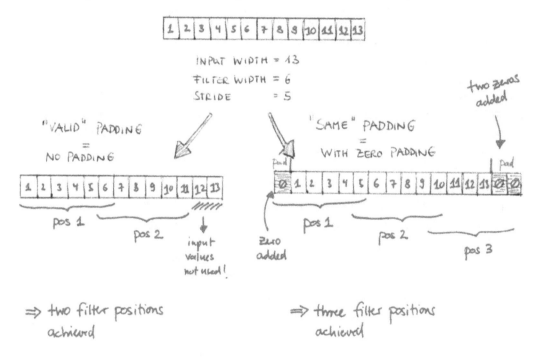

Figure 9.5: There are two possible choices for dealing with border cases in TensorFlow. The first one is not to use zero padding at all ("VALID"). The second one is to use zero padding ("SAME"). In this case TensorFlow tries to pad evenly left and right. But if the amount of columns to be added is odd, TensorFlow adds the extra column to the right.

## 9.5 How to compute the dimension of an output tensor

**Spatial dimension of an output tensor is a result of many parameters.** While we define the depth of the resulting 3D output tensor (that is the result of a convolution operation) directly by specifying the number of feature maps to use, the spatial dimension (width, height) results automatically from the spatial dimensions of the input tensor, the padding width, the filter size and the filter stride.

**Computation of the spatial dimension.** Have a look at Fig. 9.6. Here we assume that our input tensor has a depth of 1 and a spatial dimension of $W \times W$. The filter is assumed to have size $F \times F$ and the stride is set to $S$. We further assume a padding width of $P$ at the borders of the input tensor. Then we have $W + 2P$ possible positions in one row where we could put the origin of the filter, right? However, the last positions will not allow to fit the filter completely into the image since it has some extension as well. For this, there are only $(W + 2P - F) + 1$ positions such that the filter of size $F$ completely fits into the image padded to both sides with $P$ zeros. Now this computation assumes a stride $S = 1$. For a larger filter stride we have to divide the number of possible filter origins by the the stride size: $X = (W + 2P - F)/S + 1$.

**How to keep the spatial dimensions of input and output tensors the "SAME".** Imagine we want the spatial dimensions of our output tensor after the convolution operation to be the same as the spatial dimensions of the input tensor, i.e., for one dimension we want $X$ (spatial dimension of output tensor) and $W$ (spatial dimension of input tensor) to be equally. In the following computation we further assume that $S = 1$ (usually chosen):

$$
\begin{align}
D &= W \tag{9.1}\\
\Leftrightarrow \frac{W + 2P - F}{S} + 1 &= W \tag{9.2}\\
\Leftrightarrow W + 2P - F + 1 &= W \tag{9.3}\\
\Leftrightarrow 2P - F + 1 &= 0 \tag{9.4}\\
\Leftrightarrow 2P &= F - 1 \tag{9.5}\\
\Leftrightarrow P &= \frac{F - 1}{2} \tag{9.6}
\end{align}
$$

So we need to choose the padding size $P = \frac{F-1}{2}$ in order to assume that the output tensor has the same spatial dimension as the input tensor.

## 9.6   Parameters to be defined for a pooling layer

**Similar to convolution layers.** The pooling operation can be considered as a filter as well. For this, the same considerations that we did for the convolution layers hold here. First, we have to choose a filter kernel size. Usually: 2x2 pooling is done. Second, we have to choose a filter stride. Normally the filter stride for pooling is set exactly to the filter width, such that we do not have overlaps in the pooling filter positions. So normally we use a filter stride of 2x2.

## 9.7   A CNN in TensorFlow

The following code shows a complete implementation of a CNN with TensorFlow. Set the variable exp_nr in file train_cnn.py to choose one of three different CNN topologies. Also set the variable dataset_root in order to define the location of your training and testing images.

After all mini-batches have been trained the final model will be saved to a file with the filename save_filename. This model can then be restored in order for testing (inference) using the file test_cnn.py.

The file dataset_reader.py is used for easier access to the training data. The function nextBatch() can be called for retrieving the next mini-batch.

Listing 9.2: train_cnn.py

```
1  # file: train_cnn.py
2  #
3  # A CNN implementation in TensorFlow
4  #
5  # First set the variable <dataset_root>
6  # It tells the Python script where your training and
7  # validation data is.
8  #
9  # Store your training images in a sub-folder for each
10 # class in <dataset_root>/train/
11 # e.g.
12 #    <dataset_root>/train/bikes
13 #    <dataset_root>/train/cars
14 #
15 # Store your test images in a sub-folder for each
16 # class in <dataset_root>/test/
17 # e.g.
18 #    <dataset_root>/test/bikes
```

```
19  #      <dataset_root>/test/cars
20  #
21  # Then let the script run.
22  # The final trained model will be saved.
23
24  from dataset_reader import dataset
25  import tensorflow as tf
26
27  # Experiments
28  # Exp-Nr   Comment
29  # 01       10 hidden layers:
30  #          INPUT->C1->P1->C2->P2->C3->C4->C5->P3->FC1->FC2->OUT
31  #          trained 100 mini-batches of size 32
32  #          feature maps: 10-15-20-25-30
33  #
34  # 02       10 hidden layers:
35  #          INPUT->C1->P1->C2->P2->C3->C4->C5->P3->FC1->FC2->OUT
36  #          trained 1000 mini-batches of size 32
37  #          feature maps: 10-15-20-25-30
38  #
39  # 03       4 hidden layers: INPUT->C1->P1->FC1->FC2->OUT
40  #          trained 1000 mini-batches of size 32
41  #          feature maps: 10
42
43  exp_nr = 1
44  dataset_root =\
45      "V:/01_job/12_datasets/imagenet/cars_vs_bikes_prepared/"
46
47
48  # helper function to build 1st conv layer with filter size 11x11
49  # and stride 4 (in both directions) and no padding
50  def conv1st(name, l_input, filter, b):
51      cov = tf.nn.conv2d(l_input, filter,
52                         strides=[1, 4, 4, 1], padding='VALID')
53      return tf.nn.relu(tf.nn.bias_add(cov, b), name=name)
54
55
56  # in all other layers we use a stride of 1 (in both directions)
57  # and a padding such that the spatial dimension (width,height)
58  # of the output volume is the same as the spatial dimension
59  # of the input volume
60  def conv2d(name, l_input, w, b):
61      cov = tf.nn.conv2d(l_input, w,
62                         strides=[1, 1, 1, 1], padding='SAME')
63      return tf.nn.relu(tf.nn.bias_add(cov, b), name=name)
64
65  # generates a max pooling layer
66  def max_pool(name, l_input, k, s):
67      return tf.nn.max_pool(l_input,
68                            ksize=[1, k, k, 1],
```

```
69                                    strides=[1, s, s, 1],
70                                    padding='VALID', name=name)
71
72
73  # helper function to generate a CNN
74  def build_cnn_model(_X, keep_prob, n_classes, imagesize, img_channel):
75      # prepare matrices for weights
76      _weights = {
77          'wc1': tf.Variable(tf.random_normal([11, 11, img_channel, 10])),
78          'wc2': tf.Variable(tf.random_normal([5, 5, 10, 15])),
79          'wc3': tf.Variable(tf.random_normal([3, 3, 15, 20])),
80          'wc4': tf.Variable(tf.random_normal([3, 3, 20, 25])),
81          'wc5': tf.Variable(tf.random_normal([3, 3, 25, 30])),
82          'wd1': tf.Variable(tf.random_normal([6 * 6 * 30, 40])),
83          'wd2': tf.Variable(tf.random_normal([40, 40])),
84          'out': tf.Variable(tf.random_normal([40, n_classes])),
85          'exp3_wd1': tf.Variable(tf.random_normal([27 * 27 * 10, 40]))
86      }
87
88      # prepare vectors for biases
89      _biases = {
90          'bc1': tf.Variable(tf.random_normal([10])),
91          'bc2': tf.Variable(tf.random_normal([15])),
92          'bc3': tf.Variable(tf.random_normal([20])),
93          'bc4': tf.Variable(tf.random_normal([25])),
94          'bc5': tf.Variable(tf.random_normal([30])),
95          'bd1': tf.Variable(tf.random_normal([40])),
96          'bd2': tf.Variable(tf.random_normal([40])),
97          'out': tf.Variable(tf.random_normal([n_classes]))
98      }
99
100     # reshape input picture
101     _X = tf.reshape(_X, shape=[-1, imagesize, imagesize, img_channel])
102
103     if (exp_nr == 1 or exp_nr==2):
104
105         # feature hierarchy:
106         # topology:
107         # INPUT->C1->P1->C2->P2->C3->C4->C5->P3->FC1->FC2->OUT
108         conv1 =\
109             conv1st('conv1', _X, _weights['wc1'], _biases['bc1'])
110         pool1 =\
111             max_pool('pool1', conv1, k=3, s=2)
112         conv2 =\
113             conv2d('conv2', pool1, _weights['wc2'], _biases['bc2'])
114         pool2 =\
115             max_pool('pool2', conv2, k=3, s=2)
116         conv3 =\
117             conv2d('conv3', pool2, _weights['wc3'], _biases['bc3'])
118         conv4 =\
```

```
119            conv2d('conv4', conv3, _weights['wc4'], _biases['bc4'])
120        conv5 =\
121            conv2d('conv5', conv4, _weights['wc5'], _biases['bc5'])
122        pool3 =\
123            max_pool('pool3', conv5, k=3, s=2)
124
125        # classifier:
126        # fully connected layers
127        dense1 =\
128            tf.reshape(pool3,
129                       [-1, _weights['wd1'].get_shape().as_list()[0]])
130        dense1 =\
131            tf.nn.relu(tf.matmul(dense1,
132                       _weights['wd1']) + _biases['bd1'],
133                       name='fc1')
134        dense2 =\
135            tf.nn.relu(tf.matmul(dense1,
136                          _weights['wd2']) + _biases['bd2'],
137                          name='fc2')
138        out =\
139            tf.matmul(dense2, _weights['out']) + _biases['out']
140
141    elif exp_nr == 3:
142
143        # feature hierarchy:
144        # topology:
145        # INPUT->C1->P1->FC1->FC2->OUT
146        conv1 =\
147            conv1st('conv1', _X, _weights['wc1'], _biases['bc1'])
148        print("conv1 shape: ", conv1.get_shape())
149        pool1 =\
150            max_pool('pool1', conv1, k=3, s=2)
151        print("pool1 shape: ", pool1.get_shape())
152
153        # classifier:
154        # fully connected layers
155        dense1 =\
156            tf.reshape(pool1, [-1, 27*27*10])
157        dense1 =\
158            tf.nn.relu(
159                    tf.matmul(dense1,
160                          _weights['exp3_wd1']) + _biases['bd1'],
161                          name='fc1')
162        print("dense1 shape: ", dense1.get_shape())
163        dense2 =\
164            tf.nn.relu(
165                    tf.matmul(dense1,
166                          _weights['wd2']) + _biases['bd2'],
167                          name='fc2')
168        print("dense2 shape: ", dense2.get_shape())
```

```
169
170          out =\
171              tf.matmul(dense2, _weights['out']) + _biases['out']
172          print("out shape: ", out.get_shape())
173
174      return [out, _weights['wc1']]
175
176
177 # 1. create a training and testing Dataset object that stores
178 #     the training / testing images
179 training = dataset(dataset_root + "train", ".jpeg")
180 testing = dataset(dataset_root + "validation", ".jpeg")
181
182 # 2. set training parameters
183 learn_rate = 0.001
184 batch_size = 32
185 display_step = 1
186 if exp_nr==1:
187     nr_mini_batches_to_train = 100
188 elif exp_nr==2:
189     nr_mini_batches_to_train = 1000
190 elif exp_nr==3:
191     nr_mini_batches_to_train = 1000
192
193 save_filename = 'save/model.ckpt'
194 logs_path = './logfiles'
195
196 n_classes = training.num_labels
197 dropout = 0.8   # dropout (probability to keep units)
198 imagesize = 227
199 img_channel = 3
200
201 x = tf.placeholder(tf.float32, [None,
202                                 imagesize,
203                                 imagesize,
204                                 img_channel])
205 y = tf.placeholder(tf.float32, [None, n_classes])
206 keep_prob = tf.placeholder(tf.float32)   # dropout (keep probability)
207
208 [pred, filter1st] = build_cnn_model(x,
209                                     keep_prob,
210                                     n_classes,
211                                     imagesize,
212                                     img_channel)
213 cost = tf.reduce_mean(
214         tf.nn.softmax_cross_entropy_with_logits(logits=pred,
215                                                 labels=y))
216 # cost = tf.reduce_mean(tf.squared_difference(pred, y))
217
218 global_step = tf.Variable(0, trainable=False)
```

```
219
220 optimizer = tf.train.AdamOptimizer(
221              learning_rate=learn_rate).minimize(
222                  cost, global_step=global_step)
223 # optimizer = tf.train.GradientDescentOptimizer(lr).
224 #                  minimize(cost, global_step=global_step)
225
226 correct_pred = tf.equal(tf.argmax(pred, 1), tf.argmax(y, 1))
227 accuracy = tf.reduce_mean(tf.cast(correct_pred, tf.float32))
228
229 saver = tf.train.Saver()
230 tf.add_to_collection("x", x)
231 tf.add_to_collection("y", y)
232 tf.add_to_collection("keep_prob", keep_prob)
233 tf.add_to_collection("pred", pred)
234 tf.add_to_collection("accuracy", accuracy)
235
236 print("\n\n")
237 print("----------------------------------------")
238 print("I am ready to start the training...")
239 print("So I will train a CNN, starting with a"+
240      "learn rate of", learn_rate)
241 print("I will train ", nr_mini_batches_to_train,
242      "mini batches of ", batch_size, "images")
243 print("Your input images will be resized to ",
244      imagesize, "x", imagesize, "pixels")
245 print("----------------------------------------")
246
247 with tf.Session() as my_session:
248     my_session.run(tf.global_variables_initializer())
249
250     step = 1
251     while step < nr_mini_batches_to_train:
252
253         batch_ys, batch_xs = training.nextBatch(batch_size)
254         # note: batch_ys and batch_xs are tuples each
255         # batch_ys a tuple of e.g. 32 one-hot NumPy arrays
256         # batch_xs a tuple of e.g. 32 NumPy arrays of shape
257         #   (width, height, 3)
258
259
260         _ = my_session.run([optimizer],
261                     feed_dict={x: batch_xs,
262                                 y: batch_ys,
263                                 keep_prob: dropout})
264
265         if step % display_step == 0:
266             acc = my_session.run(accuracy,
267                         feed_dict={x: batch_xs,
268                                     y: batch_ys,
```

```
269                                                    keep_prob: 1.})
270            loss = my_session.run(cost, feed_dict={x: batch_xs,
271                                                    y: batch_ys,
272                                                    keep_prob: 1.})
273            print("learn rate:" + str(learn_rate) +
274                    " mini batch:" + str(step) +
275                    ", minibatch loss= " + "{:.5f}".format(loss) +
276                    ", batch accuracy= " + "{:.5f}".format(acc))
277          step += 1
278
279      print("\n")
280      print("Training of CNN model finished.")
281
282      save_filename =\
283          "saved_model_exp0" + str(exp_nr) + "/final_model.ckpt"
284      saver.save(my_session, save_filename, global_step=step)
285      print("Saved CNN model to file '",save_filename,"'")
```

Listing 9.3: test_cnn.py

```
1  # file: test.py
2  #
3  # Restores a learned CNN model and tests it.
4  #
5  # Store your test images in a sub-folder for each
6  # class in <dataset_root>/validation/
7  # e.g.
8  #     <dataset_root>/validation/bikes
9  #     <dataset_root>/validation/cars
10
11
12 from dataset_reader import dataset
13
14 dataset_root =\
15     "V:/01_job/12_datasets/imagenet/cars_vs_bikes_prepared/"
16 testing   = dataset(dataset_root + "validation", ".jpeg")
17
18 import tensorflow as tf
19 import numpy as np
20
21 # Parameters
22 batch_size = 1
23
24 ckpt = tf.train.get_checkpoint_state("saved_model_exp01")
25 saver = tf.train.import_meta_graph(
26         ckpt.model_checkpoint_path + '.meta')
27
28 pred = tf.get_collection("pred")[0]
29 x = tf.get_collection("x")[0]
30 keep_prob = tf.get_collection("keep_prob")[0]
```

```
31
32 sess = tf.Session()
33 saver.restore(sess, ckpt.model_checkpoint_path)
34
35 # test
36 step_test = 0
37 correct=0
38 while step_test * batch_size < len(testing):
39
40     # testing_ys and testing_xs are tuples
41     testing_ys, testing_xs = testing.nextBatch(batch_size)
42
43     # get first image and first ground truth vector
44     # from the tuples
45     first_img          = testing_xs[0]
46     first_groundtruth_vec = testing_ys[0]
47
48     # at first iteration:
49     # show shape of image and ground truth vector
50     if step_test == 0:
51         print("Shape of testing_xs is :",
52                 first_img.shape)
53         print("Shape of testing_ys is :",
54                 first_groundtruth_vec.shape)
55
56     # given the input image,
57     # let the CNN predict the category!
58     predict = sess.run(pred,
59                     feed_dict={x: testing_xs,
60                                 keep_prob: 1.})
61
62     # get ground truth label and
63     # predicted label from output vector
64     groundtruth_label = np.argmax(first_groundtruth_vec)
65     predicted_label = np.argmax(predict, 1)[0]
66
67     print("\nImage test: ", step_test)
68     print("Ground truth label    :",
69             testing.label2category[groundtruth_label])
70     print("Label predicted by CNN:",
71             testing.label2category[predicted_label])
72
73     if predicted_label == groundtruth_label:
74         correct+=1
75     step_test += 1
76
77 print("\n---")
78 print("Classified", correct, "images correct of",
79                     step_test,"in total.")
80 print("Classification rate in" +
```

```
81      "percent = {0:.2f}".format(correct/step_test*100.0))
```

Listing 9.4: dataset_reader.py

```
 1 # file: dataset_reader.py
 2 #
 3 # Contains helper class dataset
 4 # which is able to return mini batches of a desired
 5 # size of <label, image> pairs
 6 #
 7 # For this the class constructor needs to be passed
 8 # a imagePath in which it expects a subfolder for each
 9 # image category.
10 #
11 # It automatically will traverse each subfolder recursively
12 # in order to generate a image list of the form
13 # e.g. [['cow', 'cow8439.jpeg'], ['dog', 'dog02.jpeg'], ...]
14 #
15 # Images will be read only using OpenCV's imread() function
16 # when preparing a mini-batch.
17 # They are not loaded all at once which is good,
18 # if we want to train on several 10.000 of images.
19 # (e.g. 1024 images of 1MB each --> 1 GB already!)
20 #
21 # The code here is inspired by:
22 # Wang Xinbo's AlexNet implementation:
23 # see https://github.com/SidHard/tfAlexNet
24
25
26 import numpy as np
27 import os
28 import cv2
29
30 RESIZE_WIDTH, RESIZE_HEIGHT = 227,227
31
32 class dataset:
33
34     '''
35     Checks which image categories are stored
36     in the subfolder of <imagePath>:
37     e.g. 'cows', 'dogs'
38     Then prepares lists of filenames and label information
39     for the image files found in the imagePath
40     '''
41     def __init__(self, imagePath, extensions):
42
43         # 1. prepare image list with category information
44         #     self.data = [['cow', 'cowimg01.jpeg'],
45         #                     ['dog', 'dogimg3289.jpeg'], ...]
46         print("\n")
```

```
47    print("Searching in folder", imagePath, "for images")
48    self.data = createImageList(imagePath, extensions)
49    NrImgs = len(self.data)
50    print("Found", NrImgs, "images")
51    print("Here are the first 5 and the last 5 images and "
52          "their corresponding categories I found:")
53    for i in range(0,5):
54            print(self.data[i])
55    for i in range(NrImgs-5,NrImgs):
56            print(self.data[i])
57
58    # 2. shuffle the data
59    np.random.shuffle(self.data)
60    self.num_images = len(self.data)
61    self.next_image_nr = 0
62
63    # 3. use zip function to unzip the data into two lists
64    #     see
65    #     https://docs.python.org/3.3/library/functions.html#zip
66    self.labels, self.filenames = zip(*self.data)
67
68    # 4. show some random images
69    for i in range(0,5):
70            rnd_idx = np.random.randint(NrImgs)
71            rnd_filename = self.filenames[ rnd_idx ]
72            print("random filename = ", rnd_filename)
73            img = cv2.imread( rnd_filename )
74            img = cv2.resize(img, (RESIZE_WIDTH, RESIZE_HEIGHT))
75            img_name = "example image " + str(i)
76            cv2.imshow(img_name, img)
77            cv2.moveWindow(img_name, 300+i*250,100);
78    cv2.waitKey(5000)
79    cv2.destroyAllWindows()
80
81
82    # 5. get a list of all categories,
83    #     e.g. ['cows', 'dogs']
84    category_list = np.unique(self.labels)
85
86    # 6. how many categories are there?
87    self.num_labels = len(category_list)
88
89    # 7. prepare a dictionary to map
90    #     category names to category numbers
91    self.category2label = \
92        dict(zip(category_list, range(len(category_list))))
93
94    # 8. and the other way round:
95    #     prepare a dictionary {} to map category numbers
96    #     to category names
```

```
 97        self.label2category =\
 98            {l: c for c, l in self.category2label.items()}
 99
100        # 9. prepare list of ground truth labels
101        #    where we can find the ground truth label for
102        #    image i at the i-th position in the list
103        self.labels = [self.category2label[l] for l in self.labels]
104
105
106    '''
107    Returns the number of images
108    available by this dataset object
109    '''
110    def __len__(self):
111        return self.num_images
112
113    '''
114    Returns a onehot NumPy array,
115    where all entries are set to 0
116    but to 1 for the right category
117    '''
118    def onehot(self, label):
119        v = np.zeros(self.num_labels)
120        v[label] = 1
121        return v
122
123
124    '''
125    Are there further images available?
126    '''
127    def hasNextRecord(self):
128        return self.next_image_nr < self.num_images
129
130
131    '''
132    Resizes the specified OpenCV image to a fixed size
133    Converts it to a NumPy array
134    Converts the values from [0,255] to [0,1]
135    '''
136    def preprocess(self, img):
137
138        # preprocess image by resizing it to 227x227
139        pp = cv2.resize(img, (RESIZE_WIDTH, RESIZE_HEIGHT))
140
141        # and convert OpenCV representation to Numpy array
142        # note: asarray does not copy data!
143        #       see
144        pp = np.asarray(pp, dtype=np.float32)
145
146        # map values from [0,255] to [0,1]
```

```
147        pp /= 255
148
149        # prepare array of shape width x height x 3 array
150        pp = pp.reshape((pp.shape[0], pp.shape[1], 3))
151        return pp
152
153
154    '''
155    Returns a (label, image) tuple
156     where label is a one-hot teacher vector (list)
157     e.g. [0,1] if there are two categories
158     and
159     image is a NumPy array
160     of shape (width, height, 3)
161    '''
162    def get_next_record(self):
163
164        # will return the next training pair
165        # consisting of the input image and a
166        # one-hot/teacher label vector
167        if not self.hasNextRecord():
168
169            # Ups! We are at the end of the image list!
170
171            # So generate new random order of images
172
173            # randomly shuffle the data again
174            np.random.shuffle(self.data)
175            self.next_image_nr = 0
176            self.labels, self.filenames = zip(*self.data)
177            category = np.unique(self.labels)
178            self.num_labels = len(category)
179            self.category2label =\
180                dict(zip(category, range(len(category))))
181            self.label2category =\
182                {l: c for c,
183                 l in self.category2label.items()}
184
185            # prepare ground-truth label information for all images
186            # according to the newly shuffled order of the images
187            self.labels = [self.category2label[l] for l in self.labels]
188
189        # prepare one-hot teacher vector for the output neurons
190        label = self.onehot(self.labels[self.next_image_nr])
191
192        # read in the image using OpenCVs imread()
193        # function and then preprocess it
194        # (i.e., resize it, convert it to a NumPy array,
195        #  convert values from [0,255] to [0,1])
196        img_filename = self.filenames[self.next_image_nr]
```

```
197          img_as_np_array = self.preprocess(cv2.imread(img_filename))
198
199          # prepare next image nr to return
200          self.next_image_nr += 1
201
202          # prepare a (label, image) tuple
203          return label, img_as_np_array
204
205
206      '''
207      Given a batch size, this function
208      first creates a list of (label, image)
209      tuples called <records>
210      [(0, img-of-cow), (1, img-of-dog), (0, img-of-cow), ...]
211      and then returns the labels and images as separate
212      tuples
213      '''
214      def nextBatch(self, batch_size):
215
216          # creates a mini-batch of the desired size
217          records = []
218          for i in range(batch_size):
219              record = self.get_next_record()
220              if record is None:
221                  break
222              records.append(record)
223          labels, imgs = zip(*records)
224          return labels, imgs
225
226
227  '''
228  Helper function to provide a list of
229  all label info and image files in all
230  subfolders in the the given <imagePath>
231  '''
232  def createImageList(imagePath, extensions):
233
234      # 1. start with an empty list of labels/filenames
235      labels_and_filenames = []
236
237      # 2. each subfolder name in imagePath is considered to be
238      #    a class label in stored in categoryList
239      categoryList = [None]
240      categoryList = [c for c in sorted(os.listdir(imagePath))
241                      if c[0] != '.' and
242                      os.path.isdir(os.path.join(imagePath, c))]
243
244      # 3. for each of the categories
245      for category in categoryList:
246          print("subfolder/category found =", category)
```

```python
            if category:
                walkPath = os.path.join(imagePath, category)
            else:
                walkPath = imagePath
                category = os.path.split(imagePath)[1]

            # create a generator
            w = _walk(walkPath)

            # step through all directories and subdirectories
            while True:

                # get names of dirs and filenames of current dir
                try:
                    dirpath, dirnames, filenames = next(w)
                except StopIteration:
                    break

                # don't enter directories that begin with '.'
                for d in dirnames[:]:
                    if d.startswith('.'):
                        dirnames.remove(d)

                dirnames.sort()

                # ignore files that begin with '.'
                filenames =\
                    [f for f in filenames if not f.startswith('.')]
                # only load images with the right extension
                filenames =\
                    [f for f in filenames
                       if os.path.splitext(f)[1].lower()
                       in extensions]
                filenames.sort()

                for f in filenames:
                    labels_and_filenames.append(
                        [category, os.path.join(dirpath, f)])

        # labels_and_filenames will be a list of
        # two-tuples [category, filename]
        return labels_and_filenames


def _walk(top):
    """
    This is a (recursive) directory tree generator.
    What is a generator?
    See:
    http://stackoverflow.com/questions/231767/what-does-the-yield-keyword-
```

```
        do
297     In short:
298     - generators are iterables that can be iterated only once
299     - their values are not stored in contrast e.g. to a list
300     - 'yield' is 'like' return
301     """
302
303     # 1. collect directory names in dirs and
304     #    non-directory names (filenames) in nondirs
305     names = os.listdir(top)
306     dirs, nondirs = [], []
307     for name in names:
308         if os.path.isdir(os.path.join(top, name)):
309             dirs.append(name)
310         else:
311             nondirs.append(name)
312
313     # 2. "return" information about directory names and filenames
314     yield top, dirs, nondirs
315
316     # 3. recursively process each directory found in current top
317     #    directory
318     for name in dirs:
319         path = os.path.join(top, name)
320         for x in _walk(path):
321             yield x
```

# Computing the dimension of an output tensor

Example:
- Input area of size WxW with W=7
- Receptive field size of FxF with F=3
- Filter stride S in both directions with S=1
- Padding size P at borders with P=1

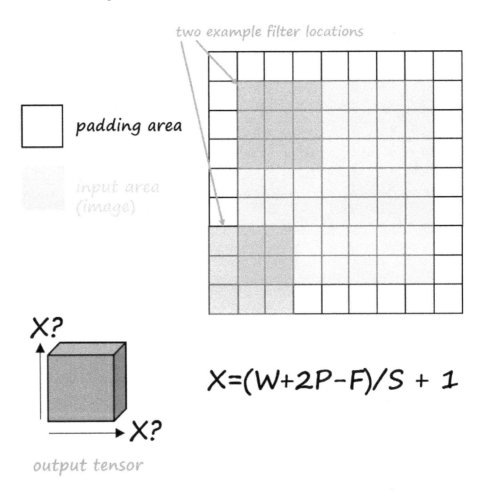

two example filter locations

padding area

input area
(image)

X?

X?

output tensor

$$X=(W+2P-F)/S + 1$$

Figure 9.6: How to compute the spatial dimension $X$ of an output tensor that results from a convolution operation.

# 10

# Deep Learning Tricks

## 10.1  Fighting against vanishing gradients

**An observation: Vanishing gradients.** A severe problem that can be observed when using Backpropagation to train deep neural networks is the observation that the absolute value of the gradient of the error function E derived into the direction of a weight $w_{kj}$ (remember that this was the starting point for deriving the Backprop weight update formulas)

$$\Delta w_{kj} = -\alpha \frac{\partial E}{\partial w_{kj}} \tag{10.1}$$

typically get smaller and smaller as we go from the higher layers of a deep neural network down to the lower layers. This is called the *vanishing gradient problem*. The Backpropagation algorithm propagates the error signals down to the lower layers. This means that the weights in the lower layers of a deep neural network keep nearly unchanged.

**Reason for vanishing gradients.** The reason of the vanishing gradient problem can be traced back to the use of *squashing activation functions* such as the logistic and the hyperbolic (tanh) transfer functions. Initially, these squashing activation functions were biologically motivated: no neuron can have negative firing rates and no neuron can fire arbitrarily fast. However, it means that a large range of possible input values for the transfer function (the activation of the neuron) will be mapped to a small range of output values. Namely to the interval (0,1) for the logistic transfer function and to the interval (-1,1) for the hyperbolic transfer function. This means that even a large change in the input to the neuron will produce a small change in the neuron's output. With other words: also the gradient of the error function will be (with high probability) small when using squashing functions, since the error will (with high probability) only change slightly when changing the input values, since the values of the output neurons only will change slightly.

And the problem becomes even worse if we use several layers of neurons with squashing transfer functions. The first layer in such a network will map a large region of the input space to a small interval, the second layer in the network will map the resulting output intervals to even smaller regions and so on. As a result, a change in the weights of the first layer will not change much the final output or with other words: the gradient of the error with respect to some weight stemming from one of the lower layers is small.

**Avoiding vanishing gradients.** So how can we tackle this problem? We can simply avoid using squashing functions which show this saturating behavior to the left and right side of the input space! One popular example is the ReLU activation function which maps an input value $x$ to $f(x) = max(0, x)$.

**Seeing the vanishing gradients.** You will better believe the above argumentation about vanishing gradients if you have seen them. How can we visualize the vanishing gradients? We could compute the average gradient length or average weight change per neuron layer (remember: the height of a weight change $w$ is the scaled negative gradient of the error function differentiated with respect to this variable $w$) in a deep MLP and display these average weight change values. This is exactly what you shall do in exercise 12 (solution can be found in the GitHub repository). Here are the average weight change values of a 2-5-5-5-5-2 MLP, i.e., a deep neural network with 2 input neurons, 2 output neurons and 5 hidden layers. If we use the logistic transfer function for the neurons in the hidden layer

```
1  my_mlp.add_layer(2, TF.identity)
2  my_mlp.add_layer(5, TF.sigmoid)
3  my_mlp.add_layer(5, TF.sigmoid)
4  my_mlp.add_layer(5, TF.sigmoid)
5  my_mlp.add_layer(5, TF.sigmoid)
6  my_mlp.add_layer(5, TF.sigmoid)
```

```
7 my_mlp.add_layer(2, TF.identity)
```

we get these average weight changes for weights to neurons to layer 1-6:

```
1 Layer # 1 : 0.000016467941743
2 Layer # 2 : 0.000069949781101
3 Layer # 3 : 0.000252670886581
4 Layer # 4 : 0.000760924226725
5 Layer # 5 : 0.002352968443448
6 Layer # 6 : 0.015992000875581
```

And if we use the ReLU transfer function for the neurons in the hidden layer

```
1 my_mlp.add_layer(2, TF.identity)
2 my_mlp.add_layer(5, TF.relu)
3 my_mlp.add_layer(5, TF.relu)
4 my_mlp.add_layer(5, TF.relu)
5 my_mlp.add_layer(5, TF.relu)
6 my_mlp.add_layer(5, TF.relu)
7 my_mlp.add_layer(2, TF.identity)
```

we get these average weight changes for weights to neurons to layer 1-6:

```
1 Layer # 1 : 0.000073625247850
2 Layer # 2 : 0.000064233540185
3 Layer # 3 : 0.000047251698986
4 Layer # 4 : 0.000073345206668
5 Layer # 5 : 0.000066667856138
6 Layer # 6 : 0.008097748184853
```

Can you see the systematics? In the first case (where we use a squashing function) the weight changes become smaller and smaller if we go towards lower layers due to fact that the gradients get smaller and smaller. In the second case (where we use the ReLU) this systematics cannot be detected.

## 10.2   Momentum optimization

**A simple observation.** Imagine a high dimensional error surface (e.g. 25 dimensions) that is induced by using a certain error metric E - also called *cost function*. At each point $\mathbf{w} \in \mathbb{R}^{25}$ of the 25 dimensional space (we assume a network here in this example with 25 weights), i.e., for each combination of the 25 weights in the network, a certain error $E(\mathbf{w})$ results. Can you see now the 25 dimensional error surface before your eyes? Good! ;-) Now imagine that there are (nearly) plateaus on this error surface with a small slope into the direction of the next local minimum. Standard Backpropagation with a fixed small learning rate will do a lot of small steps on such plateaus.

**The idea: Accumulating gradient information.** So how could we speed up gradient descent on such plateaus? The idea is quite simple. We could integrate knowledge of old gradients into the computation of the next weight change step and speed-up (increase our) steps on the error surface if gradients point successively (roughly) into the same direction. All the gradients on a plateau with a small slope will point into the same direction. So we could speed up here and hike faster downwards to the local minimum. And what is the easiest way to integrate knowledge about past gradients? Yes, we could just sum up the old weight change steps in some way. This is exactly what *Gradient descent with momentum term* does. More formally:

$$\Delta w_{kj} \;=\; -\alpha \frac{\partial E(\mathbf{w})}{\partial w_{kj}} + \beta \Delta w_{kj} \tag{10.2}$$

$$\;=\; -\alpha\, \delta_j\, y_k + \beta \Delta w_{kj} \tag{10.3}$$

So at each weight update step we do not only use the local gradient information $\frac{\partial E}{\partial w_{kj}}$, but also make use of older gradient information that has been integrated in steps before into $\Delta w_{kj}$. $E(\mathbf{w})$ is the error function evaluated for the current weight vector $w$ which is a vector of all the weights in the neural network.

Another way to describe momentum optimization is:

$$\mathbf{v} \;\leftarrow\; \beta\mathbf{v} + \alpha\nabla E(\mathbf{w}) \tag{10.4}$$

$$\mathbf{w} \;\leftarrow\; \mathbf{w} - \mathbf{v} \tag{10.5}$$

where you can think of $\mathbf{v}$ as a velocity vector which is added to the current weight vector $\mathbf{w}$ in each update step.

**Resulting behavior.** Now what will happen if we use Backpropagation with momentum term on a plateau, i.e., using the new weight change update formula 10.2 ? On a plateau with a slight slope the local gradients will point into the same direction, so we sum up gradients pointing into the same direction when applying the update formula several times. This will make the weight change value $\Delta w_{kj}$ larger and larger. Or with other words: we will speed up our steps on the error surface at locations where the gradients consistently point into the same direction.

**Momentum hyperparameter.** What is $\beta$ good for? $\beta$ is a new hyperparameter, i.e., a parameter that is not set automatically during training but has to be set manually before training. It is called *momentum* and controls how much we care about old gradients. If it is set to 0, we do not care about old gradients at all and end up with standard Backpropagation. If we set $\beta$ to large values, we care more about old gradients and less about the current local gradient. Often $\beta$ is set 0.9.

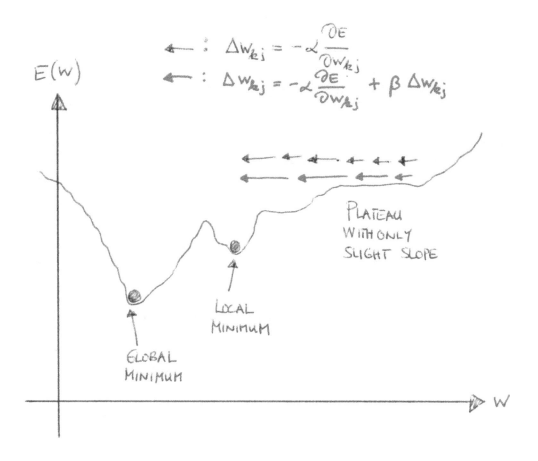

Figure 10.1: Backpropagation with momentum term can overcome plateaus much more faster than standard Backpropagation. Imagine also a perfect plateau: How could Backpropagation with momentum term be superior to standard Backpropagation here? Having still some momentum from previous weight change updates it could run over the plateau even if the plateau is perfect (i.e., without a slope), while standard Backpropagation would not be able to overcome it since the gradient is zero on a perfect plateau!

## 10.3   Nesterov Momentum Optimization

**The idea.** Normal gradient descent can be compared with a mountaineer which goes down from his current position into the direction of the steepest descent. Gradient descent with momentum can be compared with a ball that rolls down a mountain. Now imagine that the ball is rolling down towards a valley. It will increase its speed while rolling down. However, if the ball has reached a high velocity it will also overshoot the lowest point of the valley and will start to roll up a little bit on the other side of the valley. So, wouldn't it be nice, if the ball would be a little bit smarter and could look ahead into the direction in which it is rolling so that it slows down before the hill slopes up again? This is exactly the idea of *Nesterov Momentum Optimization* which is also called *Nesterov Accelerated Gradient (NAG)* and was proposed by *Yuri Nesterov* in 1983. Instead of computing the gradient at the current location **w** of the weight space, NAG "looks ahead" and computes the gradient for the next weights update step already at the next location $\mathbf{w} + \beta\mathbf{v}$ we would reach if we followed the current momentum vector **v** (which represents the accumulated gradient information from the last gradient descent steps):

$$\mathbf{v} \leftarrow \beta\mathbf{v} + \alpha\nabla E(\mathbf{w} + \beta\mathbf{v}) \tag{10.6}$$

$$\mathbf{w} \leftarrow \mathbf{w} - \mathbf{v} \tag{10.7}$$

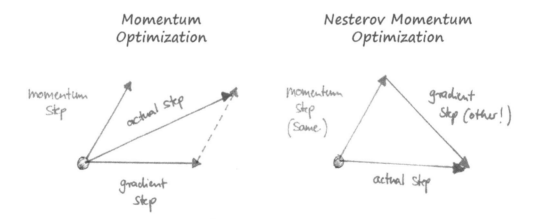

Figure 10.2: Comparison of momentum optimization (left) with Nesterov momentum optimization (right). Momentum optimization evaluates the gradient at the current location in weight space, while Nesterov optimization computes the gradient at the location in weight space we would reach after a momentum step, i.e., "looks ahead".

## 10.4 AdaGrad

**Idea 1: A learning rate per weight**. All three optimizers we know so far (standard gradient descent, momentum optimizer, Nesterov momentum optimizer) use the same learning rate $\alpha$ for all weights in the weight vector $\mathbf{w}$. However, probably not all the weights in a network will have the same impact onto the output values. There will be typically some weights in the network that will have a larger impact onto the output values than others in the sense that if you turn them up or down the output values will change much more faster compared to other weights. Perhaps it makes sense to use a smaller learning rate for such weights that have a high impact onto the output values (and in consequence also onto the errors the network makes). The current impact of a weight onto the error, i.e., how fast the error changes if we turn the weight up or down, is represented by the gradient of the error evaluated at the current location in weight space.

**Idea 2: Decrease learning rates during learning**. And perhaps it makes sense first to make large steps on the error surface and then as learning proceeds to make smaller and smaller steps on the error surface. The idea behind this is to roughly adjust the weights at the start and to do the fine-tuning at the end of the training.

**The formulas.** These two ideas are implemented by the *AdaGrad* algorithm. Instead of using an explicit learning rate for each weight which is decreased, the algorithm iteratively updates a sum vector $\mathbf{s}$ of the squared gradients $\nabla E(w) \otimes \nabla E(w)$ (where $\otimes$ means the element-wise multiplication of two vectors) and scales the current gradient vector by dividing by the root of this sum $\sqrt{\mathbf{s} + \epsilon}$. A small value $\epsilon$ (e.g. $10^{-8}$) is used to make sure the square root argument is different from zero, i.e., always valid:

$$\mathbf{s} \;\leftarrow\; \mathbf{s} + \nabla E(\mathbf{w}) \otimes \nabla E(\mathbf{w}) \tag{10.8}$$
$$\mathbf{w} \;\leftarrow\; \mathbf{w} - \alpha \nabla E(\mathbf{w}) \oslash \sqrt{\mathbf{s} + \epsilon} \tag{10.9}$$

Here $\oslash$ means the element-wise division of two vectors. Since the gradients are scaled the algorithm is called *Adaptive Gradients* or in short *AdaGrad*. The algorithm was introduced in 2011 in a paper by John Duchi et al. [9]. However, it is not the easiest paper to read due to the mathematical derivation of the algorithm presented in the paper.

**Remaining meaning of $\alpha$.** So the weights $w_1, w_2, w_3, \ldots$ in the weight vector $\mathbf{w} = (w_1, w_2, \ldots, w_N)$ are adapted individually due to the scaling of the current gradient. The individual scaling factors are computed on basis of the scaling vector $\mathbf{s} = (s_1, s_2, \ldots, s_N)$ and are given by the square root of the sum of squares of the historical gradients. An advantage of this method is, that the algorithm is not very sensitive to the overall learning rate $\alpha$. Typically it set to a value of $\alpha = 0.01$. Howver, a disadvantage of the method is that the learning rates are often decreased too quickly resulting in a stopping of the learning before the local minimum has been reached.

In TensorFlow an AdagraOptimizer node can be added to the computation graph using the following command:

```
optimizer = tf.train.AdagradOptimizer(learning_rate=0.01)
```

**Frequently vs. infrequently updated parameters.** In some sources you can read that AdaGrad is also helpful for sparse data, since it assigns a high learning to infrequently updated parameters. What does this mean? Isn't each weight updated in each step? Yes, it is. But what tis means is that some parameters (=weights in the context of neural networks) will be updated with larger changes if the current and/or last gradients are very small for this parameter, since the error on the sparse training dataset will not change much if we turn this parameter up or down. This in turn means that the corresponding argument in the accumulated sum vector $\mathbf{s}$ will be relatively small and for this the corresponding argument in the gradient vector $\nabla E(\mathbf{w}))$ will be divided only by a small number when dividing the gradient vector by $\sqrt{(\mathbf{w} + \epsilon)}$. Thus: for infrequently (not much) updated weights in the network an effective larger learning rate results.

## 10.5 RMSProp

**Similar to AdaGrad, but avoiding a major problem of it**. *RMSProp* or *Root Mean Square Propagation* is an algorithm by Tieleman and Hinton from 2012 which avoids the disadvantage of AdaGrad by accumulating only the gradients from the last steps. This in turn avoids that the vector $s$ becomes larger and larger and that the gradient $\nabla E(\mathbf{w})$ is scaled by a large denominator $\sqrt{\mathbf{s} + \epsilon}$ and that the training therefore stops since the weights are effectively not changed any more. RMSProp achieves this by multiplying the vector $\mathbf{s}$, i.e., the sum of gradients accumulated so far, with a multiplication factor $\beta$ (typically set to 0.9). Doing this iteratively will result in an exponential decay of the sum of accumulated gradients. By contrast, the current gradient $\nabla E(\mathbf{w})$ will be multiplied with $1 - \beta$, resulting in slightly different weight updates formulas compared to AdaGrad:

$$\mathbf{s} \leftarrow \beta\mathbf{s} + (1 - \beta)\nabla E(\mathbf{w}) \otimes \nabla E(\mathbf{w}) \tag{10.10}$$
$$\mathbf{w} \leftarrow \mathbf{w} - \alpha\nabla E(\mathbf{w}) \oslash \sqrt{\mathbf{s} + \epsilon} \tag{10.11}$$

The pattern where we compute the new value of **s** by multiplying the old value with $\beta$ and adding a new value multiplied with $1 - \beta$ is a special case of a *moving average* which is called an *exponential moving average (EMA)* and sometimes also called an *exponentially weighted moving average (EWMA)*.

In TensorFlow a RMSProp optimizer can be generated using the following code line:

```
optimizer = tf.train.RMSPropOptimizer(learning_rate=0.01, decay=0.9)\
            .minimize(loss)
```

## 10.6 Adam

**Combining RMSProp and Momentum optimization.** *Adam* or *Adaptive Moment Estimation* was published in 2015 by Kingma and Ba [21]. It can be seen as a combination of both RMSProp and the idea of momentum optimization. Have a look at the formulas:

$$\mathbf{v_t} \leftarrow \beta_1 \mathbf{v_{t-1}} + (1 - \beta_1)\nabla E(\mathbf{w}) \tag{10.12}$$

$$\mathbf{s_t} \leftarrow \beta_2 \mathbf{s_{t-1}} + (1 - \beta_2)\nabla E(\mathbf{w}) \otimes \nabla E(\mathbf{w}) \tag{10.13}$$

$$\hat{\mathbf{v}}_t \leftarrow \frac{\mathbf{v_t}}{1 - \beta_1^t} \tag{10.14}$$

$$\hat{\mathbf{s}}_t \leftarrow \frac{\mathbf{s_t}}{1 - \beta_2^t} \tag{10.15}$$

$$\mathbf{w} \leftarrow \mathbf{w} - \alpha\hat{\mathbf{v}}_t \oslash \sqrt{\hat{\mathbf{s}}_t + \epsilon} \tag{10.16}$$

Here $t$ is the update step number. Equation 10.12 reminds us of momentum optimization, while equation 10.13 is stolen from RMSProp. So Adam does both: it accumulates the last gradients by computing an EWMA of the past gradients (similar to momentum optimization) and it accumulates the squared gradients by computing an EWMA of the squared past gradients as RMSProp.

**Adam: A method that uses first and second moments of gradients.** With the help of the first equation we estimate the first moment (the mean) and with the help of the second equation we estimate the second moment (the uncentered variance) of the gradients respectively.

**Bias correction.** But what are equations 10.14 and 10.15 good for? Normally, **v** and **s** are initialized with zero vectors **0**. But thereby they will be biased each to zero vectors, especially during the initial time steps. In order to tackle this problem, these two equations correct for the biases. In their paper [21] (see page 2) the authors propose to set $\beta_1 = 0.9$, $\beta_2 = 0.999$ and $\epsilon = 10^{-8}$.

**Final weight update rule for Adam.** Equation 10.16 finally tells us how to update the weights according to Adam: We do a (learning rate scaled) update step into the direction of the (EWMA) mean of the past gradients, which is further scaled by the EWMA of the squared gradients.

In TensorFlow an Adam optimizer can be generated using the following code line:

```
optimizer = tf.train.RMSPropOptimizer(learning_rate=0.01, decay=0.9)\
            .minimize(loss)
```

## 10.7   Comparison of optimizers

**How to make a fair comparison.** The following comparison between the different optimizers described in the previous sections was generated using my MLP TensorFlow implementation, which can be found in the GitHub repository (solution for exercise 09): https://goo.gl/XnJubD

For a fair comparison, we need the MLP weights to be the same random start weights. This can be achieved in TensorFlow using the following command:

```
tf.set_random_seed(12345)
```

Place this command, before you generate the variables for the MLP. It initializes the pseudo random number generator with the same seed for each new start of the Python script and will allow us to start each experiment with the same weights and bias values:

```
weights = {
    'h1': tf.Variable(tf.random_normal(
        [NR_NEURONS_INPUT, NR_NEURONS_HIDDEN1])),
    'h2': tf.Variable(tf.random_normal(
        [NR_NEURONS_HIDDEN1, NR_NEURONS_HIDDEN2])),
    'out': tf.Variable(tf.random_normal(
        [NR_NEURONS_HIDDEN2, NR_NEURONS_OUTPUT]))
}
biases = {
    'b1': tf.Variable(tf.random_normal(
        [NR_NEURONS_HIDDEN1])),
```

```
12        'b2': tf.Variable(tf.random_normal(
13            [NR_NEURONS_HIDDEN2])),
14        'out': tf.Variable(tf.random_normal(
15            [NR_NEURONS_OUTPUT]))
16  }
```

even if we exchange the optimizer for the comparison:

```
 1  use_opt_nr = 5
 2
 3  if use_opt_nr==1:
 4      optimizer =\
 5          tf.train.GradientDescentOptimizer(LEARN_RATE)
 6  elif use_opt_nr==2:
 7      optimizer = \
 8          tf.train.MomentumOptimizer(learning_rate=LEARN_RATE,
 9                                     momentum=0.9)
10  elif use_opt_nr==3:
11      optimizer = \
12          tf.train.AdagradOptimizer(learning_rate=0.01)
13  elif use_opt_nr==4:
14      optimizer = \
15          tf.train.RMSPropOptimizer(learning_rate=0.01,
16                                    decay=0.9)
17  elif use_opt_nr==5:
18      optimizer = \
19          tf.train.AdamOptimizer(learning_rate=0.001,
20                                 beta1=0.9,
21                                 beta2=0.999,
22                                 epsilon=10e-8)
23
24  optimizer = optimizer.minimize(loss)
```

In the code you can set the variable use_opt_nr to 1-5 in order to compare the different optimizers. The result of this comparison can be seen in Fig. 10.3.
After 200 epochs the momentum optimizer has reached a decision boundary that better represents the underlying training data than the decision boundary learned by the gradient descent optimizer.

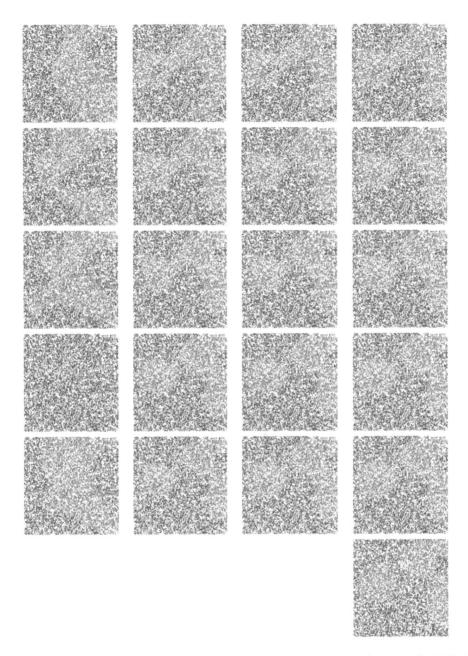

Figure 10.3: Comparison of decision boundaries learned after epochs 0,50,100,200 for a MLP with the same start weights using gradient descent (row 1), momentum optimizer (row 2), AdaGrad (row 3), RMSProp (row 4), Adam (row 5). Last row: training data used. You can see that especially RMSProp and Adam have found quite good decision boundaries. At a first glance it is therefore not that strange that RMSProp and Adam are often used to train neural networks.

## 10.8   Batch normalization

**The problem.** In a paper by Sergey Ioffe and Christian Szegedy from 2015 the authors describe the problem, that the training of deep neural networks is hard due to the fact that the distribution of the input values to a layer $l$ is changing steadily since the weights to the layer $l - 1$ before change and so the output values of the neurons in layer $l - 1$ which are the input values to the neurons in layer $l$. In their paper the authors call the problem of the changing distribution of neuron activation (and output) values the *internal covariate shift* problem.

**The remedy.** The proposed remedy for this problem is to reduce thus the amount of change in the distribution of the activation values of neurons in a layer by introducing a normalization step of these values per layer. In order to normalize the activation values of all neurons in a layer some statistical information about it will be computed, namely the mean and variance of the values. The mean is then used to shift the values such that they always have a new mean of zero. The variance in turn is used to rescale the values such that the new normalized values have a variance of 1. The shifting and rescaling of the activation values will be controlled by two new hyperparameters per layer (one for the shifting, one for the scaling). In short: Batch normalization lets the model learn the best scale and mean of the activation values in each layer $l$, such that the overall goal of reducing the error over the training dataset is reduced.

**Remember from statistics.** Remember that if $X$ is a random variable, the *standardized random variable* $\hat{X}$ can be computed by

$$\hat{X} = \frac{X - \mu}{\sigma} \qquad (10.17)$$

if $E(X) = \mu$ and $Var(X) = \sigma^2$. The new standardized random variable $\hat{X}$ has a mean of $E(\hat{X}) = 0$ and a variance $Var(\hat{X}) = 1$.

**The formulas.** Let us assume a mini-batch consists of m training samples. Batch normalization (BN) first computes the mean and variance of all the activations of neurons in a layer based on a mini-batch using the following first two equations, then normalizes the activation values using the third equation such that they have zero mean and variance 1 and computes the final new values using the scaling hyperparameter $\gamma$ and the shifting hyperparameter $\beta$ (which should not be confused with the $\beta$ hyperparameter(s) from Adam or RMSProp!).

$$\mu_{\mathbf{B}} = \frac{1}{m} \sum_{i=1}^{m} \mathbf{act}^{(i)} \tag{10.18}$$

$$\sigma_{\mathbf{B}}^2 = \frac{1}{m} \sum_{i=1}^{m} (\mathbf{act}^{(i)} - \mu_{\mathbf{B}})^2 \tag{10.19}$$

$$\hat{\mathbf{x}}^{(i)} = \frac{\mathbf{act}^{(i)} - \mu_{\mathbf{B}}}{\sqrt{\sigma_{\mathbf{B}}^2 + \epsilon}} \tag{10.20}$$

$$\mathbf{z}^{(\mathbf{i})} = \gamma \hat{\mathbf{x}}^{(i)} + \beta \tag{10.21}$$

Note that the terms $\mu_{\mathbf{B}}$, $\sigma_{\mathbf{B}}^2$, $\hat{\mathbf{x}}^{(i)}$ and $\mathbf{z}^{(\mathbf{i})}$ are all vectors!

- $\mu_{\mathbf{B}} \in \mathbb{R}^N$ is the vector that contains for each of the $N$ neurons in the layer considered its mean activation value, evaluated on the mini-batch

- $\sigma_{\mathbf{B}}^2 \in \mathbb{R}^N$ is also a vector and contains for each of the $N$ neurons in the layer considered the variance of the activation values observed while evaluating the mini-batch

- $\hat{\mathbf{x}}^{(i)} \in \mathbb{R}^N$ is the vector of normalized activation values for the $N$ neurons in the layers for the i-th sample from the mini-batch. Instead of $\mathbf{act}^{(i)}$ we use $\hat{\mathbf{x}}^{(i)}$ as an intermediate-step since it has mean 0 and variance 1 as a standardized random vector.

- $\mathbf{z}^{(\mathbf{i})} \in \mathbb{R}^N$ is what we finally use. Instead of using the actual neuron activation values in layer $l$ which are stored in the vector $\mathbf{act}^{(i)}$, Batch normalization suggests to use the vector $\mathbf{z}^{(\mathbf{i})}$, which stores a rescaled and shifted version of the original activation values. These normalized activation values are then the input for the corresponding transfer functions of the neurons.

- $\gamma$ is the re-scaling parameter for the layer considered. The value of $\gamma$ is learned during training.

- $\beta$ is the shifting parameter for the layer considered. The value of $\beta$ is learned during training.

- $\epsilon$ as usually denotes a very small number. Here it is used in order to make sure, that the denominator is not zero and thus the fraction well-defined.

**Batch normalization at test time.** During training the normalized activation values are computed with the help of the mean and variance of the activation values

of the neurons in the layer evaluated on basis of the mini-batch. But during testing
("inference") there are no mini-batches. For this, we already compute during the
training a moving average of the mean and variance of the activation values of the
neurons per layer which can then later be used in the test phase. This means that
actually we do not only need to learn $\gamma$ and $\beta$ for each layer, but also to compute
(not learn!) two moving averages per layer: a moving average of the mean of neuron
activation values and a moving average of the variance of the activation values.

# 11

# Beyond Deep Learning

At Quora - a question-and-answer site - people ask "What's next after deep learning?" and "What is the next step beyond deep learning in AI?". At the beginning of this book I wanted to underline my opinion that learning a hierarchy of local feature detectors is a good idea that can be borrowed from nature, but that there are many more helpful principles for information processing that could be exploited. In this last chapter I will present some possible further approaches, which are very promising from my point of view.

## 11.1 Principle of attention

Currently, the same training patterns are presented in each training epoch again and again. But think about how you learn about a topic. Do you invest the same time for each fact? Probably no. Probably, after some time of learning you will notice that some facts are already understood quite good and that for some other topics you need more time to understand or remember them. It seems to be a waste of time to present a model input patterns that are mapped to the desired output vectors almost perfectly. For this, a more reasonable approach could be to compile a new batch of training patterns in each epoch based on the observed errors at the output neurons. Training patterns that still produce large errors at the output side of the model should be included in the next batch with a much higher probability than training patterns that are mapped nearly flawlessly.

Of course, this approach bears a danger in itself: Overfitting. If we first train on all patterns, but then neglect some training patterns, because they are mapped already quite well, we reduce the training set towards the end of the training phase practically to a real subset. Thereby, we increase the probability of overfitting. Further, we run the risk that we even forget about things that we have learned before. However, if these possible negative effects are regarded and a solution can be found, compiling the training batches in a more clever way could give us the possibility to reduce even the training time.

## 11.2 Principle of lifelong learning

In machine learning, training and inference is divided into two distinct phases. Machine learning systems such as neural networks are trained and then the weights are froze for the inference phase. For living beings, there is no such distinction. Learning and inference happens at the same time and learning never stops. It would be interesting to design machine learning systems that can do something similar. This would probably also mean a turnaround from the domination of supervised learning approaches to unsupervised learning in order to be able to make use of a never ending input data stream at all.

In a survey paper on "Continual Lifelong Learning with Neural Networks: A Review" [34] an important problem of lifelong learning is mentioned: How can a system learn forever, i.e. stay plastic, without forgetting what it has learned before? This *plasticity vs. stability* problem is called *catastrophic forgetting* or *catastrophic interference*. Some approach is needed such that newly acquired information does not interfere with previously learned knowledge in a problematic way.

This rises a good question: How does nature solve the stability-plasticity problem? The *Complementary Learning System* (CLS) theory seems to show a direction for answering this question: The hippocampal system is able to to adapt on the short-term time scale and allows to rapidly learn new information (and does not represent old knowledge), while the neocortical system operates on a long-term time scale and learns an overlapping representation of different things learned before. The interplay between both systems is crucial: The hippocampus shows a high learning rate and can quickly adapt to new input data, but for storing the new information into the neocortical system it has to be played back into the neocortex (probably during sleep) to achieve its long-term retention.

## 11.3    Principle of incremental learning

When living beings learn a new ability, they never learn it from scratch. Take, e.g., the skill to play tennis. You will not start to learn tennis, before you have learned to walk and run, which are important ingredients of being able to play tennis. Probably you have also learned to catch a ball before, i.e., you have learned *hand-eye* and *hand-eye-object coordination* before which is helpful for moving the tennis racket into the direction of the tennis ball. Probably you have also seen a tennis match in TV. So you know, that a match is divided into sets and that these white lines on the ground show where a valid position for the tennis ball is, that the ball may only jump up once before it has to be played back, etc. Perhaps you have played a similar game as, e.g., Badminton before. So surprisingly, learning tennis means that you nearly already know how to do it!

In general, we learn things in an incremental fashion and thereby make use of previously acquired motoric and non-motoric knowledge (facts). An important question that arises here is: Which model or which architecture is needed for realizing incremental learning? Many research papers, e.g. in robotics, show that some certain ability X can be learned with a combination of certain machine learning techniques. The papers are written in a fashion similar to "We recorded N training examples of tennis returns, then used clustering technique C to identify prototypes of tennis returns, mapped each prototype to a lower-dimensional space using PCA, then modeled each tennis return using a Hidden Markov Model (HMM) and a Markov Random Field (MRF) etc.". But it is completely unclear, how such models can be reused - after being trained to model a certain ability X - in order to model also capabilities Y and Z and - perhaps even more importantly - how the learning of Y and Z can be accelerated based on what we have learned for realizing ability X.

## 11.4    Principle of embodiment

Assume you want to build a machine learning system that can be used as an emergency breaking assistant for autonomous driving cars. Perhaps you take one of the state-of-the-art CNN based object detection models like Faster R-CNN [38], YOLO [37] [36], or SSD [29] and train the model to detect object categories as persons, cyclists, cars, trucks and animals. Each time a person, cyclist, truck, or animal suddenly blocks the road you activate an emergency break. Is this enough?

What do you think if suddenly a small ball rolls out from behind a car onto the street? Probably, "Attention! A child could run out from behind the car onto the street as well without looking for cars". Unfortunately your emergency breaking assistant was not trained to detect balls, because balls are not considered as an important road user class. For this, probably no emergency break will be activated in such a situation.

The message of this example is, that some *general knowledge* is probably necessary for many machine learning applications. But then the question arises: How can we encode and learn general knowledge? The approach of *Symbolic Artificial Intelligence* (also called *Good Old-Fashioned Artificial Intelligence (GOFAI)*) was to try to manually encode general knowledge in symbolic forms, e.g., as predicates and rules. In my opinion, history has shown, that practically this approach only works for a very limited amount of general knowledge. Further, the *symbol grounding problem* arises which is the question of how these abstract symbols as "child", "ball", "to roll", "small", etc. get their meanings.

A solution to the symbol grounding problem is to associate the symbols with sensoric and actoric signals. So the symbols *are grounded* in sensoric-actoric patterns. But that in turn means that your system has to have sensors and actuators which allow the system to learn these symbol $\leftrightarrow$ sensoric-actoric associations. A system which has sensors and actuators could be a robot and many robotic researchers think that for realizing a *general artificial intelligence (GAI)* an AI needs a body. The belief that a body is very helpful for an AI to learn general knowledge is called the *embodiment thesis*. I think it is the only feasible way to give an AI general knowledge: Give it a body and let it learn like a child which objects are out there and how they can be used to manipulate the world. This learning process is called *affordance learning*, where affordances is a term which robotic researchers borrowed from psychology to describe the possibilities what a given body can do with an object.

## 11.5 Principle of prediction

The current perspective onto the brain is that it is reactive: Something happens in the world. This event is recorded by different sensors. The brain computes an reaction in order to maximize some expected reward. The computed motoric signals are send to the muscles. Next input signal, please!

A new perspective onto the brain is that the brain is more a prediction machine. Work [5] conducted in the context of the *Human Brain Project (HBB)* seems to underline this perspective. Based on what you have learned since your birth and what you have sensed in the last moments your brain predicts what will happen next. And the brain will already send signals to your muscles *just based on theses predictions*. These predictions are then compared with what really happens and either will confirm the prediction and thereby the ongoing movement or will update the prediction which in turn will alter the ongoing movement.

The latter perspective seems to be more plausible, since acting quickly and pro-actively in the world seems to give living beings an evolutionary advantage. And of course, returning a tennis ball back to your opponent is much easier or even only possible if you can predict where the tennis ball lands.

## 11.6   Cognitive architectures

Non-recurrent models as CNNs do an input to output mapping. In this book we did not discuss another important Deep Learning model, which is the Long Short Term Memory (LSTM) model. LSTMs are recurrent neural networks which have their strengths in processing time series as audio or text data, since simple cells called *memory cells* can be trained to store some information and pass it to the output when needed, i.e., features seen some steps before can influence features seen later.

However, even for these models which store some information from previous time steps it is unlikely that they can be used for realizing complex cognitive functions as reasoning about a scene in an image, or deciding which goal to achieve, developing an idea ("plan") how to achieve it and pursuing a selected goal. We need some larger, probably more complex, model that is able to realize different tasks with the same cognitive building blocks.

The idea of a *cognitive architecture* is not new. In a survey paper on cognitive architectures called "A Review of 40 Years of Cognitive Architecture Research: Focus on Perception, Attention, Learning and Applications" [23], Kotseruba et al. start their paper with a list of 84 (!) different cognitive architectures and depict in a table which cognitive architecture have been presented in which of the 16 previous surveys on cognitive architectures.

Thereby, many cognitive architectures borrow ideas from cognitive science and name *cognitive modules* in their architecture correspondingly. For example, the "old" ACT-R (by John R. Anderson, a professor for psychology at CMU) cognitive architecture models the limited working memory with the help of "buffers". Elements of information are stored as "chunks" in these buffers, where chunks consist of a set of slots with concrete values. A goal buffer e.g. encodes which goal is tried to achieve next and a retrieval buffer can store one chunk that was retrieved from the declarative memory. The procedural memory stores a set of production rules which encode cognitive processes: A single production rule tests for some conditions / contents of the buffers and if it can "fire" (i.e., if all the buffer conditions are met), describes how to change the buffer contents. By this, cognition is modeled as a sequence of firing of production rules.

Sounds good. However, to the best of my knowledge, none of these cognitive architectures has shown to produce a *cognition* that can solve *different real world problems*.

I started this chapter by telling that many people ask "What's next after deep learning?". My best guess is: A cognitive architecture that is able to learn to solve *different real world problems*. I think, cognitive architectures are a promising way.

And perhaps in the year 2024 there will be a conversation between two students similar to this one:

Jürgen: What have you done today?

Christine: I updated my robot with the new CogFlow cognitive architecture that came out last week! The robot can now do the dishes, wash and iron my clothes and play tennis with much better due to better predictions!

Jürgen: What is CogFlow?

Christine: CogFlow is the newest cognitive architecture that models cognition by coglets. Didn't you here about it?

Jürgen: Umm... No! But what are these *cocktails*?

Christine: *Coglets!* They are called *coglets*! Come on! You really should know what a coglet is if this is the evening before your oral exam in computer science! Coglets are the building blocks of all newer cognitive architectures. They model all mental processes in natural brains. After the seminal paper of Alexandrowitsch Krimkowski in 2022 coglets lead to a renaissance in interest to the old field of Deep learning when he showed a 11% performance gain on the famous MultiRealWorldTaskNet benchmark using coglets.

Jürgen: Oh. I really didn't know...

*Jürgen rapidly finishes his dinner, then goes to his room to read into cognitive architectures and coglets.*

*@Christine: I hope everything is all right again!*

# 12

# Exercises

Solutions for all the exercises can be found in the corresponding GitHub repository accompanying this book:

`https://github.com/juebrauer/Book_Introduction_to_Deep_Learning`

## 12.1  Ex. 1 - Preparing to work with Python

Go to the Python download page:
`https://www.python.org/downloads/`

You will see that there are two different versions of Python that are available: Python 3.6.3 and Python 2.7.14. Which one should I download?

It is important to know that code written in Python 3.x is not compatible with code written in Python 2.x. On the one side Python 2.7 still provides a larger set of packages which has the effect that some programmers choose to remain with Python 2.7.

On the other side Python 3 is said to be the future of the language.

Fortunately, we need not to decide and can use a tool called *conda* to remain flexible. conda allows to create *environments* which can host different versions of Python interpreters and different packages.

**Step 1:**
Go to `https://www.anaconda.com/download/` and download (Windows) *Anaconda* (64 bit, Python 3.6 version). Anaconda contains the conda package and environment manager that will allow us to create environments with different Python versions.

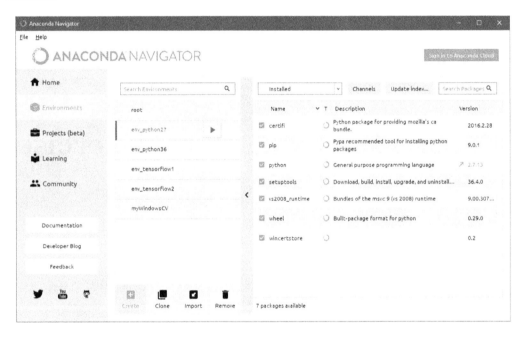

**Step 2:**
Start the *Anaconda navigator*. Then create two environments. An environment
`env_python27`
where you choose Python 2.7 as interpreter and another environment
`env_python36`
where you choose Python 3.6 as interpreter.

**Step 3:**
Install *PyCharm*, a nice Python IDE. Start PyCharm and create a project
`a_python2_project`. Open the
`File → Settings → Project Interpreter`

dialog and add the directory where conda stores the `env_python27` environment to the Project Interpreter selection box ("Add local") by choosing the Python interpreter in that environment directory. Then choose this newly added interpreter as the project interpreter.

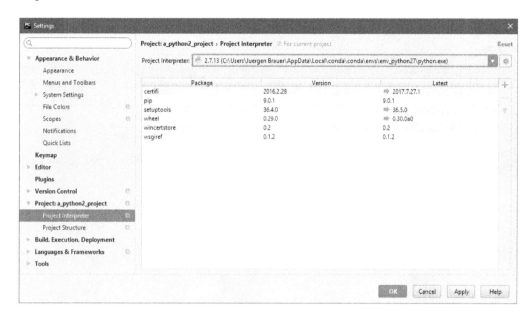

**Step 4:**
Now add a new file `python2_code.py` to the project, enter the following code and run it:

```
import sys
print "Your Python version is: " + sys.version
```

It should output something like this:
```
Your Python version is:  2.7.13 |Continuum Analytics, Inc.|
(default, May 11 2017, 13:17:26) [MSC v.1500 64 bit (AMD64)]
```

**Step 5:**
Now prepare a `a_python3_project`, choose the `env_python36` environment as project interpreter and add a `python3_code.py` source code file to this project with the following code:

```
import sys
```

```
2  print("Your Python version is: " + sys.version)
```

It should output something like this:

```
Your Python version is:  3.6.2 |Continuum Analytics, Inc.|
(default, Jul 20 2017, 12:30:02) [MSC v.1900 64 bit (AMD64)])]
```

**Step 6:**

Now search for articles in the internet describing some differences between Python2 and Python3 and augment the code in both project source files python2_code.py and python3_code.py to show and try out these differences. Try to find as many differences as possible, at least 5.

## 12.2   Ex. 2 - Python syntax

### Loops

**a)** Write a for-loop and a while-loop that print the numbers between 10 and 30 with a step size of 3 in <u>one</u> line:

```
10   13   16   19   22   25   28
10   13   16   19   22   25   28
```

**b)** Format the following code correctly such that it runs and produces the output specified:

```
counter=0
while(counter<10):
print(counter, end=' ')
counter +=1
else:
print("counter=" + str(counter))

for i in range(1, 10):
if(i%5==0):
break
print(i, end=' ')
else:
print("i=" + str(i))
```

Desired output:

```
0 1 2 3 4 5 6 7 8 9 counter=10
1 2 3 4
```

### Dynamic typing

**a)** How can you get the information which data type Python uses internally for each of the variables a-f? Print the data type for each of the variables.

```
a = 2
b = 3.1
c = 'd'
d = "a string"
```

```
5 e = [1,22,333]
6 f = (4,55,666)
```

**b)** Which output will be generated by the following program?

```
1 b = 21
2 b = b+b
3 print(b)
4 b = "3"
5 b = b+b
6 print(b)
7 print(type(int(b)))
8 print(type(str(type(int(b)))))
9 print(str(type(str(type(int(b)))))[3])
```

## Selections

**a)** Let the user enter a number. If the number is between 1-3 output "A", if it is between 4-6 output "B", if it is between 7-9 output "C". If it is not between 1-9 output "Invalid number!". The user shall be able to enter numbers till he enters the word "exit". If he enters a string that is not a number and different from the word "exit", output "Invalid command!"

Example program run:

```
1  1
2  A
3  1.384
4  A
5  5.4
6  B
7  9
8  C
9  9.0
10 C
11 9.1
12 Invalid number!
13 10
14 Invalid number!
15 -1.45
16 Invalid number!
17 test
18 Invalid command!
19 exit
```

## Functions

**a)** Define a function f1 that accepts two parameters value1 and value2, computes the sum and the product and returns both. What is the type of the "thing" that you return?

**b)** Now define a function f2 that does the same but provides default values for both arguments (e.g. default value1 = 2, default value2 = 3). So the behavior of your function f2 should look like this without specifying any of the values:

```
print(f2())
(5,6)
```

Is it possible now to call f2 without specifying value1, but only value2? How?

## Lists

**a)** Define a list which stores the strings "cheese", "milk", "water". Output the list. Then append the string "apples". Output the list. Remove the string "milk". Output the list. Iterate over the list and output each element.

**b)** What does "list comprehension" mean in Python? Use a list comprehension to generate a list of $\pi$ rounded to the first, second, third, fourth and fifth decimal and output this list:

```
[3.1, 3.14, 3.142, 3.1416, 3.14159]
```

## Classes

**a)** Define a class "car" that accepts the car's name and its maximum speed as parameters in the class constructor. Three attributes shall be stored for a car: its name, its maximum speed and its mileage. Define a method "set_speed" which allows to set the current speed. Also define a method "drive" which accepts as parameter the number of hours to drive and increases the mileage accordingly. Finally, also provide a method "show_status" which outputs the current speed and mileage. Test your class by creating two object instances.

**b)** Derive a class "convertible" that uses "car" as base class. Pass the time for letting the roof of the convertible down as an argument to the class. Overwrite the "show_status" method of the base class and output also the time to open the roof.

## 12.3 Ex. 3 - Understanding convolutions

### Learning goal

Convolutions (filtering) are the core operations of Convolutional Neural Networks (CNNs). In section 4.5 we further said, that regarding its function a single Perceptron neuron can be considered as a convolution operator or filter. The goal of this section is to give you an intuition what it means to convolute (process) a 2D input signal (an image) with a filter. You will see that we can manually "design" filter kernels that are appropriate to detect simple features in an image. Note, that in CNNs these filters will be not designed manually! The cool thing is that appropriate filters can be learned automatically in a CNN to create filters that are helpful in tasks as, e.g., classifying images into N object classes.

### Step 1: Preparing to work with OpenCV

First, we need to install the OpenCV library. You can go through the steps of this post, that explains how to install OpenCV3 under Windows with the help of Anaconda:

https://chrisconlan.com/installing-python-opencv-3-windows/

### Step 2: Test whether OpenCV works on your computer

Download a test image from the internet. Then use the following small python script in order to check whether everything works:

```python
import sys
import cv2

print("Your Python version is: " + sys.version)
print("Your OpenCV version is: " + cv2.__version__)

# Load an color image as a grayscale image
img = cv2.imread('coins.jpg',0)

# Show the image
cv2.imshow('image',img)

# Wait for user to press a key
cv2.waitKey(0)
```

In my case the result was:

```
1 Your Python version is: 3.5.4 |Continuum Analytics, Inc.| (default, Aug 14
    2017, 13:41:13) [MSC v.1900 64 bit (AMD64)]
2 Your OpenCV version is: 3.1.0
```

## Step 3: Reading from a video stream frame by frame

Download the following test video from my website:

http://www.juergenbrauer.org/teaching/deep_learning/exercises_book/
test_data/video_testpattern.mp4

and use the following code to read in the video frame by frame:

```
1 import numpy as np
2 import cv2
```

```
3
4  cap = cv2.VideoCapture('video_testpattern.mp4')
5  #cap = cv2.VideoCapture(0)
6
7  while(cap.isOpened()):
8
9      ret, frame = cap.read()
10
11     if (ret == False):
12         break
13
14     gray = cv2.cvtColor(frame, cv2.COLOR_BGR2GRAY)
15
16     cv2.imshow('frame',gray)
17
18     c = cv2.waitKey(1)
19     # 'q' pressed?
20     if (c==113):
21         break
22
23 cap.release()
```

Try out what happens on your computer if you comment (deactivate) line 4 and comment out (activate) line 5.

## Step 4: Filtering each frame with a filter

Now read in and use OpenCV's function `filter2D()` to write a Python script that filters each image frame of the video with the following filter kernel:

$$K = \begin{bmatrix} -1 & 0 & 1 \\ -1 & 0 & 1 \\ -1 & 0 & 1 \end{bmatrix}$$

Display the filter result matrix with `imshow()`: For which image structures does the filter kernel return large values?

If we consider a grayscale image with values from [0,255] and use the `filter2D()` function with the above Kernel: Which is the largest and which is the smallest possible resulting value that we could in principle observe in the filter result matrix?

Note: Make sure, that you normalize the resulting filter values such that `imshow()` can be used to display all values of the filter result matrix!

## 12.4   Ex. 4 - NumPy

*NumPy* (Numerical Python Extensions)is a Python library that is widely used whenever we need a data structure for storing n-dimensional arrays (including vectors, matrices, but also 3D arrays, etc.) and also supports linear algebra functions that can be applied onto these arrays. Its long history goes back to the year 1995 and NumPy's predecessors were the libraries Numeric and Numarray. NumPy 1.0 was released in 2006.

You can install NumPy directly with the help of the *Anaconda Navigator*. However, I recommend to install *TensorFlow* directly, which has dependencies to *NumPy* and therefore NumPy will be installed automatically as well, since we will need TensorFlow already in the next exercise.

### Version

**a)** How can you output the version of your NumPy installation?

```
Your NumPy version is 1.13.1
```

### Generating arrays

**a)** Generate an 1D array a1 that consists of 5 integers. Then output the data type used to store the entries of this array.

```
a1= [ 2  4  6  8 10]
Numbers in a1 are stored using data type int32
```

**b)** Change the data type that is used to store the numbers in a1 to float with 32 bit and make sure you did it right by outputting the data type used for storing the numbers of a1 again:

```
Numbers in a1 are now stored using data type float32
```

**c)** Generate a 2D array a2 of size 3x2 (rows x columns) with the following numbers and output it. Also output the number of dimensions of this array, the number of rows and number of columns.

```
a2= [[1 2]
```

```
2   [3 4]
3   [5 6]]
4 number of dimensions of a2:  2
5 number of rows      of a2: 3
6 number of columns of a2: 2
```

**d)** Output how much bytes are used to store a single array element of a2 and how many bytes are used in total:

```
1 nr of bytes needed to store one a2 array element : 4
2 nr of bytes needed to store all a2 array elements: 24
```

**e)** Generate the following 3D array a3. Also output the number of dimensions of a3 and the size of each dimension

```
1 a3= [[[ 1  2  3  4]
2   [ 5  6  7  8]
3   [ 9 10 11 12]]
4
5   [[13 14 15 16]
6   [17 18 19 20]
7   [21 22 23 24]]]
8 number of dimensions of a3:  3
9 number of slices   of a3: 2
10 number of rows      of a3: 3
11 number of columns of a3: 4
```

## Accessing array elements

**a)** Get and output the value of the element of a3 in the second slice, third row, fourth column:

```
1 Value of that element is  24
```

**b)** Change the value of that element to 42 and output the value again by retrieving the value at that position from array a3:

```
1 Value of that element is now 42
```

**c)** Store the first slice from the 3D array a3 in a new 2D array a4 and output it:

```
1 a4= [[ 1  2  3  4]
```

```
2  [ 5  6  7  8]
3  [ 9 10 11 12]]
```

**d)** Now retrieve from a4 the third column as a 1D array a5 and output it:

```
a5= [ 3  7 11]
```

**e)** Retrieve from a4 the second row as a 1D array a6 and output it:

```
a6= [5 6 7 8]
```

**f)** Retrieve from a4 the following 2x2 sub-matrix:

```
a7= [[ 6  7]
 [10 11]]
```

## Reshaping arrays

**a)** Generate the following 1D array A. Then reshape it to a 2D array B with 2 rows and 5 columns.

```
A= [ 1  2  3  4  5  6  7  8  9 10]
B= [[ 1  2  3  4  5]
 [ 6  7  8  9 10]]
```

**b)** Reshape the 2D array B to a 2D array C with 5 rows and 2 columns.

```
C= [[ 1  2]
 [ 3  4]
 [ 5  6]
 [ 7  8]
 [ 9 10]]
```

## Linear algebra with arrays

**a)** Define the following two matrices A and B in your code. Then compute the sum of the two matrices, the element wise multiplication result and the matrix multiplication result:

```
A=
```

```
 2   [[1 1]
 3    [0 1]]
 4  B=
 5   [[2 0]
 6    [3 4]]
 7  A+B=
 8   [[3 1]
 9    [3 5]]
10  element wise multiplication A*B=
11   [[2 0]
12    [0 4]]
13  matrix multiplication A*B=
14   [[5 4]
15    [3 4]]
```

**b)** Define the following matrix $A$. Then compute its inverse $A\_inv$. Check whether the matrix product of both matrices $A$ and $A\_inv$ really gives you the 2x2 identity matrix.

```
1  A=
2   [[ 1.   2.]
3    [ 3.   4.]]
4  A_inv=
5   [[-2.    1. ]
6    [ 1.5 -0.5]]
7  A * A_inv=
8   [[  1.00000000e+00   1.11022302e-16]
9    [  0.00000000e+00   1.00000000e+00]]
```

**c)** What does the function `numpy.eye()`?

**d)** How can we automatically check whether $A*A\_inv$ gives us the 2x2 identity matrix?

## Random arrays

**a)** How can you generate a random matrix of 5 rows and 3 columns with random float values drawn from a uniform distribution with values in the range -1 and +1? Generate such a matrix `rndA`, then output it:

```
1  rndA=
2   [[ 0.67630242 -0.49098576 -0.18706128]
3    [ 0.61222022  0.38307423  0.74869381]
4    [ 0.16949814  0.16301043 -0.77961425]
5    [-0.99861878  0.9521788  -0.55123554]
6    [ 0.92839569  0.45590548  0.09234368]]
```

**b)** How to do the same but with random int values?

```
rndB=
 [[-1  0 -1]
 [ 0 -1  0]
 [-1  0 -1]
 [ 0 -1  0]
 [ 0 -1  0]]
```

## 12.5  Ex. 5 - Perceptron

### Plotting the learning curve

Use the source code for the Perceptron from section 5.3 as a starting point. Augment the code such that it computes and plots the classification rate already during training at each 100 training steps on the test dataset. Then let your Perceptron train for 25.000 steps. Your result should look similar like this:

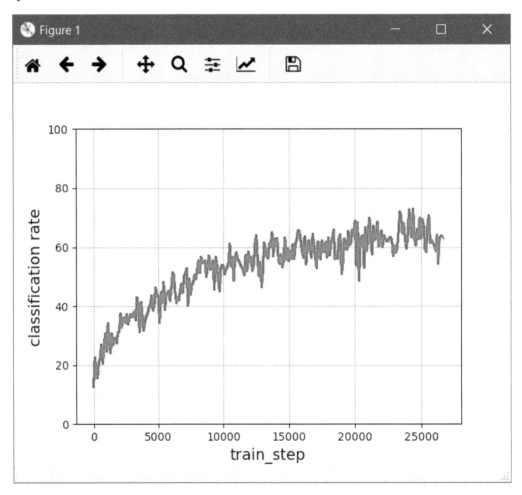

Which classification rate do you get for the Perceptron after 25.000 training steps?

### Comparing the Perceptron with a simple classifier

Think about an own idea for a simple (non-neuronal) classifier that "learns" using the MNIST training dataset. Then implement this classifier and let it learn. Then compare the classification rate of your simple classifier with the classification rate of the Perceptron that has learned for 25.000 steps. Which one has a larger classification rate?

## 12.6   Ex. 6 - Speech Recognition with a SOM

### Download the 10x10 audio dataset

I generated a simple audio dataset. The training dataset consists of 10 audio streams where I spoke a single word 10 times. Theses words are: 1. student, 2. lecture, 3. course, 4. exercises, 5. department, 6. dean, 7. professor, 8. office, 9. university, 10. exams. The test dataset consists of 10 audio stream where I spoke each word only once. So this is actually not enough to train and test a method thoroughly, but it allows to conduct first experiments in the field of speech recognition.

Download URL:

`http://www.juergenbrauer.org/teaching/deep_learning/exercises_book/test_data/`
`10x10_audio_dataset.zip`

### Complete a Python project for speech recognition

Go to

`https://github.com/juebrauer/Book_Introduction_to_Deep_Learning/tree/master/`
`exercise06_self_organizing_map/starting_point/`

and download the starting point of a small Python project that aims to use the training data of the above 10x10 audio dataset to train a SOM. However, the code is not complete. Your task is 1.) to understand and 2.) to complete the code file `audio_classifier.py` such that it uses the SOM that is trained with audio feature vectors in order to classify the 10 test audio streams. Add your code for classification here:

```
# 5. now try to classify each test audio stream
print("YOUR CODE HERE!")
for audio_nr in range(nr_test_audio_streams):
    print("\nClassifying test audio stream", audio_nr, ":")
    print("IMPLEMENT THE CLASSIFICATION HERE")
```

## 12.7 Ex. 7 - MLP with feedfoward step

With this and the next exercise the goal is to implement a Multi Layer Perceptron fully by your own. In this first part the task is just to implement the feedforward step.

More precisely: Write a Python class MLP where new layers can be added flexibly. For each new layer of neurons the `add()` method of this class shall accept the number of neurons and the type of transfer function to be used for neurons in this layer as parameters. Also write a method `feedforward()` which accepts an input vector and then computes the output values of the neurons, starting in the first layer and going to the last (output) layer step by step.

After implementing the MLP think about a test which allows to make it plausible that your implementation works correctly.

Then generate a 100-500-5000-500-10 MLP (100 input neurons, 500 neurons in layer 1, etc.) and measure how long a single feedforward step takes.

## 12.8    Ex. 8 - Backpropagation

The goal of this exercise is to understand how the Backpropagation formulas can be implemented in code. For this you have three options:

### Option 1

Take your own implementation of your MLP from Exercise 7 and augment it by a method `backprop()` that accepts a teacher vector (vector of desired output values of the output neurons) and uses the Backpropagation formulas presented in sections 7.4 - 7.6 for changing the weights to output neurons and hidden neurons. Then generate some training data and test your implementation: can your MLP map the input vectors to the desired output vectors after training?

### Option 2

Take my implementation of a MLP with the Backpropagation formulas. You can find it here:

```
https://github.com/juebrauer/Book_Introduction_to_Deep_Learning/tree/master/
code_examples_in_book/03_mlp
```

Read the code and try to understand how the Backpropagation formulas are implemented in `train()`. Also try to understand what happens in `test_mlp.py`. Then prepare to explain the code in the form of a code walk-through to your fellow students in the class.

### Option 3

Search an easy to understand implementation of the Backpropagation algorithm in Python. Understand the code at least at a level that allows to show your fellow students where and how in the code the Backpropagation formulas are implemented. Prepare to explain the code in the form of a code walk-through to your fellow students in the class. Use this implementation to train a MLP using some training data: can the MLP map the input vectors to the desired output vectors after training?

## 12.9 Ex. 9 - A MLP with TensorFlow

In section 7.9 you have seen one approach to visualize the decision boundaries of a MLP. Now use TensorFlow to implement a MLP with the same topology used in that section (2-10-6-2) with the logistic transfer function in the hidden layers. Train the MLP using stochastic gradient descent (SGD) with one sample. Compare the time needed to train one epoch of my Python implementation

```
https://github.com/juebrauer/Book_Introduction_to_Deep_Learning/tree/master/
code_examples_in_book/03_mlp
```

with the time needed of your TensorFlow implementation to train one epoch as well. Use the class `data_generator.py` of my implementation to generate the 10.000 2D training samples (= one batch) and visualize the decision boundaries learned by your TensorFlow MLP after each epoch.

## 12.10    Ex. 10 - CNN Experiments

Write a CNN using TensorFlow or find one which you can use for experiments. There a lot of implementation examples at GitHub available. Prepare your code such that you can play with different number of convolution and pooling layers. Then download ca. 1000 images (e.g. from ImageNet) for two categories (e.g. bikes vs. cars, dogs vs. cows, etc.) and split the dataset into a training, evaluation and test dataset (e.g., 80% of the images for training, 10% for evaluation, 10% for testing). Train your CNN such that you can classify images into one of these categories.

Experiment with i) different number of convolutional layers and ii) different number of features per convolution layer. For each experiment compute the classification rate of your model on the test dataset. Stop the training of your model a) if you have presented a fixed number of training images or b) if the classification error on your evaluation dataset seems not to shrink any longer. Choose a) or b) as a stop criterion.

In the exercise you should first present your implementation, then which experiments you did and finally the results of your experiments.

## 12.11 Ex. 11 - CNN for word recognition using Keras

Learning goals for this exercise:

1. Learn how to use a CNN for speech processing

2. First steps with Keras

Actually, the LSTM model and not the CNN model is the current dominating model for speech processing. However, a CNN can be used for speech recognition as well and it works quite good!

Read the following blog post by Manash Kumar Mandal:
`http://goo.gl/75EGt2`

In this post the author shows how to convert an audio signal to a MFCC (Mel Frequency Cepstral Coefficients) feature vectors computed using the help of the `librosa` library. It further shows how to use Keras to build up and train a simple CNN using just a few lines of code. With Keras using the model for prediction ("inference") similarly needs only some few lines of code.

You can use his code as a starting point:

`https://github.com/manashmndl/DeadSimpleSpeechRecognizer`

In the GitHub repository Manash already has uploaded 3 folders with ca. 1700 audio files each for the words 'cat', 'bed', 'happy' spoken by different speakers. These audio files are part of a larger dataset available at Kaggle:

`https://www.kaggle.com/c/tensorflow-speech-recognition-challenge`

The dataset is part of the "TensorFlow Speech Recognition Challenge" which takes place in January 2018.

Write a Python program that uses Manash's code snippets in order to classify the three words 'cat', 'bed', 'happy' with a CNN implemented in Keras. From the audio folder take 100 audio streams each in order to test the accuracy of your learned model.

## 12.12   Ex. 12 - Vanishing gradients problem

Take your own MLP implementation or use my slow Python implementation (without TensorFlow) from here:

```
https://github.com/juebrauer/Book_Introduction_to_Deep_Learning/tree/master/
code_examples_in_book/03_mlp
```

Then generate a 2-5-5-5-5-5-2 MLP, i.e., a deep neural network with 2 input neurons, 2 output neurons and 5 hidden layers. Let the NN learn some 2D to 2D mapping using examples of (2D input vector, 2D output vector). Then augment the MLP implementation such that you also compute the average weight change per layer. Also add a method for the MLP class such that you can output the average weight changes per layer that are applied in the Backpropagation step. Conduct two experiments: one with the logistic transfer function in the hidden neurons, one with the ReLU transfer function in the hidden neurons. Can you see some systematics when viewing the average weight change values per layer when using the ReLU transfer function? How does the average weight change values of the first experiment compare to the values in the second experiment?

## 12.13 Ex. 13 - Batch normalization in TensorFlow

Read the following blog by Rui Shu (a PhD student at Stanford):

http://ruishu.io/2016/12/27/batchnorm/

Then implement batch normalization in a MLP using TensorFlow. Compare the development of decision boundaries when batch normalization is turned off with the case that it is turned on. What is striking?

# Bibliography

[1] Frederico A. C. Azevedo et al. "Equal numbers of neuronal and nonneuronal cells make the human brain an isometrically scaled-up primate brain". In: *The Journal of Comparative Neurology* 513.5 (2009), pp. 532–541.

[2] Ladina Bezzola et al. "Training-Induced Neural Plasticity in Golf Novices". In: *Journal of Neuroscience* 31.35 (2011), pp. 12444–12448. ISSN: 0270-6474.

[3] G Bi and M Poo. "SYNAPTIC MODIFICATION BY CORRELATED ACTIVITY: Hebb's Postulate Revisited". In: *Ann. Rev Neurosci* 24 (Jan. 2001), pp. 139–66.

[4] Christopher M. Bishop. *Neural Networks for Pattern Recognition*. New York, NY, USA: Oxford University Press, Inc., 1995. ISBN: 0198538642.

[5] Kevin Casey. "Theory of predictive brain as important as evolution - Prof. Lars Muckli". In: *Horizon - The EU Research and Innovation Magazine* (2018). URL: https://horizon-magazine.eu/article/theory-predictive-brain-important-evolution-prof-lars-muckli_en.html.

[6] CBNInsights, ed. *The Race For AI: Google, Baidu, Intel, Apple In A Rush To Grab Artificial Intelligence Startups*. 2017. URL: https://www.cbinsights.com/research/top-acquirers-ai-startups-ma-timeline/.

[7] Jeff Dean and Urs Hölzle, eds. *Build and train machine learning models on our new Google Cloud TPUs*. 2017. URL: https://www.blog.google/topics/google-cloud/google-cloud-offer-tpus-machine-learning/.

[8] Bogdan Draganski et al. "Neuroplasticity: changes in grey matter induced by training". In: 427 (Feb. 2004), pp. 311–2.

[9] John Duchi, Elad Hazan, and Yoram Singer. "Adaptive Subgradient Methods for Online Learning and Stochastic Optimization". In: *The Journal of Machine Learning Research* 12 (July 2011), pp. 2121–2159. ISSN: 1532-4435.

[10] Luke Durant et al. *Inside Volta: The World's Most Advanced Data Center GPU.* 2017. URL: https://devblogs.nvidia.com/parallelforall/inside-volta/.

[11] Jon Fingas. *Apple's AI acquisition could help Siri make sense of your data.* 2017. URL: https://www.engadget.com/2017/05/13/apple-acquires-lattice-data/.

[12] Ina Fried. *Intel is paying more than 400 million dollar to buy deep-learning startup Nervana Systems.* 2016. URL: https://www.recode.net/2016/8/9/12413600/intel-buys-nervana--350-million.

[13] Kunihiko Fukushima. "Cognitron: A self-organizing multilayered neural network". In: *Biological Cybernetics* 20.3 (1975), pp. 121–136. ISSN: 1432-0770. DOI: 10.1007/BF00342633. URL: http://dx.doi.org/10.1007/BF00342633.

[14] Kunihiko Fukushima. "Neocognitron: A self-organizing neural network model for a mechanism of pattern recognition unaffected by shift in position". In: *Biological Cybernetics* 36.4 (1980), pp. 193–202. ISSN: 1432-0770. DOI: 10.1007/BF00344251. URL: http://dx.doi.org/10.1007/BF00344251.

[15] Gordon D. Goldstein. "Perceptron Mark I". In: *Digital Computer Newsletter of the Office of Naval Research* (1960).

[16] Donald O. Hebb. *The Organization of Behavior: A Neuropsychological Theory.* New Ed. New York: Wiley, June 1949. ISBN: 0805843000. URL: http://www.amazon.com/exec/obidos/redirect?tag=citeulike07-20\&path=ASIN/0805843000.

[17] J.C. Horton and DL Adams. "The cortical column: a structure without a function." In: *Philosophical Transactions of the Royal Society* (2005), pp. 837–682.

[18] Norm Jouppi. *Google supercharges machine learning tasks with TPU custom chip.* 2016. URL: https://cloudplatform.googleblog.com/2016/05/Google-supercharges-machine-learning-tasks-with-custom-chip.html.

[19] Norman P. Jouppi et al. "In-Datacenter Performance Analysis of a Tensor Processing Unit". In: 2017. URL: https://arxiv.org/pdf/1704.04760.pdf.

[20] KhanAcademy, ed. *Neuron action potentials: The creation of a brain signal.* URL: https://www.khanacademy.org/test-prep/mcat/organ-systems/neuron-membrane-potentials/a/neuron-action-potentials-the-creation-of-a-brain-signal.

[21] D.P. Kingma and J. Ba. "Adam: A Method for Stochastic Optimization". In: *Proc. of International Conference on Learning Representations (ICLR)* (2015).

[22]  Teuvo Kohonen. "Self-Organized Formation of Topologically Correct Feature Maps". In: *Biologically Cybernetics* (1982).

[23]  Iuliia Kotseruba, Oscar J. Avella Gonzalez, and John K. Tsotsos. "A Review of 40 Years of Cognitive Architecture Research: Focus on Perception, Attention, Learning and Applications". In: *CoRR* abs/1610.08602 (2016). arXiv: 1610.08602. URL: http://arxiv.org/abs/1610.08602.

[24]  Alex Krizhevsky, Ilya Sutskever, and Geoffrey E Hinton. "ImageNet Classification with Deep Convolutional Neural Networks". In: *Advances in Neural Information Processing Systems 25*. Ed. by F. Pereira et al. Curran Associates, Inc., 2012, pp. 1097–1105. URL: http://papers.nips.cc/paper/4824-imagenet-classification-with-deep-convolutional-neural-networks.pdf.

[25]  Nicolas Langer et al. "Effects of limb immobilization on brain plasticity". In: 78 (Jan. 2012), pp. 182–8.

[26]  Frederic Lardinois. *How Google's Acquisition Of DNNresearch Allowed It To Build Its Impressive Google+ Photo Search In 6 Months*. 2013. URL: https://techcrunch.com/2013/06/12/how-googles-acquisition-of-dnnresearch-allowed-it-to-build-its-impressive-google-photo-search-in-6-months/.

[27]  Y. LeCun et al. "Backpropagation Applied to Handwritten Zip Code Recognition". In: *Neural Computation* 1.4 (Dec. 1989), pp. 541–551. ISSN: 0899-7667. DOI: 10.1162/neco.1989.1.4.541. URL: http://dx.doi.org/10.1162/neco.1989.1.4.541.

[28]  Yann LeCun et al. "Gradient-based learning applied to document recognition". In: *Proceedings of the IEEE*. 1998, pp. 2278–2324.

[29]  Wei Liu et al. "SSD: Single Shot MultiBox Detector". In: *CoRR* abs/1512.02325 (2015). arXiv: 1512.02325. URL: http://arxiv.org/abs/1512.02325.

[30]  C. von der Malsburg. *The correlation theory of brain function*. 1981.

[31]  Christopher D. Manning. "Computational Linguistics and Deep Learning". In: *Computational Linguistics* 41(4) (2015), pp. 701–707.

[32]  Marvin Minsky and Seymour Papert. *Perceptrons: An Introduction to Computational Geometry*. Cambridge, MA, USA: MIT Press, 1969.

[33]  Vernon B. Mountcastle. "Modality and topographic properties of single neurons of cats somatic sensory cortex". In: *Journal of Neurophysiology* 20.4 (1957), pp. 408–434. ISSN: 0022-3077. eprint: http://jn.physiology.org/content/20/4/408.full.pdf. URL: http://jn.physiology.org/content/20/4/408.

[34] German I. Parisi et al. "Continual Lifelong Learning with Neural Networks: A Review". In: *arXiv:1802.07569* (2018). https://arxiv.org/abs/1802.07569. URL: `https://www2.informatik.uni-hamburg.de/wtm/publications/2018/PKPKW18/`.

[35] James Randerson. *How many neurons make a human brain? Billions fewer than we thought*. 2012. URL: `https://www.theguardian.com/science/blog/2012/feb/28/how-many-neurons-human-brain`.

[36] Joseph Redmon and Ali Farhadi. "YOLO9000: Better, Faster, Stronger". In: *CoRR* abs/1612.08242 (2016). arXiv: `1612.08242`. URL: `http://arxiv.org/abs/1612.08242`.

[37] Joseph Redmon et al. "You Only Look Once: Unified, Real-Time Object Detection". In: *CoRR* abs/1506.02640 (2015). arXiv: `1506.02640`. URL: `http://arxiv.org/abs/1506.02640`.

[38] Shaoqing Ren et al. "Faster R-CNN: Towards Real-Time Object Detection with Region Proposal Networks". In: *CoRR* abs/1506.01497 (2015). arXiv: `1506.01497`. URL: `http://arxiv.org/abs/1506.01497`.

[39] Gerard Rinkus. "A cortical sparse distributed coding model linking mini- and macrocolumn-scale functionality". In: *Frontiers in Neuroanatomy* 4 (2010), p. 17. ISSN: 1662-5129. DOI: `10.3389/fnana.2010.00017`. URL: `https://www.frontiersin.org/article/10.3389/fnana.2010.00017`.

[40] Frank Rösler. *Psychophysiologie der Kognition - Eine Einführung in die Koginitive Neurowissenschaft*. Spektrum Akademischer Verlag, 2011.

[41] Yichuan Tang. "Deep Learning using Linear Support Vector Machines". In: *ICML Challenges in Representation Learning Workshop* (2013).

[42] The Economic Times, ed. *The 11 most important Google acquisitions ever*. 2014. URL: `http://economictimes.indiatimes.com/slideshows/tech-life/the-11-most-important-google-acquisitions-ever/dnnresearch-inc-neural-networks/slideshow/40253843.cms`.

[43] Wikipedia, ed. *List of mergers and acquisitions by Alphabet*. URL: `https://en.wikipedia.org/wiki/List_of_mergers_and_acquisitions_by_Alphabet`.